Theory and Interpretation of Narrative
James Phelan and Peter J. Rabinowitz, Series Editors

NARRATIVE CAUSALITIES

EMMA KAFALENOS

The Ohio State University Press
Columbus

Copyright © 2006 by The Ohio State University.
All rights reserved.

Library of Congress Cataloging-in-Publication Data

Kafalenos, Emma, 1939–
  Narrative causalities / Emma Kafalenos.
    p. cm.
  Includes bibliographical references and index.
  ISBN 0-8142-1025-2 (cloth : alk. paper) — ISBN 0-8142-9102-3 (cd-rom) 1. Literature, Modern—History and criticism.
2. Narration (Rhetoric) 3. Causation in literature. I. Title.
  PN701.K34 2006
  808—dc22

                                2005034750

Cover design by DesignSmith.
Type set in Sabon.
Printed by Thomson-Shore, Inc.

"The Princess and the Pea" from *The Complete Fairy Tales and Stories* by Hans Christian Andersen, translated by Eric Haugaard, copyright © 1974 by Eric Christian Haugaard. Used by permission of Random House Children's Books, a division of Random House, Inc.
"A Third Tale" and "The Pea Test" from *The Complete Fairy Tales of the Brothers Grimm* by Jack Zipes, Translator, copyright © 1987 by Jack Zipes. Used by permission of Bantam Books, a division of Random House, Inc.

The paper used in this publication meets the minimum requirements of the American National Standard for Information Sciences—Permanence of Paper for Printed Library Materials. ANSI Z39.48–1992.

9 8 7 6 5 4 3 2 1

CONTENTS

Preface   vii

Chapter 1   Reading Narrative Causalities: Functions and
Functional Polyvalence   1

Chapter 2   The Princess and the Pea(s): Two Versions,
Different Causalities   27

Chapter 3   Nonchronological Narration:
Poe's "The Assignation" and Browning's
"My Last Duchess"   44

Chapter 4   The Comforts That Function C Brings:
Shakespeare's *Hamlet*, Racine's *Phaedra*,
and James's *Daisy Miller*   62

Chapter 5   Lingering at Functions D, E, and F:
James's *The Ambassadors* and Kafka's
"Before the Law"   104

Chapter 6   Sequential Perception: James's *The Turn of
the Screw* and Balzac's *Sarrasine*   126

Chapter 7   Narrative Borderlands I: The Lyric, the Image,
and the Isolated Moment as Temporal Hinge 157

Chapter 8   Narrative Borderlands II: The Image Where
Stories Proliferate in Novels by Robbe-Grillet
and Others   179

Glossary   197

Notes   203

Works Cited   235

Index   243

PREFACE

Josef Albers's *Homage to the Square: Aurora,* which is reproduced on the cover of this book, is one of the paintings of squares super-imposed on squares by which Albers demonstrates that percep-tions of color are influenced by context. In experiments beginning at Black Mountain College in 1949 and continuing during the 1950s at Yale, the artist showed that a given pigment will be seen sometimes as one color and at other times as a surprisingly differ-ent color.[1] To experience this effect when we look at one of Albers's paintings, we pick a square other than the innermost or the outer-most. Then we look at an area of that square that is adjacent to the next square inside. We see one color. Then we shift our focus and look at our same square but this time at an area that is adja-cent to the next square outside. This time we see a different color. The pigment of a given square is the same throughout, but the color we perceive when we look at the pigment depends on whether we are seeing it in relation to the pigment of the outer square or of the inner square.

Albers proves that interpretations of the color of a pigment depend on the context in which the pigment is perceived. Similarly, interpretations of the causes and effects of something someone does or something that happens depend on the context in which the action or happening is considered. In narrative studies, some-thing someone does or something that happens is referred to as an *event.* Like interpretations of the color of a pigment, interpreta-tions of the causality of an event are contextual and depend on the other events in relation to which the event is perceived.

Narratives determine the context in relation to which we inter-pret the events they report. When we read a novel, scan a newspa-per account about events in our world, watch a film, or listen to a friend who is telling us about her problems at work, we are receiv-ing information sequentially about sequential events; we are read-ing or viewing or listening to a narrative. A *narrative,* according to the definition I use (which I discuss in more detail in chapter 1), is a sequential representation of sequential events, fictional or other-wise, in any medium. As we shall see in the chapters that follow, both sequences—the sequence in which we receive information and the chronological sequence in which the events are reported to have occurred—contribute to the formation of the context that a narrative establishes.

The sequence in which the events are reported to have occurred not only positions individual events chronologically in relation to prior and subsequent events. Because narratives reach an end and conclude, the set of events that a given narrative reports is finite. This chronologically ordered, finite set provides the context in relation to which we interpret the causes and consequences of individual reported events. Because all narratives establish a chronologically ordered, finite set of events, *all narratives* unavoidably shape readers' (listeners', viewers') interpretations of the causes and effects of those events. This shaping of perceivers' interpretations of causality, which is the effect of the context that a narrative provides, occurs, I will argue, whether the writer or speaker intends to guide causal interpretations or not.

Furthermore, because narratives are represented sequentially, we receive information increment by increment. In other words, the context a narrative provides—and in relation to which we interpret the causes and effects of revealed events—changes and expands as information about subsequent and sometimes about prior events is revealed. The sequential representation of events in narratives, along with the concomitant sequential perception of events for readers (viewers, listeners), can have varied epistemo-logical and aesthetic effects, which will be considered in detail in the chapters that follow. In response to most narratives, I suggest, almost as soon as we begin to read (or listen, or watch), we start to analyze the causal relations among the events we have learned about thus far. That is to say, our first interpretations are made in relation to a context that is necessarily more limited than it will be after we read on. Some narratives, as we shall see, guide us to retain our first interpretation until information that is revealed only in the concluding words or moments forces us to recognize that that interpretation was incorrect. Other narratives shape and reshape our interpretation, leading us from a first interpretation of the causes and effects of an event to another interpretation and yet another interpretation. Sometimes, I will argue (particularly in chapter 6), in the interaction between a given narrative and a given reader (listener, viewer), our first interpretation of causality becomes so firmly fixed in our minds that we retain that interpretation even after we have received additional information that would lead us, if only we recognized the need to reinterpret, to a new interpretation.

A *function,* as I use the term, names a position in a causal sequence. The ten functions I define in chapter 1 provide a vocabulary to talk about interpretations and reinterpretations of causal relations between a given event and other events that the interpreter considers related. I use functions, for example, to record readers' interpretations as they develop and change (or fail to change) during the process of reading, to compare interpretations among characters, between characters and narrators, and between readers and characters or readers and narrators, as well as, more generally, to show how the context in which an event is perceived affects interpretations of its causes and consequences.

Moreover, we process events we observe in our world in the same way we process events reported in narratives—by interpreting their causes and consequences in relation to other events we consider related. Thus a vocabulary of functions can name and compare interpretations of real-world events, interpretations of events in narratives that report real-world events, and interpretations of events in literary narratives. In addition to exploring one source of the power of literary texts, function analysis serves two real-world purposes: first, to show that the different contexts in which events are viewed can lead people (in our world), as well as characters (in a fictional world), to quite different interpretations of the causes and effects of a given event; and, second, to demonstrate how seriously any telling, by establishing one rather than another context, unavoidably guides readers' (viewers', listeners') interpretations of the events it reports. The real-world danger to which my analysis draws attention is that as readers (listeners, viewers) of narratives, we may not recognize the extent to which the reports through which we learn about events can shape—and are shaping—our interpretation of the causes and effects of those events.

A constant thread throughout this book is the epistemological question of what we can know—but in a slightly reformulated version. I focus on epistemology in relation to narratives, which are the source of most of the information we receive. I ask what we can know if a narrative is the source of our information—or, in other words, how the information we receive through narratives is shaped by the representation through which we receive it. To

address this question I draw widely from the rich store of presently available narrative theory—a corpus that my study is designed
to complement. Although I am equally interested in the effects on
interpretations of narratives about events in our world as of literary narratives, I take most of my examples from literature, mainly because of the advantage for epistemological analysis of fictional worlds for which (with notable Postmodern exceptions) all
information is contained between the covers of one book.

This project began more than a decade ago when I developed a
vocabulary of functions for talking about interpretations of
causality. Using that vocabulary to analyze responses to narratives, I became increasingly aware both that context shapes interpretations of causality and that narratives determine context. As a
result, this book demonstrates both a methodology (the vocabulary of functions as a tool for analysis) and the results of one
application (my own) of that methodology. As closely related as
the methodology and the findings are in the chapters that follow,
they can be conceived separately, and each, I think, can be incor-
porated into other projects and developed without reference to the
other.

The chapters are arranged approximately in the sequence in
which I have identified ways of using functions to analyze narratives, which is also the sequence in which I find ways to use functions to show, on the one hand, how open events are to plural
interpretations of their causes and consequences—for characters
in their world and for us in our world—and, on the other hand,
the degree to which context determines interpretations of causality. I choose this sequence as the clearest demonstration of my
argument that narratives unavoidably shape interpretations of the
events they represent. Even so, this book is designed to enable
readers, after they read chapter 1 (and perhaps with reference to
the Glossary at the end of this book), to turn to a chapter on a
topic that attracts their interest. Thus chapter 1 presents the basic
theory underlying all the later chapters.

After introducing in chapter 1 the vocabulary of functions and
the idea of functional polyvalence, I present in chapter 2 a first test
case: a comparison of two versions of a fairy tale that guide readers to two different interpretations of which characters' actions
bring about the happy ending. In chapter 3 I look at Poe's "The
Assignation" and Browning's "My Last Duchess"—both influenced by Romanticism and both told in a sequence other than
chronological sequence—to investigate the strong emotional

effects for readers that nonchronological narration can elicit by guiding readers initially to misinterpret causal relations among the reported events.

In chapter 4 I argue that information about a character's decision to try to ameliorate a situation brings comfort—both as a thematics and as a hermeneutic device—to readers (listeners, viewers). My examples in this chapter are Shakespeare's *Hamlet,* Racine's *Phaedra,* and James's *Daisy Miller.* Then in chapter 5 I take as my examples narratives that deny us these forms of comfort: James's *The Ambassadors* and Kafka's "Before the Law." In this chapter I trace the many interpretations of causality that we try out as we progress through these two twentieth-century narratives, drawing attention to how difficult the process of interpreting where we are in a causal sequence can be—for readers of certain modern stories and novels, and also for characters in fictional worlds and for people in our world—without the guidance that the familiar shape of traditional narratives provides.

Returning to the issue of nonchronological narration in chapter 6, I examine two narratives in which, within a frame story, another story is told: Balzac's *Sarrasine* and James's *The Turn of the Screw.* In both narratives some of the same events are perceived by characters, character narrators, and readers—but not in the same sequence. Thus readers' and several of the characters' interpretations of these events are made in relation to contexts that vary. A comparison of these interpretations shows the effect of sequential perception on context, and of context on interpretations of causality, as unequivocally as Albers's experiments demonstrate the effect of context on interpretations of the color of a pigment.

The power of sequential perception to shape interpretations of causality, in our response to life as well as to narratives, leads me to turn to what I think of as the narrative borderlands, to explore separately, to the extent possible, the effects of sequential events, in chapter 7, and of sequential representation, in chapter 8. To do this, in chapter 7 I look at representations of an isolated moment, both the lyric poem and the discrete image, and find, on the one hand, that information about just one prior or subsequent event provides sufficient context to determine our interpretation of the function of the represented moment and that language (the medium of the lyric and of captions to the image) easily specifies that one event. A moment fully cut from the temporal continuum, on the other hand, is open to divergent interpretations of its causes and consequences—even to the extent that it can sometimes be interpreted as a *hinge* in a sequence that, like a palindrome, can be read as beginning at either end. But while a palindrome reads the same in either direction, causality is dependent on sequence. When a sequence of events is reversed, our interpretation of the function of the events—their consequences and causes—changes too.

In the concluding chapter I turn to novels from the second half of the twentieth century that, according to my definition, are not narratives; the events they represent cannot be ordered in chronological sequence. Because I want to consider what novels can teach us about how we read images and how we read discrete events in our world, I choose for analysis in chapter 8 novels that include visual representations, or anecdotes that are interpretations of visual representations, of an isolated moment. Drawing attention to a recognized phenomenon—the many novels published in the second half of the twentieth century that include images or descriptions of images—I speculate that by incorporating visual material and interpretations of visual material, novelists have found a way to open the experience of reading novels to widely divergent interpretations of causality. In this way, these and other novels that are not narratives offer an experience that is closer than narratives offer to the experience of living in our world.

■

Jack Zipes and Erik Christian Haugaard have graciously granted permission to publish in the CD-ROM version of this book their translations of (respectively) Grimms' and Andersen's fairy tales. I thank them. Earlier versions of chapters 3, 5, and 6 have previously appeared in print under these titles: "Functions after Propp: Words to Talk About How We Read Narrative" in *Poetics Today* 18.4 (Winter 1997): 469–94; "Lingering Along the Narrative Path: Extended Functions in Kafka and Henry James" in *Narrative* 3.2 (May 1995): 117–38; and "Not (Yet) Knowing: Epistemological Effects of Deferred and Suppressed Information in Narrative" in *Narratologies: New Perspectives on Narrative Analysis,* edited by David Herman and published in 1999 by The Ohio State University Press. The suggestions made by readers prior to the publication of each article were very useful to the development of my ideas. I have also benefited from and appreciate the responses (the casual comments, the discussions, the e-mail correspondences) from readers of these articles once they were published and from conference attendees who listened to the many papers where I first tried out ideas that appear in this book.

In addition to generations of students at Washington University in St. Louis (and at the St. Louis Conservatory of Music until its unfortunate demise), who have helped me to work out in the classroom my ideas about functions and many of my ideas about narratives, I am greatly indebted to a number of people who have listened to and contributed to my ideas. Let me name—and express my great appreciation for their careful reading and thoughtful, invaluable comments—David Herman, Brian McHale, Peter J. Rabinowitz, Meir Sternberg, and my colleague at Washington University Nancy Berg, all of whom read earlier versions of one or several (or even all eight) of these chapters.

My very special gratitude goes to three colleagues without whose contributions and encouragement this book might not have come to be: to the composer and music theorist Roland Jordan, my colleague at Washington University, who shared with me the early stages of my journey toward understanding how narratives communicate; to Gerald Prince, who was the first narratologist to reassure me, many years ago when I needed that reassurance, that what I was saying was of interest to specialists in the field; and to James Phelan, who has supported and guided this project at every stage since its inception many years ago.

CHAPTER 1

READING NARRATIVE CAUSALITIES:

Functions and Functional Polyvalence

Whenever something that happens attracts our attention, everyone everywhere engages in more or less the same initial interpretive process. Once our attention is focused, however briefly, on something that happens or something someone does, we begin to interpret the action we noticed by considering what may have motivated it and (or or) what that action may make happen. If we see a child scratching her arm, and she is outdoors at nightfall during mosquito season, we may interpret her gesture of scratching as motivated by a desire to ease the discomfort of a mosquito bite she has just received. In this interpretation the child's action is a response to a prior event. On the other hand, watching the child, we may worry that she will hurt herself by scratching, and be uncomfortable for days. In this interpretation, the child's action is a potential cause of a later condition. Both interpretations represent an effort to understand an action, to give it meaning by exploring its possible causes and consequences. As I am using the terms, *meaning* is an interpretation of the relations between a given action (or happening or situation) and other actions (happenings, situations) in a causal sequence. *Interpretation*, in the restricted sense in which I use the word in this study, refers to the process of analyzing the causal relations between an action or happening and other actions, happenings, and situations one thinks of as related.

Something someone does and something that happens, in narrative studies, are referred to as *events*. To be able to engage in interpretation and give meaning to events, we need to have internalized an abstract pattern of a causal sequence. The cognitive theorist Mark Turner argues that the human mind is predisposed to interpret the events he calls "small spatial stories"—"a child throws a rock, a

1

mother pours milk into a glass, a whale swims through the water"—as the motivated action of an agent (*The Literary Mind*, 13).[1] Generally at an early point in our intellectual development, I maintain, we create for ourselves and internalize a pattern of causality that extends (in the versions most of us constitute) from the onset of a problem through stages that potentially can lead to its resolution. When something someone does catches our attention, we interpret the person's action by considering it in relation to this pattern. We place (tentatively, at least) the action that we noticed in one or another position in our internalized causal sequence, and then we consider what other events (possible causes, possible effects) to place in other positions in the sequence.

This interpretive process is fundamental to what Gérard Genette has called "narrative competence" (*Narrative Discourse*, 77). While narrative competence may vary from individual to individual as well as from culture to culture, being able to read or listen to a reported sequence of events and make sense of it necessitates, I will argue, two conceptual leaps. The first is to conceive the reported events as temporally related (occurring one after another in a chronological sequence), and the second, equally important, is to conceive them as potentially causally related. Probably human beings develop narrative competence by listening to stories and (in literate cultures) reading stories. If this is the case, it would help to explain why every culture has had its narratives. When children listen to and later read the stories that in their cultures are significant, they would then be learning, in addition to cultural data, the abstract patterns that underlie chronological and causal relations. The similarity between interpreting the situations and events that we perceive in our world, and interpreting the situations and events that are reported in narratives— whether literary narratives or reports of events in our world—suggests that both procedures require narrative competence, and that practice in either procedure can enhance a person's skills in both.

A *narrative*, in the definition I use, is a sequential representation of a sequence of events. This definition, formulated by Meir Sternberg, emphasizes narrative's two paths as its distinctive feature: the chronological path in which the events are reported to have occurred, which readers (listeners, viewers) with narrative competence construct in response to the information they are given, and the path of the representation, which we perceive incrementally, segment by segment. According to this definition, narratives include representations of events that take place in fictional worlds (novels, stories) and our world (biographies, newspaper articles), representations that show (drama) and those that tell (stories), verbal representations and those in other media—film, ballet, comics, photonovels—that represent sequentially two or three or more events or a situation and an event that changes it.[2] I am claiming that human beings engage in the same initial interpretive process in response to the events in our world that attract our attention and to those that are brought to our attention in narratives, and that, in response to narratives, we bring the same interpretive process (if at times more soberly) to the events in our world that are reported in newspapers and on the nightly news and to the events that take place in fictional worlds that are reported in television series, films, and novels. In all these cases, when an event attracts our attention, whether the event is in our world or in a fictional world, we explore its meaning by analyzing the causal relations between a perceived or a reported event and other events or situations we think of as related. Moreover, characters in fictional worlds and narrators who report the events that take place in fictional worlds engage in this same initial interpretive process.

A theory of interpretive sites, or *functions,* that I have developed gives names to these interpretations. In response to the poststructuralist interest in interpretation, I adopt and adapt the term *function,* which has generally been associated with Formalist and structuralist thought, to create a tool to trace shifts in individuals' and communities' interpretations over time and differences in interpretations from perceiver to perceiver. As I define the term, a function names a position in an abstract causal sequence. I identify ten positions (sites, stages) in a causal sequence that begins at the onset of a problem and leads to its resolution. By naming these positions, functions facilitate analyzing and comparing people's and narrators' and characters' interpretations of causal relations as they develop and change (or fail to change) in response to new information.

In this chapter, after briefly introducing the ten functions I identify, I demonstrate in a close reading of a very short story (one of the shortest of the stories collected by the Brothers Grimm) some of the differences that distinguish one interpretation from another and that functions can name, and I begin to suggest the kinds of information that analyzing the function of events guides interpreters to consider. Throughout this book, when I speak of "readers (listeners, viewers)," I am talking about human beings—not hypothetical constructs—and I am interested in the correlations between the way human beings interpret events in narratives and in our world. Nonetheless, with few exceptions I analyze novels and stories. I do this in part to draw attention to the richness and complexity inherent in even our initial interpretive response—our interpretations of causal relations, which is my topic—to works of literature that I love. But I also appreciate the advantages for analysis both of the medium of the printed page, which readers can digest at their own pace and revisit and find unchanged, and, for fictional worlds, of a finite source of information. I nonetheless assume that our initial interpretive response to novels and stories is so analogous that it can be taken as a pattern for analyzing our initial interpretive response to events in our world, to narratives that represent events in our world, and to narrative representations in other media. After this chapter, this book is designed to allow its readers to move freely to any subsequent chapter. But to avoid repetition, the subsequent chapters are written for readers who are familiar with the ideas and vocabulary introduced in this chapter.

Readers (listeners, viewers) of a narrative travel along the path of the representation, receiving information sequentially. If one conceives this path as an undifferentiated flow, without landmarks or signposts or buoys, then the process of traveling along the path is exceedingly difficult to describe or even to consider. A vocabulary of functions that name positions (sites, stages) in a causal sequence enables describing and comparing individual experiences of moving through a narrative. My theory of functions is developed from ideas, which I see as interrelated, introduced by narrative theorists Tzvetan Todorov and Vladimir Propp.

Todorov, who analyzed the plots of the stories in Boccaccio's *Decameron* in the late 1960s, recognized that in many of these stories periods of equilibrium (or stability) alternate with periods of imbalance (or instability). An *equilibrium,* in Todorov's words, is "the existence of a stable but not static relation between the members of a society." During a period of equilibrium, as I use the term, the characters whose lives are represented consider the prevailing situation acceptable. Periods of equilibrium, Todorov sees, "are separated by a period of imbalance, which is composed of a process of degeneration and a process of improvement" ("Structural Analysis of Narrative," 328). During a period of imbalance, in other words, the characters whose lives are represented consider the prevailing situation unacceptable and as needing to be changed. The pattern of alternation that Todorov perceived in the *Decameron* offers signposts to look for—signs that indicate an equilibrium and signs that indicate imbalance—that enable readers (listeners, viewers) of any narrative to talk about where they are, or (at least) where they think they are and where they think they are going, as they make their way along a narrative path.

Specifically, Todorov discerned in the stories he analyzed a recurrent cyclical unit: the movement from one equilibrium, through a period of imbalance, to a new equilibrium that is similar but not identical to the first ("La Grammaire du récit," 96). Initially calling this unit a "minimal plot," Todorov then introduces a term that I too use: the *sequence* (96, 101). I cite Todorov's analysis that indicates that he conceives the sequence, as I do, as an abstraction, in relation to which to view and describe the varying shapes of real narratives. In Boccaccio's *Decameron,* he reports, "One story coincides often, but not always, with one sequence: a story can contain several sequences, or contain only a part of one sequence" (101).[3] Stories that contain only a part of a sequence, he specifies later in the article, may move from an equilibrium only to an imbalance, or may begin at an imbalance and move to an equilibrium (101–2).

Todorov's discovery that the plots of the stories in the *Decameron* can be perceived as alternating cyclically from periods of equilibrium to periods of imbalance and back to an equilibrium opens the possibility of looking at all narratives not as an undifferentiated flow of information but as a cyclical path in which periods of equilibrium alternate with periods of imbalance. I am proposing that during the process of moving through any narrative, readers (listeners, viewers) interpret (tentatively) a given scene as a relatively stable equilibrium (and wonder what will disrupt it), and another scene as a crucial disruption (and wonder how and whether stability can be restored). Along this path that alternates between equilibrium and disruption, perceived by Todorov, the functions that Propp discerned situate and name additional positions or stages.

In his *Morphology of the Folktale,* published in 1928, Propp reported the thirty-one functions he found in the Russian tales he analyzed. From the thirty-one, I select ten that recur in narratives of various periods and genres, and, for these ten, I provide definitions that are more abstract than Propp's, and that are designed to reveal the general situations that underlie the specific circumstances of the stories he studied.[4] Although I have derived these ten functions from Propp's work and, like Propp, from analyzing narratives, I conceive my ten-function model as denoting positions (sites, stages) in an abstract causal sequence—a logical pattern that readers (listeners, viewers) with narrative competence bring to the analysis of the narratives they encounter.[5]

For Propp, a function is "an act of a character, defined from the point of view of its significance for the course of the action" (21), or defined "according to its consequences" (67). Propp does not specify who defines the significance or consequences of the act. Perhaps he even understands and is saying that any given narrative "defines"—by revealing—the consequences of reported events. As I understand the word, however, if readers or characters or narrators "define" an event according to its consequences, or its significance, they are interpreting its consequences or significance. In my terms, functions represent events that change a prevailing situation and initiate a new situation. A vocabulary of functions enables identifying, naming, and comparing interpretations of an event's consequences and causes.

Because the causal relations between a given event and related events and situations depend on which events or situations the interpreter considers related, and on the given event's chronological position among the related events and situations, an event can express one function in one narrative and another function in another narrative. This attribute of the event—that it is subject to interpretations that may shift according to the context in which it is perceived—is *functional polyvalence,* Lubomír Dole el's term (*Occidental Poetics,* 144) for the phenomenon Propp discovered.[6] Functions name an interpretation of an event in the context in which it is perceived. I argue in this book that narratives determine the context in which events are perceived and that, by doing so, intentionally or otherwise, guide interpretations of the events' causes and effects: their function.

The ten functions that name positions in a causal sequence, in the model I have developed (figure 1), offer an abstract pattern—like Todorov's sequence but more detailed—in relation to which to view and describe the varying shapes of real narratives. Immediately following an initial equilibrium (EQ), I place Propp's function A or function (lower-case) a. Function A represents an action or a happening that disrupts an equilibrium and by changing a situation introduces a period of imbalance. Function a represents a reevaluation that reveals instability in an otherwise unchanged situation. Either a function-A or a function-a event, by disrupting a prevailing equilibrium, initiates a period of imbalance—a function-A or function-a situation—in the cyclical alternation between equilibrium and imbalance that Todorov observed.

A   (*or* a) destabilizing event (*or* reevaluation that reveals instability)

      B   request that someone alleviate A (*or* a)

C   decision by C-actant to attempt to alleviate A (*or* a)
   (The C-actant is the character who performs function C.)

C' C-actant's initial act to alleviate A (*or* a)

      D   C-actant is tested
      E   C-actant responds to test
      F   C-actant acquires empowerment

      G   C-actant arrives at the place, or time, for H

H   C-actant's primary action to alleviate A (*or* a)

I   (*or* I_{neg}) success (*or* failure) of H

A function is a position in a causal sequence. The ten functions locate positions (sites, stages) along a path that leads from the disruption of an equilibrium to a new equilibrium. A complete sequence—from the onset of imbalance to its resolution—will include all five key functions (A, C, C', H, I) and may include any or all of the five additional functions (B, D, E, F, G).

Functions represent events that change a prevailing situation and initiate a new situation.

Figure 1: THE TEN FUNCTIONS

With the addition of functions B through I, which I adopt from Propp, the functions that I identify enable analyses that are more specific than Todorov's sequence allows. Functions B through I name positions or stages along a logical path of motivated action that is undertaken in response to a disruptive event (function A, or a) and designed to resolve the effects of the disruptive event and establish a new equilibrium. As we shall see, not every function is embodied in every narrative. Some functions are useful in illuminating causal relations in certain narratives and not in others; the usefulness of other functions becomes apparent when we interpret other narratives.[7]

Clearly readers vary in what they pay attention to as they read. We know this from our students' responses, from discussions with colleagues, and from reading literary criticism. Nonetheless most readers (listeners, viewers), I suggest, are particularly alert to signs that they read as indicating five key moments along the logical path that leads from one equilibrium to a new equilibrium. Function A (or a) marks the first of these key moments. The next two are marked by functions C and C' (pronounced "C prime"): the decision (C) and the initial motivated action (C') to attempt to resolve the function-A (or function-a) disruption. I will return to the distinction between C and C' later in this chapter and again in chapter 4. Functions C and C' represent actions performed by an intelligent being (human or anthropomorphic) that I call the C-actant: the character who performs function C. Like the word *protagonist,* which is a related term but not synonymous, "C-actant" avoids the evaluation that the word *hero* implies. The final two key moments are marked by function H and function I or I_{neg}: the C-actant's primary action (H) to resolve the function-A or function-a disruption, and the conclusion of that action, whether in success (I) or failure (I_{neg}).

When the five key moments are considered sequentially, the logical relations among them are evident.

Prevailing Equilibrium

(1) Function A (an event that disrupts the equilibrium) or a (a reevaluation that discerns instability)

(2 and 3) Functions C and C' (the decision to act and the beginning of action to resolve a function-A disruption and potentially establish a new equilibrium)

(4 and 5) Functions H and I or I_{neg} (the primary action to

resolve a function-A disruption, and its successful or unsuccessful conclusion)

New Equilibrium

In a complete sequence, a C-actant responds to a function-A or
function-a situation by deciding to undertake action (function C)
that begins (function C'), continues (function H), and concludes
(function I or I_{neg}).[8] Just as these functions lead logically from one
situation to the next, in narratives that include events which one
or more of the additional functions interpret, those functions too
contribute to the logical progression. In the next section we will
look at examples of all ten functions, and consider the kinds of
information that an analysis of the function of events can uncover,
even in a very short and relatively simple narrative.

The following story is one of the shorter ones in Jack Zipes's fine
translation of the stories collected by the Brothers Grimm. Titled
only "A Third Tale" (in a group of stories about elves), it provides
a relatively straightforward example to explore readers' interpretations of the key moments and to begin to consider the usefulness
of the additional functions.

> The elves had stolen a mother's child from the cradle and
> had replaced the baby with a changeling who had a fat head
> and glaring eyes and would do nothing but eat and drink. In
> her distress the mother went to her neighbor and asked for
> advice. The neighbor told her to carry the changeling into
> the kitchen, put him down on the hearth, start a fire, and
> boil water in two eggshells. That would make the changeling
> laugh, and when he laughed, he would lose his power. The
> woman did everything the neighbor said, and when she put
> the eggshells filled with water on the fire, the blockhead said:
>
> "Now I'm as old
> as the Westerwald,
> and in all my life I've never seen
> eggshells cooked as these have been."
>
> And the changeling began to laugh. As soon as he laughed,

a bunch of elves appeared. They had brought the right child
with them and put him down on the hearth and took the
changeling away. (I, 166)

Judging by the response of the students with whom I have read this
story, most readers interpret the theft of the child (and the arrival
of the changeling) as a disruptive event (function A), and the return
of the child (and the removal of the changeling) as a successful resolution (function I) that will establish a new equilibrium.

Once we recognize that the story begins with a disruptive function-A event, readers who are thinking about Todorov's cyclical
sequence or my sequence of functions will recognize that no prior
equilibrium is represented. The story could have begun, after all,
with a statement such as this: "Throughout the first winter after the
baby's birth, mother and child lived in great contentment. Then one
day, the elves stole the mother's child and replaced it with a
changeling." Similarly, the story concludes by indicating that the disruptive situation is successfully resolved (function I: the child is
returned), but without representing a resultant equilibrium—even by
including the familiar words "and they all lived happily ever after."

This story gives us no glimpse of the narrative world (the world
in which the characters act and interact) either prior to the theft
of the baby or after the baby's return. The effect of information
that is not included in a story is a topic to which I will return
repeatedly in this book. Here, let me suggest that even in this tiny
story the lack of representation of prior and subsequent periods of
equilibrium can affect readers' experience. If readers were shown
mother and child during a happy period before and after the
events represented in the story, they might think more about the
emotional impact for the mother of the theft of the child and the
child's return, might thus care more that the child is returned, and
might even read more analytically to ascertain how and by whom
the return of the child was accomplished.

When I ask my students, they disagree about which character,
the mother or the neighbor, is the C-actant: the character who
decides to act to try to alleviate the function-A situation and, in
this story, whose motivated actions successfully get the baby
returned. Initially, as many students credit the neighbor as the
mother. Functions provide a vocabulary to talk about what our
interpretations of agency may mean. To demonstrate, I draw
examples from the familiar plots about knights and princesses and
dragons, where agency, like right and wrong, is rarely ambiguous.

A dragon carries off a princess (function A). These three patterns of response are common:

(1)   The knight whom the princess is to marry catches sight of her in the clutches of the dragon. He leaps on his horse and follows.

In this example, the knight is the C-actant who immediately decides (function C) to save the princess and sets off in pursuit (function C'). (Function C is the pivot that connects the motivating event I call function A to the beginning of the action it motivates, function C'. The move from C to C' marks the important step from deciding to act to beginning to act.)

(2)   The king sees his daughter in the clutches of the dragon. He asks his best knight to save the princess. The knight agrees and rides off.

In this example, the king's request that someone else—the knight—perform the primary action to resolve the disruption is an example of function B. The knight, as in the previous example, is the C-actant who performs function C (decides to save the princess) and function C' (rides off to save the princess). In the previous example, no function-B event is necessary to forward the plot because the knight already has sufficient motivation to take on the C-actant role (he is to marry the princess) and already knows that a function-A event has occurred (he sees the princess in the dragon's clutches).

(3a) The knight either sees the princess in the clutches of the dragon or is asked by the king to save her. He decides to save her (function C). But his horse is lame, so the knight takes off on foot (function C'). Just down the road he meets a frog, who asks to be carried to a nearby pond (function D; the C-actant is tested). The knight carries the frog to the pond (function E; the C-actant responds to the test). Immediately the frog turns into a winged horse that offers to carry the knight in pursuit of the dragon (function F; the C-actant acquires a form of empowerment he lacks and will need to achieve his goal).

(3b) Or, without a horse (as above), the knight takes off on foot (function C'). Just down the road he meets a winged horse that offers to take him in pursuit of the dragon (function F). In this case without having to earn it, the C-actant acquires a needed form of empowerment.

In the Grimms' story about the baby who is carried off by elves, the mother responds to the baby's disappearance by going to her neighbor and asking for advice—the event that is reported in the second sentence. In determining whether the mother or the neighbor is the C-actant, the core issue is how to interpret this event in relation to the other events that the story reports. Is the mother's request comparable logically to the king's request to the knight, in example 2 above, or to the knight's taking off after the dragon on foot, in example 3?

If we say that the mother's going to her neighbor and asking for advice is comparable to the king's request to the knight, we are interpreting the mother's action as function B. That is, we are indicating that the mother's role in forwarding the plot is to bring the problem to the attention of her neighbor and ask for her neighbor's help. If that is the extent of the mother's role, then the primary action that leads to resolving the function-A theft of the baby is done by the neighbor, and in that case the neighbor is the C-actant (the C-actant is the character who performs function C).

If we say that the mother's going to her neighbor and asking for advice is comparable to the knight's taking off after the dragon on foot, we are interpreting the mother's action as function C'. That is, we are indicating that we think that the mother has made a decision to try to save her baby (even though the story does not report in so many words that she makes a decision), and that going to ask her neighbor for advice is the mother's first step toward carrying out that decision. According to this interpretation, the mother is the C-actant (the character who performs function C). The neighbor is the *donor*. Like the frog (in example 3a above) who empowers the knight by turning into a winged horse, the neighbor empowers the mother by giving her advice (function F) so that the mother can do what needs to be done to get the baby back (function H). When the baby returns, we know that the mother has succeeded (function I).

Retrospectively, after discussing the story, my students general-ly opt for the second interpretation—that the mother, rather than the neighbor, is the C-actant. The following sequence of functions represents, I suggest, most readers' considered interpretations:

A   baby is carried off and replaced by a changeling (disrup-tive event)

[C] mother decides to try to save baby (C-actant's decision, inferred)

C' mother goes to neighbor and asks for advice (C-actant's initial act)

F   neighbor gives mother the information she needs (empow-ering the mother)

G   mother brings changeling into the kitchen (the scene of the primary action)

H   mother boils water in two eggshells (the primary action)

I   baby is returned and the changeling taken away (success)

Function G, which has not previously been introduced, is self-explanatory. Function C is in brackets to indicate that the act it interprets is not reported in the text, but inferred by readers. Since function C is the crucial link between the motivating event (func-tion A or a) and the actions it motivates (function C' and function H), I like to indicate function C when we infer it. In narratives that explore characters' mental acts, a function-C decision is often reported explicitly, in so many words. In response to narratives that report only the actions that can be seen by someone who is watching—and, often, in response to events in our world—when-ever we interpret someone's act as motivated, *we are inferring that the actor has made a function-C decision that causally links the act to an existing situation it is to alleviate.*

After thinking about a relatively simple story like this one, read-ers will almost always agree on interpretations of the causal rela-tions among the primary events. Even so, the vocabulary of func-tions brings precision to discussions of issues such as heroism (does heroism require action? motivation? are all heroes C-actants?); knowledge (is knowledge a body of information? the ability to acquire the information or skill or tool one needs?); the comparative value of knowledge and action (is knowing how to get rid of a changeling more or less valuable than the act of boil-ing water in eggs?)—all of which are issues that can be historicized or considered in relation to the culture they reflect. Throughout this book, however, I will be drawing attention to ways that events lend themselves to more than one interpretation of their function, and ways that a representation—for novels and stories, the words of the text—unavoidably (whether correctly or incorrectly, intentionally or not) guides readers' interpretations of the function of the represented events.

In the Grimms' story, for instance, the words *went* and *asked* (in the second sentence) may suggest divergent interpretations. The verb *to ask,* after all, is the word most commonly used in English to denote a request for help. In a context in which most readers will not be able to imagine that the mother herself will be able to effect the baby's return, her act of asking can easily be misinterpreted as a request for help (comparable to asking a neighbor to use his own hammer—to be the C-actant and make something), rather than as a request for empowerment (comparable to asking a neighbor to lend his hammer—to the C-actant, so that the C-actant can make something). The verb *to go,* on the other hand, draws attention to someone's physical movement, in this case the mother's. For readers who have come to recognize, from the many narratives they have previously read, that mention of a character's change of position or preparations to change position often signals that character's adoption of the C-actant role (got on his horse, put on her shoes, ran to the street), the information that the mother went to her neighbor may suggest that the mother is taking on the C-actant role.

Language is also a way in which narratives guide readers to adopt a given character's perspective. Here, for instance, the baby is initially described as "a *mother's* child." Since all babies (at least initially) have mothers, the effect of the word *mother's* is not to add information about the baby but to align readers' perspective and thus sympathy with the mother whose baby is lost. Other ways that this story guides readers to share the mother's experience are the withholding by the narrator of everyone's motivations except the mother's ("In her distress"), and the selection by the narrator of the moment at which readers are introduced to the narrative world. Because the theft of the baby is presented at the beginning of the story as a *fait accompli,* as it seems to have been for the mother when she discovered it, readers share with the mother the experience of confronting a changeling in place of her child. In these diverse ways, even this brief story guides readers to consider the reported events from the mother's perspective and thus to interpret the function of events as the mother does: that the loss of the baby is a primary function-A disruptive event that must be alleviated, and that the return of the baby marks a successful resolution of the situation.

At the beginning of this chapter I introduced the definition of narrative I use: a sequential representation of sequential events. I call the sequential representation a *representation,* and the sequential events (once chronologically ordered) a *fabula.* The words of a text, the perspective from which the reported events are shown to readers (listeners, viewers), and how much and what kind of information is revealed or withheld (for instance, about characters' feelings) are aspects of the representation. A fabula includes the events that a representation either explicitly represents as having occurred or provides information that permits a reader (listener, viewer) to deduce as having occurred.[9] A fabula—as I define the term—is made by readers (listeners, viewers) from information found in a representation, or from information perceived in our world. Readers (listeners, viewers) make a fabula by assembling in chronological sequence the events they discern in a representation.

The fabula we make from the Grimms' story contains basically only four events.

(1) The baby is stolen and the changeling left in its place.
(2) The mother talks to the neighbor.
(3) The mother makes the changeling laugh.
(4) The baby is returned and the changeling taken away.

Now let us imagine a different representation of these four events—told this time from the perspective of the elves and including additional information known to the elves. In a story that I am imagining, one day the Queen of the elves confides to her most powerful minister how much she longs for a human baby to raise as her own child and heir. The minister, wanting to please her and to stabilize the kingdom by ensuring an heir, steals a baby, leaving a changeling in its place, and brings the baby to the Queen. The Queen is so pleased that she rewards the minister by naming him the baby's tutor and sets the date for a ceremony to name the baby her heir apparent—when, suddenly the baby disappears from the royal nursery and a changeling is found in its place.

Readers of this representation that I am imagining will interpret the events it shares with the Grimms' story very differently than they do when they consider those events in the context of the Grimms' story.

a   minister learns that Queen longs for a baby and heir (lower-case a represents a reevaluation of an otherwise unchanged situation)

C   minister decides to find a baby for the Queen

C' minister sets out to find a baby

G   minister arrives at a house with a baby

H   minister steals the baby and leaves a changeling in its place

I   minister brings baby to Queen

EQ Queen has a baby; minister is rewarded; the kingdom has an heir

A   baby disappears; Queen is distraught; her people are in turmoil over the succession

The events that in my imagined story express the motivating function a (the Queen's desire for a baby and the Elven kingdom's need for an heir) are not included in the story the Grimms collected, which does not explain the elves' motivation. That story begins with the report of the theft of the baby, which we interpret as function A in that story and as function H in my imagined story. In my imagined story, the mother's actions are not known; only their effect is apparent: the return of the baby. In the Grimms' story, which is told from the perspective of the mother, the baby's return is interpreted by the mother and by readers as function I: the successful result of a motivated action. But to the Queen and the Elven kingdom, the baby's return to its mother is a catastrophic loss that leaves Queen and kingdom seriously disrupted.

We see here examples of functional polyvalence that demonstrate how radically interpretations of a given event can vary, depending on the perspective from which the event is perceived and the other events and situations in relation to which it is interpreted. We interpret one event (the theft of the baby) as function A in the Grimms' story and function H in my imagined story, and another event (the return of the baby) as function I in the Grimms' story and as function A in my imagined story. Moreover, the meaning of an event is subject to interpretations that can vary for people in our world as well as for characters in fictional worlds, and also for readers (listeners, viewers). But the consequences of interpretations are not the same for readers (listeners, viewers) of fictional narratives as they are for characters in fictional worlds and people in our world.[10]

In the fictional world that the Grimms' story represents, the elves steal a child. Since theft is a purposeful act, it seems fair to assume that the elves acted purposefully (even if only to amuse themselves, or to pester humans), and succeeded. Their success, we know, is the mother's traumatic loss, which motivates her action. Her success may then reverse whatever the theft of the child accomplished for the elves. A feud, in our world or in a fictional world, illustrates the degree to which, in life as in fiction, one person's or character's successful reestablishment of an equilibrium can be interpreted by another person or character as a disruptive event that motivates further action. In fictional worlds and in our world, functional polyvalence is a motor that can generate action and endless reaction. When we stop to reflect, everyone who has acquired narrative competence understands that this is the case.

Readers of the Grimms' story, however, customarily adopt the mother's—rather than the elves'—interpretation of the theft of the child: that it is a traumatic loss that must be reversed at all costs. Presumably we interpret the events as the mother does in part because we think of the mother and baby as of our species, and of the bond between mother and baby as sacrosanct. But part of our response is determined by aspects of the representation: the alignment of the information we receive with the information the mother receives, and the withholding of information about everyone's motivation except the mother's. Even this tiny story not only tells us about something that happened but also, subtly but surely, guides our interpretation of the events it reports.

For readers (listeners, viewers) of fictional narratives, being guided to interpret the reported events from one perspective rather than another does not lead us to undertake action in the fictional world, because the ontological boundary makes that impossible. But because fictional narratives offer reports of narrative worlds about which the available information is finite,[11] fiction offers an ideal laboratory for analyzing the ways in which narrative representations shape the events they report. The vocabulary of functions brings a new specificity to studies that show that—and how—narratives shape interpretations. Understanding how fictional narratives shape our interpretations of reported events can make us more competent readers of narratives that report events in our world (in response to which we may need to act, or to refrain from acting), and more competent interpreters of the events we observe in our world (in response to which we may need to decide whether to intervene).

The one narrative we have analyzed thus far—the Grimms' story—traces a path from function A to function I. Some narratives trace paths that include a number of sequences, some just one, some less than one. There is no necessary correlation between the length of a narrative and the number of sequences its path traces. A comparison of two generic forms of the novel, the *Bildungsroman* and the picaresque novel, will show this, and will show one of the ways that paths from one equilibrium to another equilibrium vary.

A *Bildungsroman* (a novel about a character's development into adulthood) begins at a point where the protagonist (the main character), while still young, begins to be aware of herself as an individual in a world that includes other individuals, and traces that character's development to a point that she interprets as the milestone marking her entrance into the adult life for which she has been preparing: entrance to a career, earning enough money to be able to contribute to her younger siblings' education, getting married, etc. The path that a *Bildungsroman* traces, typically, is a single sequence that includes numerous recurrences of the donor events (functions D, E, and F), each of which provides for the protagonist experiences that allow her to develop the qualifications or attributes she needs to become the person she wants to be.

EQ	protagonist is comfortable in her world
a	protagonist becomes aware that she lacks attributes or qualifications she will need to accomplish her goals
C	protagonist decides to try to become the person she wants to be
C'	protagonist takes first steps (sits down to study, requests a college catalog, goes to batting practice, etc.)
$(D\ E\ F)^n$	again and again, protagonist is challenged, meets challenge, and develops in ways that help her become a person who can accomplish her goals [I use the superscript 'n' to indicate that this series of events is repeated an indeterminate number of times.]
G	protagonist reaches time and place of milestone event
H	milestone event: protagonist plays in the finals at Wimbledon, becomes a partner in a prestigious law firm, gets married, hands parents a check, etc.
I	protagonist has achieved her goal
EQ	equilibrium is reestablished

In a *Bildungsroman,* the protagonist has many experiences, all of which contribute to and enable reaching the long-term goal of becoming someone with a certain set of qualifications and attributes. A reader's interest tends to be focused on how the protagonist's experiences are changing her and helping her become a person who can accomplish her goals.

In contrast, a *picaresque* novel follows a protagonist (the *pícaro,* or rogue) who proceeds from adventure to adventure, and from place to place. Often described as "episodic," a picaresque novel typically moves from episode to episode, or, in my terms, traces a path that moves along one sequence, and then another and another sequence. Typically, the protagonist arrives in a town where he is unknown. Taking advantage of his anonymity, he engages in mildly illegal or inappropriate behavior that brings him something that he enjoys, and then he is punished. Perhaps he steals a flask of wine, or orders in a tavern a meal that he cannot pay for, or seduces a woman who is willing but married. The pleasant situation that he is enjoying (EQ) is disrupted by the townspeople's attempts to punish him. Perhaps he is put in prison, or the tavern-keeper or the woman's husband grabs a cudgel and chases after him (function A).[12] He decides to save himself (function C), then, for instance, escapes from jail or hides under a barrel (function C'), and finally gets away (function H), perhaps by stealing a horse, or hiding in a cart that is headed to another town.

The protagonist's success in getting away and reaching a town where he is unknown (function I) allows him to take advantage of his anonymity to engage in behavior that brings him something he enjoys (EQ), for which he is punished (function A). Again he escapes to another town (functions C, C', H, I) where he takes advantage of his anonymity to engage in behavior that brings him pleasure (EQ). Each new town brings the anonymity that the protagonist needs to engage in behavior that brings him pleasure; each time he is punished (function A), initiating a new sequence. The protagonist of a picaresque novel—unlike the protagonist of a *Bildungsroman*—typically does not develop his abilities as a result of his experiences. Instead, in each new town he engages in reckless actions to fulfill his immediate desires, and, when punishment is threatened, he displays the same quick strategy-planning and physical agility to escape to a new town. A reader's interest tends to be focused on the protagonist's audacity, the variety of the situations in which he becomes embroiled, and his skill in escaping an often well-deserved punishment.

Described generically, the two patterns are readily distinguished and depict contrasting personality types. Analyzed from a global perspective, a picaresque novel traces a path that includes many sequences, while a full-length *Bildungsroman* includes only one sequence. In a picaresque novel, although the protagonist engages in new experiences from sequence to sequence, he does not fundamentally change. In the *Bildungsroman,* with its single sequence that includes multiple occurrences of the donor functions (D, E, and F), the protagonist's experiences contribute to a personal development (intellectual, physical, moral, etc.) that enables meeting some larger teleological goal. (The *Bildungsroman,* not surprisingly, is the newer form, its origins generally ascribed to a late-eighteenth-century novel, Goethe's *Wilhelm Meister's Apprenticeship.*)

In practice, however, the distinction between the two forms can become a matter of interpretation. For instance, Cervantes's *Don Quixote* has been categorized by some critics as a picaresque novel and by other critics as a parody of picaresque novels. Like the picaresque rogue, Cervantes's knight falls into one problematic adventure after another, without there being any resultant fundamental change in his behavior or his view of the world. He rides from place to place, and in each place disrupts a stable situation (in the best-known example, by attacking a windmill)—a function-A disruption—escapes punishment by riding away, or is punished by being chased away, to some other place. There he again undertakes action that disrupts a stable situation (function A), thus initiating a new sequence.

But the knight's interpretation of what he is doing is quite different. From his perspective, in fact, his behavior is comparable to that of a character in a *Bildungsroman.* Imitating the knight-errants about whom he has read, Cervantes's knight rides out (function C'), motivated by his lack of fame and fortune (function a) and with the intention (function C) of bettering the world, earning fame and honor, and thereby winning the attention of the woman he renames Dulcinea. His actions are not only well intentioned but subsumed to the larger goal. When he comes upon the windmill that to his eyes appears to be a giant, he interprets the situation as a test (function D), to which he responds courageously as a good knight must (function E), expecting to earn as a result honor and glory (function F). Each subsequent adventure, from his perspective, is a further test. The two interpretations of his courageous but disruptive interventions—as function E (his interpretation) or function A—illustrate functional polyvalence. For readers, the greatness of the novel can be found in part in the tension between the two interpretations.

Joyce's *Portrait of the Artist as a Young Man* provides an example of a somewhat different interpretive issue. The novel is generally considered an example of a *Bildungsroman* (or a *Künstlerroman*, the sub-type of *Bildungsroman* in which the protagonist's goal is to become an artist). The protagonist Stephen Dedalus experiences a new set of problems in each chapter, and by the novel's conclusion he has made the decision to leave home and devote himself to working as an artist. According to this interpretation, each chapter presents a test (function D) to which Stephen responds appropriately (function E) and thereby develops or reinforces attributes (function F) that will be of use to him in his larger purpose of becoming an artist. As satisfactory as this interpretation may seem from a global perspective (for instance, to a reader who has finished reading the novel, or to a reader who read the novel some months or years previously and remembers the general outline but not the details), during the process of reading, a first-time reader who does not know how the novel will conclude, or any reader who gets caught up in the immediate problem that Stephen faces in each chapter, is likely to think of each chapter as a separate sequence. In this interpretation, each chapter of Joyce's *Portrait,* like each episode in a picaresque novel, introduces a new problem (function A), which Stephen thinks about and finally undertakes to resolve (functions C, C', H).

As these two examples indicate, the shape and the number of sequences one discerns can vary from reader to reader and from reader to character. Among readers, interpretations of how many or how few sequences a given novel or story includes are probably more varied than interpretations of the function of a given event. Different reading and interpretive situations lend themselves at times to a global view (to see a novel as one extended sequence) and at times to recognizing local detail (an event as small as answering the telephone can be interpreted as an entire sequence that is initiated by the ringing, which creates a function-A disruption). Context matters; in certain contexts, even answering a telephone can effect global change. But a variation in interpretations of the shape and the number of sequences by no means invalidates the usefulness of analyzing the varying interpretations. On the contrary, subdividing a material is an important step in the process of understanding it. Analyzing the number of sequences that readers

discern, and locating the signposts that readers interpret as indications that a new sequence is beginning, offers a means to investigate the thought processes readers adopt in response to narratives.[13]

In the only narrative form we have considered that includes multiple sequences (the picaresque novel), sequences follow one another sequentially, one after the other. When sequences are combined
sequentially, either the event that resolves one sequence initiates a
new sequence (the event that we interpret as function I we then reinterpret as function A), or, as in the picaresque novel, as soon as one
sequence is resolved, some new event (that we interpret as function
A) disrupts the incipient equilibrium and initiates a new sequence.
Tzvetan Todorov recognized, both in his book on the *Decameron*
(*Grammaire du Décaméron,* 68–69) and in his earlier analysis of
the novel *Les Liaisons dangereuses* ("Les Catégories du récit littéraire," 140–41), that there were three patterns in which multiple
sequences could be represented in a linear medium like language,
which listeners and readers can grasp only one word (sentence,
paragraph) at a time. In addition to a *sequential* pattern in which
one sequence is followed by another ("Enchaînement"), Todorov
described patterns of *alternating* sequences ("Alternance") and
embedded sequences ("Enchâssement").

In an alternating pattern, a segment of one sequence is followed
by a segment of a second sequence, which is followed by another
segment of the first sequence, and then another segment of the second sequence, and so on. A pattern of alternating sequences is
often used to tell two characters' stories occurring at different
times (a daughter's experiences as a teenager, her mother's experiences as a teenager, the daughter's experiences in her twenties, her
mother's experiences in her twenties, the daughter's experiences in
her thirties, her mother's experiences in her thirties); two characters' stories occurring at the same time (but perhaps in different
cities); or one character's experiences as an adult interspersed with
that character's experiences as a child. In Tolstoy's *Anna
Karenina*—considered from a global perspective—one sequence
follows Anna's and Vronsky's developing relationship, and another sequence follows Kitty's and Levin's developing relationship.
Throughout the novel, sections on Anna's and Vronsky's activities
alternate with sections on Kitty's and Levin's activities.

In the third pattern, embedding, one sequence is included within another sequence: a segment of a first sequence (a framing
sequence) is followed by an entire second sequence, after which

the first sequence (the framing sequence) concludes. In Chaucer's *Canterbury Tales,* all the stories that the pilgrims tell are embedded within the framing sequence. In the framing sequence, the tedium of riding silently is the motivating function-a situation. The group decision by the pilgrims to amuse themselves and relieve the tedium by telling stories is function C. (Since all the pilgrims decide to participate in the storytelling designed to relieve the function-a tedium, *The Canterbury Tales* offers an example of a joint C-actant, all of them working together to accomplish a common goal.) The pilgrims draw lots (function C') to determine the order in which they will tell their stories. And then the Knight, who is selected as the first speaker, begins to tell his story (function H_1), and one by one the other pilgrims tell their stories (H_2, H_3, H_4, etc.). Generally, when a framing sequence represents a situation of storytelling, the embedded stories that characters tell express function H (the C-actant's primary action) in the framing sequence.

The three patterns Todorov discerned are sometimes found in combination. In *The Arabian Nights,* Scheherazade's stories, like Chaucer's pilgrims' stories, express function H in the framing sequence. (The king's practice of requiring that a virgin be brought to him every evening, then executing her the next morning, expresses function A. Scheherazade decides—function C—to try to stop the practice, and begins to act—function C'—by arranging that her sister Dunyazade will be brought to the bedchamber and will ask Scheherazade to tell a story.) But many of the stories that Scheherazade tells also embed other stories, forming a pattern of a sequence in a sequence in a sequence.[14] According to Todorov's analysis of *Les liaisons dangereuses,* that novel includes two alternating sequences (the story of Tourvel and the story of Cecile), which are both embedded within the story of the couple Merteuil-Valmont ("Les Catégories du récit littéraire," 140).

■

To conclude this first chapter that is intended to serve as an introduction to all the subsequent chapters, I return to the idea with which this chapter began: that *meaning* (in the sense that I use the term) is an interpretation of the causal relations between an event and the other events and situations one thinks of as related. Brian Richardson discerns the close relationship between interpretation and causality: "In many respects, interpretation and causality are two sides of the same coin. Confronted by multiple and mutually exclusive explanatory options, characters and readers alike are impelled to weigh the evidence, take hermeneutical stands, and adjust prior expectations to meet anomalous incidents" (*Unlikely Stories: Causality and the Nature of Modern Narrative,* 43). It can be argued (it has been argued) that causality *is* an interpretation, and even that causality is an invention to give meaning to otherwise meaningless activities.[15]

In an early contribution to contemporary studies of historiography, "'Plain' and 'Significant' Narrative in History," W. H. Walsh distinguishes between "description and elucidation," between "establishing facts [and] establishing connections" (483), between "the chronicle [and] history proper," or, in the terms he introduces, between "'plain' and 'significant' narrative in history" (479). Investigating, as he puts it, "in a provisional way, what the historian is concerned with and what he hopes to achieve" (479), Walsh considers:

> the two possibilities that historical narrative might be "plain" or "significant." The adjectives . . . suggest . . . (a) a description of the facts restricted to a straightforward statement of what occurred, (b) an account of them which brought out their connections. If historians were content with plain narrative they would, I thought, confine themselves to stating . . ."precisely what happened"; if their aim was rather to produce the sort of narrative I call "significant" they would seek to make clear not only what happened, but why it happened too. I had, and have, no doubt that the second alternative is correct. (480)

For Walsh, a "plain" historical narrative, like the chronicle, reports sequential events, and a "significant" historical narrative explores causal relations ("why it happened") too.

As Walsh points out, not every narrative (a sequential representation of sequential events) includes indications of causality—although readers (listeners, viewers) will strive to locate causal relations, I suggest, and, failing to do so, will generally soon lose interest. Let us take as an example this short narrative:

> John went to the party. While he was there he talked to Mary, Nancy, and Elizabeth, and then he went home.

Given only this information, we have no reason to think that a prevailing situation has changed or is about to change. We can label the prevailing situation an equilibrium (EQ). Probably we are not very interested in John or Mary or Nancy or Elizabeth. Of course, if we happen to know that John suffers from agoraphobia (a function-A situation), we will interpret his attendance at the party as a motivated (function C) and successful (functions C', H, I) endeavor on his part to overcome his malady. Or if we learn that Elizabeth, when she was talking to John, told him that her husband, Ed, John's best friend, had stayed home to try to repair the clogged drain in the kitchen sink, we may interpret John's departure as function C' and assume that he has gone to help Ed open the drain (function H). Or, if we find out that among the early guests at the party was John's ex-wife, Frances, whom he had recently divorced, then we may interpret John's arrival at the party—at least from Frances's perspective—as a disruptive event (function A_1), exacerbated by his departure without speaking to her (function A_2). Any information that guides us to explore causal relations arguably makes a narrative more interesting as well as more meaningful.[16]

While Walsh recognizes that historical narratives may address either what happened or what happened and why it happened too, he calls for the latter procedure, deeming the combination of what and why "significant." Similarly, the ability that readers (listeners, viewers) of narratives develop to make sense of a reported sequence of events—narrative competence—requires analyzing not only the chronological but also the causal relations among the reported events. The element that, according to Walsh, makes historical narrative "significant"—the connections between events—is the element that functions name. For historians, for individuals perceiving events in our world, for characters perceiving events in fictional worlds, and for readers (listeners, viewers) of narratives, meaning is an interpretation of the causal relations among a chronologically ordered sequence of events. Functions offer a uniform vocabulary to denote these interpretations—inside and outside of narratives, at any ontological level.

A uniform vocabulary permits comparisons that illuminate differences in interpretations. In studies of narratives and in analyses of events in the world, a vocabulary of functions offers a means to explore the functional polyvalence of events and to show the degree to which, even when events can be known, their meanings may diverge. In studies of narratives, a vocabulary of functions allows analysts (1) to compare and contrast perceivers' and narrators' and characters' interpretations of causal relations among events; (2) to trace when, and whether, shifts in interpretation occur in response to new information, whether by perceivers, characters, or narrators; (3) to analyze and contrast the varying patterns of sequences and of key and additional functions in sequences that specific narratives take; and (4), most broadly, to investigate the ways in which narratives by representing events in a context inevitably shape interpretations of those events.

Narrative studies is a mature discipline that has developed a broad and sophisticated body of work to elucidate narrative as a mode of communication, and to analyze how individual narratives communicate. My theory of functions focuses on only one aspect of narrative communication—how interpretations of causality vary and how representations shape interpretations of causality—and can complement, but certainly not replace, other approaches to narrative analysis. Admittedly, too, there are nuances to causal relations that a vocabulary of ten functions cannot represent. In addition, I have selected the ten functions I define because of their recurrence in mainly nineteenth- and twentieth-century narratives from Western cultures. I have looked at the causal relations in narratives from other cultures and eras only enough to ascertain that, in certain cases, patterns that differ from the range of patterns I analyze in this book will sometimes be found. The ten functions, however, I think can be used to express those differences. Even more problematic is that any terminology, once introduced, can shape not only expression but thought. Functions nonetheless provide a powerful tool to explore interpretations of events perceived sequentially, and the shaping of those interpretations by sequential representation.

CHAPTER 2

THE PRINCESS AND THE PEA(S):

Two Versions, Different Causalities

Both Hans Christian Andersen and the Brothers Grimm collected and published in slightly different versions the familiar tale about a princess who cannot sleep because of the pea(s) under her many mattresses.[1] Telling more or less the same story but telling it differently, and with different effects, the two versions illustrate some of the ways that a representation—the way that events are recounted—can affect interpretations of causality. In response to either of the two tellings, readers will construct a similar fabula (the chronologically ordered sequence of events that perceivers make in response to a representation). But the two representations elicit different interpretations of which characters are responsible for the successful outcome and, more generally, of the apparent power structure in the narrative world in which the characters exist and act.[2]

The fabulas that readers construct from the two tellings are almost identical. In both fabulas, a prince desires to marry a princess. Initial efforts to locate a princess are unsuccessful, but a princess finally arrives. The king greets her. The queen devises a test to prove that she is a princess. In the end, the prince has found his princess. As similar as the two fabulas are, however, readers' interpretations of which characters' agency brings about the happy ending and which characters wield the most power in the narrative world will vary according to whether they are reading the Grimms' version or Andersen's version. Analyzing and comparing readers' interpretations of the function of events in the two stories illuminates the degree to which, and some of the means by which, a representation guides readers' (listeners', viewers') interpretations of causality.

27

Let us look first at Andersen's "The Princess and the Pea" (translated by Erik Christian Haugaard):

> Once upon a time there was a prince who wanted to marry a princess, but she would have to be a real one. He traveled around the whole world looking for her; but every time he met a princess there was always something amiss. There were plenty of princesses but not one of them was quite to his taste. Something was always the matter: they just weren't real princesses. So he returned home very sad and sorry, for he had set his heart on marrying a real princess.

The story continues:

> One evening a storm broke over the kingdom. The lightning flashed, the thunder roared, and the rain came down in bucketfuls. In the midst of this horrible storm, someone knocked on the city gate; and the king himself went down to open it.
>
> On the other side of the gate stood a princess. But goodness, how wet she was! Water ran down her hair and her clothes in streams. It flowed in through the heels of her shoes and out through the toes. But she said that she was a real princess.
>
> "We'll find that out quickly enough," thought the old queen, but she didn't say a word out loud. She hurried to the guest room and took all the bedclothes off the bed; then on the bare bedstead she put a pea. On top of the pea she put twenty mattresses; and on top of the mattresses, twenty eiderdown quilts. That was the bed on which the princess had to sleep.
>
> In the morning, when someone asked her how she had slept, she replied, "Oh, just wretchedly! I didn't close my eyes once, the whole night through. God knows what was in that bed; but it was something hard, and I am black and blue all over."
>
> Now they knew that she was a real princess, since she had felt the pea that was lying on the bedstead through twenty mattresses and twenty eiderdown quilts. Only a real princess could be so sensitive!
>
> The prince married her. The pea was exhibited in the royal museum; and you can go there and see it, if it hasn't been stolen.
>
> Now that was a real story! (20–21)

Andersen's story begins by reporting the prince's desire for a princess. If we interpret the prince's desire as a function a, we are saying that we assume that his desire for a princess will motivate intentional action designed to satisfy his desire. The difference between the two types of motivating A functions is that an upper-case function A represents an event that changes the narrative world, while a lower-case function a represents a reevaluation—a change in perception—of an otherwise unchanged narrative world. If the prince had lost his wife, the narrative world would have changed, and we would interpret the event as function A. But in "The Princess and the Pea," the prince's world has not changed. He has not lost a wife; he has reached a stage in his life in which he realizes that he would like to have a wife. So we interpret his desire to marry as creating a lower-case function-a situation.

Andersen's prince is a C-actant. Wanting a princess, he decides to find one, and begins his search. In the analysis below, I bracket function C because we infer that he has decided to act from the actions we are told that he takes:

a   prince wants to marry a real princess
[C] prince decides to find himself a real princess
C'   prince travels, looking for a real princess

Once the prince leaves to look for a princess, most readers assume that he will find one (function H), marry her (function I), and thereby achieve a new equilibrium (Eq)—an equilibrium that is similar but not identical to the one that was disrupted when he realized that he wanted to marry a princess. But Andersen's prince cannot locate a princess.

In the comparison I drew in chapter 1 between the picaresque novel and the *Bildungsroman,* I distinguished between C-actants who, when they make the decision to act (function C), already have the power (skills, strength, knowledge, money, maturity, etc.) to accomplish their endeavor, and C-actants who undertake action (function C) without yet being sufficiently competent to accomplish it. In the former case much of the representation is generally devoted to the events of function H: direct action to alter the function-A situation. In the latter, some—and sometimes most—of the representation is devoted to events designed to empower the C-actant: the acquisition in a fairy tale of a magical talisman, the events of a *Bildungsroman* that lead to increased maturity.

Events that are designed to empower the C-actant to accomplish function H are interpreted by the functions of the donor section (functions D, E, and F). Function F marks the C-actant's acquisition of the power to accomplish function H. Function F_{neg} marks the C-actant's inability to acquire power needed to accomplish function H. Andersen's prince returns home, having discovered that he lacks the ability (F_{neg}) to find a real princess. The process of resolution toward a new equilibrium comes to a stop before the motivating function-a situation has been resolved. Moreover, at the end of the first paragraph, Andersen's story reiterates (even more emphatically than it is initially stated) that the prince is "very sad and sorry, for he had set his heart on marrying a real princess"—reminding readers that the initiating function-a situation remains unresolved.

    a   prince wants to marry a real princess
    [C] prince decides to find one: prince is C-actant
    C'   prince travels, looking for a real princess
    F_{neg} prince cannot locate a real princess
    a   prince still wants to marry a real princess

As Andersen's story continues, three characters' actions empower the prince to accomplish his primary endeavor (function H): to find a real princess. A princess arrives, the king opens the gate to admit her, and the queen provides the pea and the pea test to discern a real princess. As a result, the process of resolution can continue and a new equilibrium can be established.

    a   prince wants to marry a real princess
    [C] prince decides to find one: prince is C-actant
    C'   prince travels, looking for a real princess
    F_{neg} prince cannot locate a real princess
    F_1 princess arrives
    F_2 king admits princess
    F_3 queen provides pea and pea test to verify princesses
    H   prince marries princess, and enshrines pea in museum
    I   prince has a princess, and a pea to test princesses
    Eq equilibrium is restored

As a result of the actions of his prospective bride and both parents, the prince succeeds in satisfying his desire to marry a real princess. The pea, as I interpret it, is a talisman that empowers the possessor to discern a real princess. Handed down from mother to son, and enshrined in the royal museum where the prince will always have access to it, the pea enables the prince in the future, should the need arise, to discern a real princess without further assistance from the queen.[3] By the end of the story, according to this interpretation, the prince has acquired what we might describe as a mature level of discernment (function F), as well as satisfying his desire for a real princess (functions H and I).

Andersen's prince is ultimately successful, but his satisfaction is achieved only with the help of every other character mentioned in the story. Nor are the contributions of the other three characters presented as equal. When Andersen's prince traveled to look for a bride, we remember, he found many princesses, but he could not find a real princess. Thus the arrival of a princess and the king's admitting her into the city (functions F_1 and F_2) merely replicate the portion of the undertaking that the prince has been able to accomplish. To complete the undertaking, the princess must also be deemed real. This is what the queen accomplishes. The way Andersen's story is told guides readers to focus their attention on the queen's actions, more than the princess's or the king's.

The perspective from which Andersen's story is told remains situated in the vicinity of the prince—leaving when he does, and after he returns staying firmly within the gates—thereby suppressing all information about how and why the princess arrived at the gate, and why in this instance the king opens the gate himself. But Andersen's story reports motivations twice: the prince's in the first sentence (his desire to marry a princess), and the queen's in the fourth paragraph. As we have seen, the knowledge that the prince wants to marry a princess guides readers to interpret his journey to look for a princess as a C-actant's motivated action. The effect of information about the queen's thoughts, for many readers, is similar. Immediately after we learn that the very wet princess claims to be a real princess, we read: "'We'll find that out quickly enough,' thought the old queen." Knowing the queen's thoughts guides many readers to interpret her subsequent behavior as motivated action to test the validity of the princess's claim.

a_2 princess's claim may be invalid
C queen decides to discern whether princess is real
C' queen's first act (she keeps quiet, careful not to reveal her plan)
G queen enters bedroom—where H is to occur
H queen uses pea to test princess
I queen successfully tests princess (princess is real)

The queen's sequence reaches a successful conclusion, but the story continues. Now that the princess has been determined to be a real princess, the prince takes her as his wife, and puts the pea in a museum, completing the initiating a_1 sequence. As I interpret the causal relations of the events as Andersen reports them, the queen's a_2 sequence provides the final empowerment the prince needs to complete his a_1 sequence; the queen's sequence in its entirety is embedded as function F in the prince's sequence.

a_1 prince desires a princess
C   prince decides to find one (prince is C-actant)
C'   prince travels, looking for princesses
F_{neg} prince cannot discern a real princess
F_1 princess arrives
F_2 king admits princess
F_3 queen's a_2 sequence proves princess is real:

> a_2 princess's claim may be invalid
> C   queen decides to discern whether princess is real
> C' queen's first act (she keeps quiet, careful not to reveal her plan)
> G   queen enters bedroom—where H is to occur
> H   queen uses pea to test princess
> I   queen successfully tests princess (princess is real)

H   prince marries princess and enshrines pea in museum
I   prince has a princess (and the means to find another)
Eq   equilibrium is restored

As we have seen, readers' interpretations of causal relations are guided by the specific words of a text (the reiteration at the end of the first paragraph, for instance, of the prince's continuing desire), and the perspective through which readers are permitted to perceive the events (Andersen's narrator knows and reveals the motivations of the prince and the queen, but either does not know or suppresses the other characters' thoughts). Other textual strategies that accentuate or de-emphasize specific events and the effects of characters' actions include the sequence in which events are reported in a given representation, and the respective duration of events in the telling.[4] In Andersen's story the importance of the prince's role is emphasized by being reported at the very beginning. But after the first paragraph, the prince's actions are mentioned in only one further sentence near the end of the story: "The prince married her." The queen's test and its results, on the other hand, fill three full paragraphs.

As I interpret the causal relations in Andersen's story, the prince is a C-actant who does do something toward accomplishing his goal (he searches, and he gives credence to the results of his mother's test). But his role as a C-actant is de-emphasized by the assistance he receives from his parents and his future bride, and particularly by the emphasis that Andersen's story gives to the queen's role by revealing her motivation and by devoting three paragraphs of this very short story to describing her actions and their successful results. If Andersen's prince is a C-actant, his position as such is not unique; he is one of two. In addition, the centrality of his role is less the result of anything he himself does than of the suppression in the representation of information about the king's and the princess's motivations, and of the subordination of the queen's motivated action to enabling the prince to complete his undertaking.

Andersen's prince is no traditional hero. He leaves home, but returns defeated and in despair. Only at home, under the aegis of his parents—where his father can open doors, and his mother can use her magic talisman to show him that the locally available woman is a real princess—can he mature and begin to establish his own household. From what we see of his kingdom, it is small and family centered: a domestic world in which a woman can play a significant, if ultimately subsidiary, role. But the narrative world in which this family experiences the younger generation's transition to adulthood is still nominally a patriarchy. With his bride and his pea in his possession, Andersen's prince is in on his way to becoming a king.

■

With only a couple of exceptions, the version that Jacob and Wilhelm Grimm published as "The Pea Test" (translated by Jack Zipes) reveals the same fabula as Andersen's version, but the Grimms' story is likely to elicit from readers a much different interpretation of which characters' agency brings about the successful conclusion and of how the hierarchy of power in the narrative world is structured.

> Once upon a time there was a king whose only son was very
> eager to get married, and he asked his father for a wife.
> "Your wish shall be fulfilled, my son," said the king, "but

it's only fitting that you marry no one less than a princess, and there are none to be had in the vicinity. Therefore, I shall issue a proclamation and perhaps a princess will come from afar."

Soon a written proclamation was circulated, and it did not take long before numerous princesses arrived at the court. Almost every day a new one appeared, but when the princesses were asked about their birth and lineage, it always turned out that they were not princesses at all, and they were sent away without having achieved their purpose.

"If everything continues like this," the son said, "I'll never get a wife in the end."

"Calm yourself, my son," said the queen. "Before you know it, she'll be here. Happiness is often standing just outside the door. One only needs to open it."

And it was really just as the queen had predicted.

Soon after, on a stormy evening when the wind and rain were beating on the windows, there was a loud knocking on the gate of the royal palace. The servants opened the gate, and a beautiful maiden entered. She demanded to be led directly before the king, who was surprised by such a late visit and asked her where she had come from, who she was, and what she desired.

"I've come from a distant country," she answered, "and I'm the daughter of a mighty king. When your proclamation with the portrait of your son arrived in my father's kingdom, I felt a strong love for your son and immediately set out on my way with the intention of becoming his bride."

"I'm somewhat skeptical about what you've told me," said the king. "Besides, you don't look like a princess. Since when does a princess travel alone without an escort and in such poor clothes?"

"An escort would have only delayed me," she replied. "The color of my clothes faded in the sun, and the rain washed it out completely. If you don't believe I'm a princess, just send a messenger to my father."

"That's too far and too complicated," said the king. "A delegation cannot ride as fast as you. The people must have the necessary time for such a journey. Years would pass before they returned. If you can't prove in some other way that you're a princess, then fortune will not shine upon you, and you'd do well to head for home, the sooner the better."

"Let her stay," the queen said. "I'll put her to a test and know soon enough whether she's a princess."

The queen herself climbed up into the tower and had a bed made up for the maiden in a splendid room. When the mattress was carried into the room, she placed three peas on it, one on top, one in the middle, and one below. Then six other soft mattresses were stacked on top along with linen sheets and a cover made of eiderdown. When everything was ready, she led the maiden upstairs into the bedroom.

"After such a long trip, you must be tired, my child," she said. "Get some sleep. Tomorrow we'll continue talking."

At the break of day the queen climbed up to the room in the tower. She thought the maiden would still be in a deep sleep, but the maiden was awake.

"How did you sleep, my little daughter?" she asked.

"Miserably," replied the princess. "I couldn't sleep a wink the whole night."

"Why, my child? Wasn't the bed good enough?"

"In all my days I've never lain in such a bed. It was hard from my head to my feet. It seemed as if I were lying on nothing but peas."

"Now I know for sure," said the queen, "that you're a genuine princess. I shall send some royal garments up to you with pearls and jewels. Dress yourself as a bride, for we shall celebrate your wedding this very day." (2: 377–78)

Like Andersen's "The Princess and the Pea," the Grimms' "The Pea Test" begins by revealing the prince's desire for a princess (function a). But in the Grimms' version, the prince does not leave home to look for one. This is the main difference in the fabulas of the two versions—that Andersen's prince travels to find a princess (even though his traveling does not contribute to finding one), whereas the Grimms' prince stays home. Differences between the two representations also, however, contribute right from the beginning to establishing the character of the prince differently. In Andersen's story the prince is described as determined to marry only a real princess, whereas in the Grimms' story the prince asks for a wife and it is the king who introduces the requirement that the prince's bride must be a princess. In addition, in Andersen's version the prince is called the "prince." In the Grimms' version, the young man in question is designated throughout in relation to one or the other of his parents; he is introduced as the "only son" of a king, called "my son" by the queen, and described as "your

son" by the princess when she is speaking to the king. In the Grimms'
story, the word "prince" does not occur.

Denoting the prince only as someone's son, as the Grimms' version does, can be interpreted by readers as indicating, on the part
of the prince, the same lack of independence that is suggested by
his asking for a wife and then doing nothing further to acquire
one. Andersen's prince, after all, however unprepared he is at the
time and however unsuccessful his efforts are, leaves home to look
for a princess. Interpreting his actions as functions, we saw
Andersen's prince as a C-actant who undertook (at least in the
beginning) to find himself a wife. The Grimms' prince is not a C-
actant.

The Grimms' story illustrates a narrative path that includes
function B. In many narratives, a character who is affected by, or
knows about, a function-A (or function-a) event decides to try to
ameliorate the situation and in doing so becomes a C-actant.
Andersen's story is an example. In other narratives, a character
who is affected by a function-A (or function-a) event, or knows
about a function-A (or function-a) event, requests another character to be the C-actant and to attempt to ameliorate the situation.
That request that someone else be a C-actant expresses function B.
The Grimms' prince, instead of riding off to find a bride, asks his
father to provide one. The function of the proclamation the king
issues—its effect in forwarding the action—is to amplify the
prince's request, so that it can be heard at a greater distance. We
interpret the proclamation as a second function B: a request that
a princess come from afar to be the wife of the prince.

a   prince desires a wife
B_1 prince asks king for a wife
B_2 king issues proclamation requesting a princess

There is as yet no C-actant. Narrative logic leads us to assume that
a C-actant will emerge from among the distant peoples whom the
king's proclamation reaches.

As a result, when potential princesses begin to arrive, we
assume that they do so in response to the king's function-B proclamation. Logically, this means that each of the false princesses, having heard the king's proclamation, has decided (function C) that
she wants to marry the prince, and has set out to travel to the
court (function C'). But the Grimms' story guides us in recognizing that these princesses are not real princesses by suppressing

every indication of their function-C and function-C' intentional acts. In the analysis below, I bracket functions C and C' to indicate that the events they represent are not mentioned in the story. I interpret the arrival of the princesses at the court as function G, the test by which they attempt to prove their princesshood as function H, and their failure as function I_{neg}. Because numerous princesses arrive and fail, I put the whole sequence in parentheses and indicate by the superscript "n" an indeterminate number of recurrences.

a	prince desires a wife
B_1	prince asks king for a wife
B_2	king issues proclamation requesting a princess
$([C, C'] \, G \, H \, I_{neg})^n$	numerous princesses arrive and fail

The Grimms' representation shifts at this point to scenic treatment (unlike Andersen's version in which the only words spoken aloud are those the princess speaks when she describes the terrible effects of the pea), and includes two scenes that Andersen's version does not include: the prince's petulant outburst to his mother and the king's interview with the princess. Neither scene moves the situation toward resolution—the prince's because he merely complains; the king's because his test for princesses proves invalid—but both scenes provide the kind of information that scenic treatment generally provides. By being permitted to hear characters' conversations among themselves, readers gain information about the characters' personalities and values and how they interact with each other.

The prince's outburst, in the fourth paragraph, reminds us that the initial function-a situation is still in effect: the prince continues to want a wife. But the scene also permits the introduction of the queen, giving us, as our first view of her, her interaction with her son, whom she placates by assuring him that his bride will soon arrive. The narrator's confirmation that it was "just as [she] predicted" inspires readers' belief in the queen's wisdom and guides readers to expect immediate progress toward resolving the function-a situation. Given this information, when a beautiful maiden enters (function G), we have no doubt that she is the C-actant who will be successful. And in fact, during her interview with the king, the princess tells her story in words that reveal her C-actant role: after the proclamation and the accompanying portrait of the prince arrived (function B), she explains, "I felt a strong love for your son [function C, the decision] and immediately set out on my way [function C'] with the intention of becoming his bride."

a	prince desires a wife
B_1	prince asks king for a wife
B_2	king issues proclamation requesting a princess
$([C, C'] \, G \, H \, I_{neg})^n$	numerous princesses arrive and fail
C	princess feels love for prince (princess is C-actant)
C'	princess sets out for court
G	princess arrives at court (where H is to occur)

Like the prince's outburst, the scene in which the king interviews the princess to test her (function H_1) does not move the situation toward resolution, but it offers readers an opportunity to hear about the difficulties of the princess's long journey and her motivation for undertaking it, and also to learn something about the king. The princess fails the king's test (function I_{neg}), not as a result of any lack on her part but rather because of the king's limited powers of discernment. The princess fails the king's test because the king is too distracted by her faded clothes to understand her amazing accomplishment or even to pay attention to her explanation for the way she is dressed. "The color of my clothes," she says, "faded in the sun, and the rain washed it out completely." The story reaches a successful completion because the queen's test, which ensues, permits the princess to prove her princesshood by her inability to sleep on peas (function H_2). At this point the queen pronounces her a genuine princess (function I), and promises her clothes for the wedding.

a	prince desires a wife
B_1	prince asks king for a wife
B_2	king issues proclamation requesting a princess
$([C, C'] \, G \, H \, I_{neg})^n$	numerous princesses arrive and fail
C	princess feels love for prince (princess is C-actant)
C'	princess sets out for court
G	princess arrives at court (where H is to occur)

H_1	king tests princess
I_{neg}	princess fails king's test
H_2	queen tests princess
I	princess proclaimed a princess (wedding to occur, prince will have a wife)

But while the conclusion of the story leaves no doubt that the wedding will take place, the Grimms' version stops before the wedding occurs. Instead of a wedding, the final scene is a private meeting between the princess and the queen, in which the queen promises the princess royal garments and jewels—those signs of princesshood that are the only ones that the king, we remember, is able to read. By stopping at this point, the representation that the Grimms write emphasizes the women's roles. Whereas Andersen's version ends with a wedding and an enshrined pea, and a prince who has needed help but by the end of the story has made great strides toward achieving maturity, the Grimms' version concludes with what I read as the queen's move to ensure the king's approval of the princess she has selected, and perhaps a symbolic offer by the queen to share with the princess her power to manipulate the king and the prince, along with the clothes and jewels that are the visible signs of her power.

Further supporting the importance of the women's roles in the Grimms' version is the early disappearance from the text of the prince, who does not reappear after the fifth paragraph, and of the king, whom we do not see again after the eleventh of the twenty paragraphs. In addition, the scenic treatment in the Grimms' version lets readers observe both the prince's petulance and the king's inability to discern a princess, and also the positive attributes the women display. The queen's wisdom, in contrast to the king's lack of discernment, permits her to construct a test for princesses that is accepted as valid. The princess displays the feminine softness that is traditionally a requisite of princesses, and also the traditionally masculine traits of decisiveness, courage, and endurance, which she demonstrates in her journey to the court.

The biggest difference between Andersen's version and the Grimms' version is that in the latter the princess's motivation is revealed, and, as a result, readers interpret her behavior as that of a C-actant. The difference between the two versions is not in the princess's actions, I emphasize, but in how the two stories are told and how, as a result of the different reporting strategies, readers interpret the functions of events. In both versions, when the

princess arrives she is unrecognized, and wet. From this information readers of both versions can construct a fabula in which a
princess has traveled from some other place and through a storm.

In Andersen's version, the narrator summarizes the princess's
statements, reporting only that she claimed to be a real princess.
Readers are given no information about why she was outside the
gates of this particular city during this particular storm. In the
Grimms' version, the scenic treatment of the new arrival's interview with the king permits readers to hear how the princess
explains her presence to the king. Only in the Grimms' version are
readers, first, guided to expect the arrival of a princess by the
king's function-B proclamation that invites one to come from afar,
and, second, allowed to hear the princess tell that, motivated by
the prince's portrait that accompanied the proclamation, she had
fallen in love with the prince and traveled to the palace to be his
bride. The two versions illustrate the effect that information about
motivation can have on a reader's (or a perceiver's) interpretation
of the function of an event. Readers of Andersen's story do not
know why the princess arrived at so fortuitous a moment, and
may choose to explain it as a happy accident, as supernaturally
inspired, or as motivated by the princess's or someone else's
knowledge that the prince lacks a wife. The information about
motivation that the Grimms' readers are given guides readers to
contemplate a highly motivated, courageous princess.

■

As differently as Andersen's version and the Grimms' version
shape readers' interpretations of the princess's role, let us imagine
yet another version: a third version that reveals exactly the same
fabula as the Grimms' version, but that emphasizes the princess's
C-actant role by providing information about her experiences as
she traveled. To distinguish the C-actant in instances in which two
characters leave home, Vladimir Propp advises, "the route followed by the story and on which the action is developed is actually the route of the seeker [the C-actant, in my terminology]"
(*Morphology of the Folktale*, 39). In the third version I am imagining, the events will be reported in the sequence in which the
princess experiences them. Seeing the prince's portrait she is
entranced and immediately sets out. Day by day and difficulty
after difficulty, the third version will follow the route of the
princess during her journey, lingering over her repeated exposure

to the sun and the rain—information that the Grimms' version includes but only as a summary, to explain the state of the princess's faded clothes.

An account that, by leaving the court and following the princess's route, emphasized the difficulties of her journey would draw readers' attention to the events that express functions C and C', permitting readers to perceive the softness the princess demonstrates in the pea incident as even more amazing in contrast to the discomfort we would be aware that she had recently borne. Such an account would strengthen readers' recognition of the princess's function-C intent, and the effectiveness of her intentional acts in satisfying the prince's and the king's need for a princess to come from afar. I introduce this imagined third version to show that, while the Grimms' version provides information about the princess's motivation and her journey, and Andersen's does not, the Grimms' version by no means emphasizes the princess's C-actant role as much as it could. In the Grimms' version the narrator's perspective is spatially restricted to the cloistered locus of the court. The one glimpse we are permitted of the outside world comes from the princess herself, when she tells the king her story in her own words. The account that we are allowed to hear her tell, moreover, is both modestly undetailed (suppressing the painful experiences of the journey that in a sentimental account would draw an emotional response) and retrospective (removing suspense and the emotions readers would feel while waiting to learn whether she would arrive safely).

Instead of emphasizing the princess's heroism and enhancing readers' concern for her in these ways, the Grimms' version moves on immediately from her interview with the king to the scene in which the queen prepares and carries out her test for princesses. In contrast to the two paragraphs in which the princess talks to the king about her journey, the Grimms' version devotes the last nine of its twenty paragraphs to describing sequentially the stages of the test by which the queen determines that the princess is real. The princess's only reported activity in this section is her statement that she was unable to sleep, whereas the queen is the active figure who watches over the preparations, the test, and its results. In addition, the Grimms' version ends before the princess is given the promised finery. If we envision the concluding scene as if it were staged, the queen in her appropriate garb is the dominant figure; the princess has only her faded clothes.

The Grimms' version distracts readers' attention from the

princess's C-actant role and enhances the queen's role in two very effective ways. The first, as we have seen, is the long duration that is accorded to the queen's test in the representation and the placement of the test as the final scene. The second is by suggesting—by enabling speculation—that the queen is a C-actant too. The queen's speech to the prince in the fifth paragraph, in which she tells him that a princess will soon arrive, suggests a motivation that we have not considered. If we conceive her words as revealing an intent (function C) to ensure that the prince will have a bride, then we can interpret her test for princesses as function H: a ritual designed to anoint the next young woman who arrives, whoever she is, as princess and bride. According to this reading this queen—like Andersen's queen—can be perceived as a C-actant (although this queen would be motivated by her son's desire for a bride, while Andersen's queen is motivated by her desire to prove whether the princess's claim to be a real princess is true). For readers who interpret the Grimms' queen as a C-actant, then resolution is effected by the motivated action of *two* C-actants: the queen and the princess. But the Grimms' version is admittedly ambiguous in regard to the queen's intent. While her words to her son offer reassurance that a princess will soon arrive, she does not say that she *intends* to ensure that the next princess who arrives will be deemed a real princess. The narrative allows thoughtful readers to interpret the queen's actions in two ways.

But in either case—given either interpretation—the Grimms' version de-emphasizes the princess's role by suppressing the events of her journey and emphasizes the queen's role by providing the details of the pea test, thus underscoring the complementary nature of the two women's contributions to bringing about the successful outcome. In fact, the Grimms' version shifts readers' attention from a princess with extraordinary abilities to the value of collective action within a household by women who support each other's goals. In Andersen's version, the prince needs the assistance that each of the other three characters provides, but Andersen's story represents a relatively traditional view of the location of power in the world. With the assistance he receives, Andersen's prince seems prepared to become a responsible leader. In the Grimms' more subversive telling of almost the same fabula, the women's roles are larger than the men's. The king and his son are no match for these two women. The view of the location of power that the Grimms' version represents, as I read it, is that, at least within the household, there is no limit to what competent and courageous women working together can bring about. Analyzing the interpretations of the function of events that readers reach in response to stories that report almost the same fabula provides a way to demonstrate some of the ways and the degree to which a representation can affect interpretations of causality.

CHAPTER 3

NONCHRONOLOGICAL NARRATION:

Poe's "The Assignation" and Browning's "My Last Duchess"

In the first half of the nineteenth century, the effects of Romanticism include a new interest in the variety of human experience and in the strong emotional response that uncommon and extraordinary events can elicit—directly, in someone who experiences them, and indirectly through aesthetic representations, both visual art and narrative fiction. In narratives of the period, the emotional effect for readers is sometimes enhanced by nonchronological representation: the recounting of events in a sequence other than chronological sequence. Nonchronological narration in the nineteenth century is usually realistically motivated; a character narrator recounts the events either in the sequence in which he or she learns about them or retrospectively, from the temporal perspective of the character's "now." A function analysis of these narratives can show that the sequence in which we learn about events affects our interpretation of their causes and consequences. When new information forces us to rethink a reported situation that we thought we understood, our response is often strongly emotional. Since it is very common in our world that we learn about events when something noteworthy occurs, rather than when the first provocations that led to the occurrence began, investigating the effects of nonchronological narration provides, in addition to information about the effects of narrative techniques developed at the period, guidance in understanding the effects of the sequence in which we learn about personal and political events in our lives.

As we saw in chapter 1, the narrative sequence as Tzvetan Todorov defines it extends from one equilibrium, through a period of imbalance, to a new equilibrium. This shape can be perceived, in its entirety or in part, in representations as well as in fabulas. As a result, the same set of functions can name the stages of the narrative sequence in representations and in fabulas. The possibility of using one set of terms to analyze both trajectories is the direct result of the principle that underlies the definition of the function. Because a function expresses an interpretation of an event in the sequence in which it is perceived, a given event can be interpreted as a function in any sequence in which the event occurs. This principle permits comparisons not only between two or more representations of the same fabula, as the analysis in chapter 2 of two versions of a fairy tale indicates, but also between a representation and the fabula it reveals, and between a segment of a representation and the segment of fabula it reveals.

Since events are functionally polyvalent, and their function depends on their consequences, readers often change their interpretation of the function of an event as they read, page by page, and acquire further information. For example, when we read the beginning of a narrative, we recognize that an absence or lack (of a parent, spouse, position, money, etc.), to which a character or a narrator draws attention, may indicate that a recent reevaluation of the seriousness of the lack will motivate a narrative sequence. In my terms, function a (lower-case) represents an absence or lack that readers interpret as a motivating situation. But as we read on, we may discover that the absence or lack, rather than serving as the primary motivation, may do no more than enable the occurrence of a disruptive event that will motivate a narrative sequence. In this case, we label the disruptive event function A, and shift our interpretation of the prior situation from the primary motivation (function a) to a merely preparatory state of affairs.

In narratives in which the sequence of the representation is different from the chronology of fabula, readers' interpretation of the function of individual events will be guided by the sequence in which the events are arranged. Thus the event that seems the primary motivation and is interpreted as function A (or a) in the representation may be entirely different from the one that is interpreted as function A (or a) in the fabula. To explore this phenomenon, I have chosen for analysis two nonchronological narratives from the first half of the nineteenth century: Edgar Allan Poe's "The Assignation" (1834) and Robert Browning's "My Last Duchess" (1842).

As we read Poe's "The Assignation," we follow the perspective of
the narrator as he perceives events, interprets events as functions,
and reinterprets events as he (and readers) continues to learn more
about what is happening. In this story the narrator who tells the
story is also the *focalizer*, the character whose perceptions and
resulting conceptions readers are permitted to know.[1] When we
reach the end of the story, we construct its fabula and again reinterpret events as functions, this time in the chronological sequence
of fabula. Menakhem Perry recognizes that representations that
depart from "the 'natural' sequence of an 'external' occurrence"
generally follow one of two patterns: "the 'natural' sequence of a
character's consciousness, [or] the sequence within a block of
information transmitted from one character to another" (39–40).
Poe's story illustrates both patterns. Structured according to the
sequence of the narrator's perceptions, the representation incorporates, when the narrator reads it, a text written by the protagonist
that offers information essential to constructing a fabula.

In the second paragraph of the story the narration moves from
a generalized invocation to a fully depicted scene that takes place
at a specific time—the "third or fourth" meeting between the first-
person narrator and an unnamed man who has "fallen in the
flames of . . . youth" (Poe, 193)—and provides indications of the
scene: Venice, the Grand Canal, midnight, the narrator in a gondola. The equilibrium of the peaceful evening is disrupted by the
scream of a woman's voice, which the narrator (together with
most readers) immediately interprets as a function-A event. The
narrator leaps to his feet—in order to rescue the woman who
screamed, readers probably assume. The narrator's and many
readers' first interpretation of the initial events can be represented
by these functions:

EQ the calm of the canal at midnight
A   woman screams
[C] narrator decides to rescue woman (narrator is C-actant)
C' narrator leaps to his feet

According to this function analysis, the woman's scream is a disruptive event that will motivate a narrative sequence (function A);
the narrator makes the C-actant decision to go to the woman's rescue (function C; bracketed because the event is revealed only by
its effect: the narrator's movement); the narrator leaps to his feet
as his initial act (function C').

For readers who have interpreted the narrator's leap to his feet as the beginning of action by him to rescue the woman (function C'), the next event in the representation blocks this interpretive sequence. When (or because) the narrator leaps to his feet, the gondolier drops his oar into the canal and in the darkness cannot recover it. Instead of gaining power (function F) to alleviate the function-A situation, the narrator loses even the ability to steer the gondola (F_{neg}). The narrator and the reader recognize simultaneously that the narrator's plan to rescue the woman (to perform the role of the C-actant and alleviate the function-A situation indicated by her scream) cannot succeed, and that their interpretation of events as functions has created the beginning of a narrative sequence that has reached an impasse and cannot continue to a successful conclusion: A [C] C' F_{neg}. Readers who perceive the futility of the narrator's initial act may expect the entrance of an additional character, one who is better qualified for the role of the C-actant.

As the gondola drifts in the canal, the narrator discovers the reason for the woman's scream: she is the Marchesa Aphrodite, and her child has fallen into the canal. As a result, the narrator and the reader shift their interpretation of the initial events. The opening scream is not function A but function B. The child's fall is the disruptive event that will motivate a narrative sequence; I bracket it to indicate that it precedes chronologically the first scene in the representation (the scream).

> EQ the calm of the canal at midnight
> [A] child falls into canal (bracketed because it precedes the initial scene)
> B   Aphrodite screams for help

After a number of swimmers search for the child in vain, and while Aphrodite's husband, the Marchese Mentoni, strums his guitar, a man the narrator calls "the stranger" dives into the canal and emerges, next to Aphrodite, carrying the still-breathing child. The narrator and most readers immediately conclude that the stranger is the C-actant, who has just performed the primary C-actant functions (C, C', H). We probably assume that equilibrium has been restored, since the child has been saved.

> EQ the calm of the canal at midnight
> [A] child falls into canal (bracketed because it precedes the initial scene)

B   Aphrodite screams for help
[C] stranger decides to save the child (bracketed because
      revealed by C')
C' stranger dives into canal
H   stranger saves child
I   stranger returns child to mother
EQ new equilibrium

For the narrator and probably for many readers, this interpretation of events as functions seems accurate. The narrator's conviction that he has understood the situation correctly is revealed, in
fact, by the surprise he expresses as he narrates the next several
events: the child is taken not by its mother but by someone else
who carries it off; Aphrodite blushes; her words to the stranger are
unexpected: "'thou hast conquered—one hour after sunrise—we
shall meet—so let it be!'" (197).[2]

Although the reader, like the narrator, may have expected a
scene in which the new equilibrium is reinforced—Aphrodite, for
example, could have caressed the child with delight and profusely
thanked the stranger—neither the reader nor the narrator antici-
pates further events that would alter their present interpretation of
the functions of the events they have perceived. When the narrator arrives at the stranger's apartment early the next morning, at
the stranger's request, the narrator seems to expect—and thus we
expect—to receive information that will fill out and elucidate the
pattern of functions that has already been revealed. Along with
the narrator, in the room to which he is shown in the stranger's
Palazzo, we examine the art objects, find an underlined passage in
a book, and read a poem written in English in the stranger's hand.
When the stranger proposes a toast, drinks, and collapses, and
when a servant enters to announce that Aphrodite has died of poison, we discover with the narrator that the stranger too is dead.
At that moment, for the narrator, in the words with which the
story concludes, "a consciousness of the entire and terrible truth
flashed suddenly over my soul." Readers who are reading the
story for the first time are often, when they finish the story, nearly speechless with surprise and confusion. For readers, illumina-
tion equivalent to the narrator's generally requires extensive
rereading and analysis.

When the effect of Poe's ending dissipates sufficiently to permit
reflection, we understand the double signification of the word
assignation in the story's title: the agreement to meet (Aphrodite's

cryptic "one hour after sunrise" [197]), and the meeting itself (to which the participants of the double suicide expect it to lead). Knowing that we have now been given the concluding events in a finite sequence, we begin to reevaluate our interpretations of events as functions. An analysis of what is probably many readers' initial understanding of the causal relations among the reported events, immediately after reading the story for the first time, might look like this:

EQ   the calm of the canal at midnight
[A]   child falls into canal (bracketed because it precedes the initial scene)
B   Aphrodite screams for help
[C]   stranger decides to respond to Aphrodite's need (bracketed because revealed by C')
C'   stranger saves child
F   stranger acquires empowerment (when Aphrodite agrees to the assignation)
G   stranger arrives at the place and time where H will occur
H   stranger and Aphrodite poison themselves
I   success of suicide: both die
[EQ] new equilibrium: the expected reunion in death (bracketed because it is subsequent to the concluding scene)

Because the child's fall is positioned at the beginning of the narrative, and is the only clearly disruptive event until the final moments of the story, we retain that event as function A. Our reading of the stranger as the C-actant remains unchanged as well. But since we now know that the stranger's primary undertaking is a joint suicide to achieve eternal union with Aphrodite, we interpret the suicide as function H. Retrospectively we understand that Aphrodite's agreement to the assignation is the empowerment (function F) that permits the double suicide to occur, and we retain the stranger's retrieval of the child from the water as his initial act (function C'), because it is the first act we see him undertake. Function A and the concluding equilibrium are bracketed because the events that they interpret do not occur within the temporal limits demarcated by the initial scene and the concluding scene in the representation.

One reason that readers generally respond to the double suicide at the end of the representation with surprise is that it is only at the end of the story that we are forced to recognize that the narrator's focalization and voice are temporally separated. The focalization (the narrator's perceptions and resultant conceptions) is located at the time when the events he watched were occurring, while the voice (the narrator's recounting of the events) is located at the later time of his retrospective narration.[3] The temporal gap between focalization and voice permits the narrator to express amazement, which enhances our own.

But the fact that we have not anticipated the double suicide is only one element in the strong effect Poe's story generally creates on first reading. The sequence of functions that represents our interpretation immediately after reading the story reveals a logical gap. The suicide does not save the child; function H does not alleviate function A. The shock with which we respond to the final event is created primarily by this gap; we cannot understand how the child's fall into the canal can have caused the double suicide. The placement of the child's fall at the beginning of the representation is what leads us to interpret that event as the function-A disruption that will motivate the rest of the narrative sequence. The effect of Poe's story is in large part created by the sequence in which the events are recounted.

Once we recognize the inadequacy of the child's fall to motivate the double suicide, we rethink (and reread) the story to find the fabula it reveals. Within the representation, in which the order of events is determined by the sequence of the narrator's experience, we find an embedded representation like that which Perry describes as "the sequence within a block of information transmitted from one character to another" (39–40): the poem the narrator finds in the stranger's apartment, handwritten in English, with the word *London* inscribed on the page but crossed out (*sous rature*). A focalization framed by a focalization, the poem provides readers with a momentary glimpse of the relationship between the stranger and Aphrodite, through the stranger's focalization and at an earlier time: a glimpse that offers an opportunity to discover elements of fabula not otherwise revealed. The first four stanzas of the poem, which Poe published separately under the title "To One in Paradise" (Philip Van Doren Stern, 204n), invoke a beloved and describe a "dream too bright to last." The final fifth stanza, which appears only in the story, reads:

> Alas! for that accursed time
> > They bore thee o'er the billow,
> From Love to titled age and crime,

And an unholy pillow—
From me, and from our misty clime,
Where weeps the silver willow! (204)

Reading the poem as the primary source of information about events that precede the child's fall, we construct a fabula that we interpret according to the following sequence of functions:

EQ the stranger and Aphrodite are happy together in London
A   Aphrodite is carried over the waves to Venice to marry the Marchese Mentoni
C   stranger decides to attempt reunion with Aphrodite
C' stranger follows Aphrodite to Venice
D   stranger is tested: Aphrodite screams for help
E   stranger passes test: saves child
F   stranger acquires empowerment: Aphrodite agrees to assignation
G   stranger arrives at the place and time where function H will occur
H   double suicide
I   success of suicide: both die
EQ new equilibrium: the expected reunion in death

The last four functions and the concluding equilibrium of this fabula analysis (from F to EQ) are filled by the same events as the last four functions and the concluding equilibrium (from F to EQ) of our probable initial understanding immediately after we finish reading the story for the first time. In both analyses, the stranger is the C-actant. But whereas, when we read the representation for the first time, the event we interpret as the motivating function A is the child's fall, once we have constructed the chronological sequence of fabula the event we interpret as function A is the forced separation of Aphrodite and the stranger. As a result, in the fabula, the stranger's decision to attempt reunion with Aphrodite is the event that fills the C function. Moreover, now that we have constructed a fabula, we shift our interpretation of Aphrodite's scream, which we initially read as function A (the disruptive event), and then as function B (a call for help), to function D, the first function of the donor sequence.[4] In the fabula, Aphrodite's scream functions as a test (function D), to which the stranger responds successfully (function E), thereby gaining the power (function F) to accomplish the primary conflict (function H, the double suicide). By providing words to talk about interpretations of causal relations, functions enable analysis of readers' shifting interpretations in response to the further information a narrative provides as it continues.

In addition, a function analysis of a nonchronological narrative permits comparing the shape of the two trajectories: the fabula and the representation. Looking again at the analysis above of the fabula of "The Assignation," we see that the fabula traces one complete narrative sequence. The fabula includes every function except function B, as it moves through an entire narrative sequence from an initial equilibrium to a disruptive function A to a new equilibrium. Looking again at this analysis of the fabula, we can also see that the segment of the fabula that the representation traces—from Aphrodite's scream in the opening scene to the double suicide of the conclusion—is less than a complete narrative sequence; the representation traces the part of the fabula that moves through the six functions from function D to function I.

The exposition in a narrative, as Meir Sternberg has shown, extends from the beginning of the fabula (*Expositional Modes,* 13) to "that point in time which marks the beginning of the *fictive present*" in the representation (21). In "The Assignation," Aphrodite's scream marks the beginning of the fictive present. For the scene that marks the beginning of the fictive present and the end of the exposition, Sternberg perceives, "[t]he author's finding it to be the first time-section that is 'of consequence enough' to deserve full scenic treatment turns it, implicitly but clearly, into a conspicuous signpost, signifying that this is precisely the point in time that the author has decided, for whatever reason, to make the reader regard as the beginning of the action proper" (20).

What Poe has done in "The Assignation," by selecting the scene that begins with Aphrodite's scream as the first to receive full scenic treatment, is to guide readers to perceive everything that is chronologically prior to Aphrodite's scream as exposition—even though the chronologically prior events include the events that in the fabula constitute the primary motivating event (function A) and the initial actions of the C-actant (functions C and C'). Poe's placement of the scene in which the child nearly drowns as the first scene that receives scenic treatment is, of course, the reason that, as we read, we interpret the child's falling into the canal as a function-A event that motivates everything that follows.

For a writer to choose to deviate from "the straight chronological order of presentation" is, as Sternberg observes, "clearly an

indication of artistic purpose" (33). In nonchronological narratives in which a scene that occurs late in the chronology of fabula
is presented as the opening scene in the representation, the differences in duration between a fabula and its representation have
been described since Aristotle's *Poetics* as a temporal proportion:
the less than twenty-four hours that the trajectory of the representation of, for example, *Oedipus Rex* traces, to the years required
for the events of the fabula to unroll. Sternberg's recognition that
the exposition of a narrative can be delimited only with reference
to both the fabula and the representation enables his analyses of
the aesthetic effects of the ways in which elements of fabula are
distributed in a representation (*Expositional Modes*), but also permits a comparison of the two trajectories that reveals the specific
events in a fabula that a representation relegates to exposition. A
function analysis permits us to perceive the causal effects—the
function—of the events in fabula that a representation consigns to
exposition, and to specify the instances in which the positioning of
an event in a representation leads us to interpret it as one function
in the representation and a different function in the fabula. These
instances of functional polyvalence are among the artistic effects
that a compressed representation can produce.

In reading "The Assignation," even after we have determined that
the child's fall into the water is not the function-A event that motivates all that follows, the scene in which the child is in danger and
then rescued retains a heightened quality in our memories that
reflects the causal implications of our initial interpretation. In considering the story retrospectively, we remain able to envision this scene
in detail—in a way that we cannot envision the chronologically prior
events, including the enforced separation in London of Aphrodite
and the stranger—and the initial scene remains tinged in our minds
with the strong emotions with which we initially perceived it.

The emotional effect of the functional polyvalence of an event,
in instances in which we interpret a given event as one function in
the representation and a different function in the fabula, is perhaps
strongest immediately after we have concluded our reading and
completed the process of constructing a fabula, and gradually
fades as we forget both the effects of the representation and the
represented events. But the emotional effect of the representation
endures, I propose, until the representation is forgotten, and can
be reactivated by rereading. By shaping readers' interpretations of
the function of events, a representation can elicit a strong emotional response.

■

In Poe's "The Assignation" and Browning's "My Last Duchess," nonchronological narration is naturalized in different ways: in Poe's story by recounting the events in the sequence and at the time that the character narrator watches them occur, and in Browning's poem by recounting the events retrospectively from the temporal perspective of the character narrator's "now." The focalizer in Poe's story does not know as the story progresses how the events will turn out, whereas Browning's Duke knows exactly what has occurred. In "The Assignation," the focalization that permits the narrator's expression of surprise at the story's conclusion, in conjunction with the sequence of the telling that effectively veils the causal events in fabula until a careful second reading, creates for readers the same shock that Poe's narrator experiences when he discovers that the stranger is dead. Readers of "My Last Duchess" are also made to experience surprise, but primarily from the contrast between the seeming serenity of the opening scene and the violence that we slowly learn has brought about the present situation and that poisons the ongoing negotiations. If readers of the poem identify their response with that of anyone in the poem, that character is the Count's messenger, the narratee to whom the Duke is speaking, who readers may assume shares our shocked response.[5]

Browning's poem opens, as I read it, by suggesting a stable, calm equilibrium: the Duke is ensconced at his family seat, entertaining the narratee, the Count's messenger, by showing him the Duchess's portrait. The locus of the event places the Duke against the backdrop of his inherited wealth, and in a social situation in which his confidence bespeaks his entrenched power in the represented world. Browning creates this equilibrium through the selection of the time and place—the segment of fabula—that the opening lines of the poem depict. The meeting between the Duke and the narratee, which is the one scene represented in the poem, is the final event in the fabula that readers slowly construct; thus the Duke narrates a retrospective account of events he has witnessed. The juncture of voice and focalization, which is assigned to the Duke and—unlike Poe's narrator—at the time at which he speaks, lends credence to the Duke's words.[6]

But the Duke's focalization, in two passages early in the poem, contains other focalizations: the unvoiced response of the narratee (and previous viewers) to the Duchess's portrait, and the portrait itself, which is the visual representation of the painter's perception of the Duchess. Because a contained focalization can be colored by the focalization through which it is perceived, a contained focalization cannot confirm—but may subvert—the focalization that contains it. In the poem, the first of the contained focalizations may lead readers to wonder what possible expression anyone could read on the faces of viewers of the painting as seeming, in the Duke's words, "as they would ask me, if they durst, / How such a glance came there" (Browning, lines 11–12). Readers who question, in this passage, the validity of the Duke's interpretation of the represented world are prepared, when the Duke's account turns from responses to the painting to the painting itself, to doubt the accuracy of the Duke's ascription of the depicted lady's painted charms to her pleasure in the painter's compliments, and to distrust his judgment (perhaps reached under the influence of the painted woman's fixed smile) of his wife as having had "A heart . . . too soon made glad" (line 22).

At this point in the representation, as I read the poem, the equilibrium of the opening moments has been undermined sufficiently that most readers, during the following section in which the Duke continues to speak disapprovingly of the Duchess's behavior (lines 23–34), will decide that the motivating situation (function a) for the Duke is his perception that his wife smiles too readily at other men—a disruption that is intensified for readers who suspect that the Duke's interpretation of his wife's behavior may not be accurate. For readers, the knowledge of already having read more than half the poem (34 of 56 lines) reinforces an interpretation that the depicted situation, rather than an event yet to be revealed, is function a.

It is just at this moment that the poem turns to the Duke's ruminations on whether it is appropriate to "stoop . . . to make your will / Quite clear to such an one" (lines 34, 36–37), a passage that represents in the present the Duke's mental process of deciding (function C) whether and how to respond to the disruptive function-a situation. As shocking as the resultant events remain, even after repeated readings, the sequence of functions they fulfill is absolutely logical. Eight words, "I gave commands; / Then all smiles stopped together" (lines 45–46), reveal the events that fill three functions: function C' (the commands), function H (the murder; the word is not spoken but the event is understood because of its result), and function I (the successful alleviation of the function-a situation: the Duchess no longer smiles at other men).

The Duchess's no longer being alive, however, is doubly interpreted by the Duke: as the successful resolution of the initial disruption (function I in the first narrative sequence), and as motivation to remarry (function a in the second narrative sequence, which the poem reveals only through the marriage negotiations). The two sequential sequences of Browning's representation can be interpreted by these functions:

EQ   the apparent serenity of the scene
a   Duchess's (painted and real) smiles disturb Duke
C   Duke decides not to be disturbed
C'   Duke gives commands
[H]   Duke's henchmen murder Duchess (revealed by Duchess's being killed)
I   Duchess is dead: she no longer smiles

I = [a] Duchess is dead: Duke lacks a wife (revealed by marriage negotiations)
[C]   Duke decides to marry (revealed by marriage negotiations)
[C']   Duke approaches Count (revealed by marriage negotiations)
H   Duke negotiates marriage contract with narratee

If we remove the brackets that indicate the suppression of an event in the representation, these two narrative sequences also represent the poem's fabula. This congruence of functions in the representation and the fabula occurs because the causal events are revealed in the poem in chronological sequence. Browning accomplishes this—while placing the Duke's retrospective account within the concluding event of the fabula—by moving directly from the final moments of the fabula to the first event of the fabula, through the metonymical shift from the painted Duchess (lines 1–12) to the process of painting her ("How such a glance came there" [line 13]). As a result of this strategy, only the situation of the initial equilibrium is different in the representation than in the fabula. In the fabula it represents a state of affairs prior to the Duke's concern that his wife smiles too freely; in the representation it is a product of the Duke's confidence, during his meeting with the narratee who is the Count's emissary, that his negotiations to marry the Count's daughter are about to reach a successful conclusion.

But the initial equilibrium as Browning constructs it is highly effective, because the Duke's supreme confidence that the opening of the representation portrays increases, in retrospect, the abhorrence with which readers regard the Duke at the poem's conclusion. In contrast, imagine the sympathy for the Duke one might feel if the poem began with a scene from an earlier, happier time in their marriage in which the Duchess smiled at the Duke, and he was pleased. But Browning portrays the Duke in the opening scene as coldly confident, rather than loving, and further intensifies readers' dislike for the Duke by delaying the revelation that the Duke is responsible for the Duchess's death, adding the element of surprise to enhance our disapproval.[7] Browning postpones this information by extending the events of the first two functions (functions a and C of the first narrative sequence) for 44 lines (more than 75 percent of the 56-line poem). The Duke's commands are revealed in line 45, and the events of the seven functions that complete the first sequence and represent the second (from the first C' through the second H) are compressed within the final 12 lines. By extending the apparent initial equilibrium and by withholding and then compressing information about the events that so forcefully require readers to reinterpret the opening scene, Browning, like Poe, guides first-time readers to experience a strong mixture of surprise and shock.

Although the second sequence is technically left open, stopping at function H, my response to the poem's conclusion is that the Duke's power and confidence in the marriage negotiations that the representation portrays (the scene that in fabula fills function H) are such that the sequence must reach successful completion (function I): the Duke will marry the Count's daughter, he will again have a Duchess. If other readers respond as I do, then by suppressing an account of the marriage, Browning increases his readers' dislike of the Duke by making us write for ourselves the abhorrent but inevitable conclusion.[8] In addition, although the restriction of focalization to the Duke permits the suppression of some data (for example, how the Duchess dies), the Duke's own proud acknowledgment of his crime and its motivation leaves readers in a position to determine that, even if his interpretation of the Duchess's behavior is accurate, his motivation is insufficient for his crime. Although readers' shocked response to Browning's poem, as to Poe's story, is in part an effect of the events reported—the double suicide in Poe's story and the murder of the Duke's wife in Browning's poem—the emotion we feel is guided and intensified by the sequence and the tempo in which events are revealed in the representation.

■

As I hope to have demonstrated in the sections of this chapter devoted to Browning's poem and Poe's story, the distinction between fabula and representation is essential to analyzing the effects of the sequence of the representation. The two trajectories that I call the *representation* and the *fabula* were identified and named in the early 1920s by the Russian Formalists.[9] Since then, narrative theorists and readers who have been introduced to narrative theory have generally recognized that whenever we read a story or a novel or a historical account, or watch a film, or listen to a child's account of something that happened in the playground, we construct in our minds as a first step in the interpretive process a chronological account: a fabula. If information about sequence is not immediately available, we read on to find it, or, if the account is about our world, we turn elsewhere for information. With our children we ask questions to try to establish sequence: for instance, "Who started the fight?"

The two trajectories of narrative, as I conceive them, are as interdependent as the signifier and the signified.[10] Like the two parts of the verbal sign—the signifier (the sound of the word) and the signified (a concept attached by agreement to the sound)—of the two trajectories of narrative only one—the representation—has material form (written language, oral speech, or gestures, which we can see or hear or view).[11] Because the fabula, like the signified, exists as a concept in readers' or listeners' or viewers' minds, and cannot be seen or heard or viewed, its existence is less obvious than the existence of a representation is, and has at times been questioned.

Most famously, Jonathan Culler has argued that the relationship between a representation and its fabula is hierarchical, and thus subject to deconstruction through a demonstration that the hierarchy can be reversed ("Story and Discourse in the Analysis of Narrative," 183). Postulating that narratology gives priority to fabula, he contends that the priority implies "a hierarchy [of the fabula over the representation] which the functioning of narratives often subverts by presenting events not as givens but as the products of [the representation's] discursive forces or requirements" (172). As an example of what he sees as an event produced by "discursive forces," Culler points to the gap that exists in the fabula of Sophocles' *Oedipus Rex* because Oedipus does not ask the surviving witness whether Laius was murdered by one or many. Although, Culler concludes, readers are convinced of Oedipus's guilt:

> our conviction does not come from the revelation of the deed. Instead of the revelation of a prior deed determining meaning, we could say that it is meaning, the convergence of meaning in the narrative discourse [representation], that leads us to posit this deed as its appropriate manifestation. (174)

First, Culler's postulate that narratology gives priority to fabula is questionable. Ontologically, as we have seen, a representation has a material form that a fabula lacks. Temporally, a representation is prior for readers to the fabula it gradually reveals.[12] Second, the "convergence of meaning" that implies that Oedipus murdered Laius does not make the deed occur; it makes it significant. An effect does not cause a prior event. An effect indicates the significance of a prior event—its function—by placing it in a sequence in which the prior event can be interpreted according to its consequences. The "discursive forces" of the representation that Culler discerns do not alter the principles of causality; they guide perceivers' interpretation of the function of the event in question by indicating the event's consequences. The "discursive forces" of the representation guide interpretations of the function of an event, as we have seen in this chapter, largely by controlling which elements of fabula a reader (viewer, listener) knows and does not know at each moment as a representation unrolls.[13]

In an important study of negation and difference in narrative representations, Gerald Prince establishes three categories of discrepancies between the set of events included in a narration and the set of events that take place in the represented world ("The Disnarrated"). These categories can also help to explain how events included in a representation may not occur in its fabula, and how events that occur in a fabula may not be included in its representation.[14] Of the three categories that Prince discerns, two—the *unnarratable* and the *unnarrated*—include elements of the represented world that are suppressed in the narration. The *unnarratable* "comprises everything that *according to a given narrative* cannot be narrated or is not worth narrating" (28; Prince's emphasis).

In a given narrative, the focalization—which in the definition I use is an element of the representation—may offer reasons that a given event in the fabula will not be narrated. In the function analysis above of Poe's representation, the stranger's decision to respond to Aphrodite's need (function C) is placed in brackets, because it is revealed only by its effect, the rescue of the child. The decision cannot be narrated because it is not in the purview of the focalizer; although it is suppressed in the representation, its effect reveals it, to the narrator and to readers, as an event in fabula. In Browning's poem, the Duchess's murder is suppressed in the representation because the Duke chooses not to describe it, but it is revealed as an event in fabula through the cessation of her smiles. Similarly, Oedipus's murder of Laius is *unnarratable*—except by Tiresias, whose vision exceeds the limits of human sight—because the surviving witness is too frightened to speak, or, if he should speak, to be believed.

The questioning of the surviving witness, on the other hand, which is Culler's focus, falls under Prince's third category, the *disnarrated*: "events that *do not* happen [in the narrative world, but] are nonetheless referred to (in a negative or hypothetical mode) by the narrative text" (30; Prince's emphasis). Oedipus's hypothetical questioning of the surviving witness about Laius's murder creates an aesthetic effect. The idea that Oedipus should question the witness is proposed just after the middle of the play, at a moment when Oedipus and the audience are so certain he killed Laius that, unless some element to postpone closure is introduced, the play will end. By the time the witness arrives, Oedipus's guilt in the murder of Laius is subsumed by his guilt in his relationship with Jocasta. Further testimony about the murder would be anticlimactic, in addition to lacking credence because of the witness's fear.

The act of reading (or viewing, or listening to) a narrative includes, in addition to identifying events as they are revealed, a process of creating hypotheses about the causal relations among the revealed events and other events that may be revealed as one continues to read. The power of a representation to guide interpretations of functionally polyvalent events lies in large part in the sequence in which it dispenses information to readers. Functions provide a vocabulary to analyze the provisional fabulas and segments of fabulas readers construct from the set of events that are discernible at any moment in the process of reading, and to trace the shifting interpretations of the consequences of events that readers formulate as they move through a representation page by page. In this chapter I have considered primarily the emotional impact that nonchronological narration can elicit. When I return to the issue of nonchronological narration in chapter 6, it will be to emphasize the epistemological effects of the temporary gaps that all nonchronological narratives create and the permanent gaps in many narratives, chronological as well as nonchronological.

CHAPTER 4

THE COMFORTS THAT FUNCTION C BRINGS:

Shakespeare's *Hamlet*, Racine's *Phaedra*, and James's *Daisy Miller*

During the great floods in the Midwest in the summer of 1993, the local television newscasts in St. Louis devoted seemingly inordinate attention to sandbaggers: announcements of locations where sandbaggers were needed, interviews with sandbaggers, pictures of areas that sandbaggers had saved—and of other areas that in spite of the sandbaggers' efforts had succumbed to the flooding. Watching the nightly news, I wondered why a medium that aspires to satisfy a broad audience would devote more time to sandbaggers than to flood victims. Turning to narrative theory to find an answer, I began to analyze the function of the activities of the sandbaggers in the narratives that the evening newscasts constructed from each day's events. A function analysis of these stories leads me to suggest two ways—as a thematics and as a hermeneutic device—that function C brings comfort to viewers (listeners, readers). In the first section of this chapter I analyze the pivotal position of function C in a narrative sequence and describe the two forms of comfort that I am proposing that function C brings. Then I look at several literary examples that have been received with broad success to examine how function C is represented and the ways it brings comfort in each.

In the narratives about the flooding that the evening newscasts recounted repeatedly over a period of weeks, the sandbaggers are C-actants. A C-actant is a person (in our world, or in a narrative about our world), or a human or anthropomorphic character (in a fictional world), who decides (function C) to take action to try to alleviate a function-A situation.

A	rising flood waters threaten homes and businesses
B	authorities put out a call for sandbaggers
C	prospective sandbaggers decide to sandbag to try to protect homes and businesses
C'	sandbaggers go to announced meeting places where buses await them
G	sandbaggers arrive by bus at sites where the rising water threatens homes or businesses
H	sandbaggers sandbag
I (or I_{neg})	sandbaggers succeed (or do not succeed) in protecting the site they sandbagged

Becoming a sandbagger is an easily understood three-stage process. To become a sandbagger, one decides to be a sandbagger (function C), makes the journey to a place where sandbagging is needed (function C'), and begins to sandbag (function H): to put sand in bags, and then place the bags along a segment of the perimeter of the rising waters. The word *sandbagger* is not the one we choose when we want to describe someone who aimlessly puts sand in containers—in a sandbox, for instance. Rather, *sandbagger* denotes someone who engages in all three stages: the decision to sandbag and the journey to a site, as well as the activity of making and positioning sandbags. Sandbagging is an intentional act.

In addition, when we speak of someone as a sandbagger, we are indicating that the person's function-C decision to become a sandbagger is a response to her or his interpretation of the flooding as a disruptive function-A situation to be alleviated. A function-C decision is motivated by a function-A situation. The narratives about the sandbaggers that the evening newscasts constructed illustrate the pivotal position of function C in a narrative sequence. The decision to become a sandbagger links the activity (sandbagging) to the motivation (the flooding), and links the motivation (the flooding) to the activity (sandbagging). Function C creates the causal link between the C-actant's intentional action (functions C' through H) and the situation that motivates that action (function A). This characteristic of function C—that it is the pivotal event, or fulcrum, between function A and functions C' through H—is the basis of both forms of comfort that I am proposing function C brings.

But before looking at the ways that function C brings comfort to viewers (listeners, readers), I want first to rule out any simple correlation between a successful outcome and the comforts that function C brings. The narratives that the newscasts reported often ended in failure. For that matter, during the worst of the flooding only two outcomes were possible: a given endangered area was flooded (function I_{neg}) or provisionally spared (tentatively, function I). Even in the segments of the newscasts devoted to the sandbaggers, as much attention was given to those whose efforts had been insufficient as to those whose work had thus far restrained the rising flood waters. Assuming, as I do, that the newscasts succeeded in appealing to a broad audience, clearly a successful outcome is not necessary to the success of a narrative—a position that is corroborated by the pleasure that readers and viewers so often take in novels and stories that end with the protagonist's death, in tragedies played out on the stage, and in biographies that cover a subject's life to its end.

Moreover, if the outcome were the only consideration, the newscasts could have focused on the A-experiencers—the many individuals whose lives were disrupted and whose property was endangered by the flooding—rather than the sandbaggers. The difference between narratives about victims or potential victims and narratives about sandbaggers is not in the outcome: some people lost their property; others did not. The difference is in the lingering attention given, in the narratives about sandbaggers, to the functions performed by the C-actant: the sandbaggers.

In chapter 1, I describe Tzvetan Todorov's idea that the underlying pattern of narrative is the movement from an equilibrium (EQ), through a period of imbalance (in my terms, a function-A situation), to another equilibrium (EQ). Alternating periods of equilibrium and imbalance provide a pattern to interpret events in the world, as well as in narratives. But in the world, it is a given that both shifts—the disruptive move from an equilibrium to a function-A situation and the ameliorative move from a function-A situation to a new equilibrium—may happen as a result of unmotivated events. Both moves can be brought about by random forces (heavy rains cause flooding, heavy rains bring a forest fire under control), by unintentional actions (someone's campfire causes a forest fire, someone's campfire provides a beacon that draws a lost child to safety), or, for that matter, by actions motivated by someone other than the doer (an army destroys a city, a chain gang builds a road).[1]

The cognitive theorist Mark Turner points out, in *The Literary Mind,* that interpreting unmotivated events as intentional acts is a very common human thought process. In Turner's usage, "[a]n action is an event with an actor"; the pattern that he and George Lakoff name "events are actions" denotes interpreting unmotivated events as motivated actions (26). As Turner perceives, we regularly use the pattern "events are actions" to turn "everyday event-stories [that] lack causal actors . . . into action-stories: We complete the event-story to include a causal actor by projecting the actor in the action-story onto a nonactor in the event-story. . . . The sun becomes a *torturer*. The wind becomes a *savage and merciless beater*" (28).

Turner describes "events are actions" as one of the "fundamental patterns of parable that are essential to everyday thought, reasoning, and action." He claims, moreover, that these fundamental patterns—including "events are actions"—"show up in literary examples for the reason that literature takes its instruments from the everyday mind" (26).[2] Without doubt, in narratives about our world as well as in literary narratives, events are often represented as the result of motivated action. Moreover, I find convincing Turner's explanation that there is a correlation between the human predilection for interpreting events as motivated actions and the prevalence in literary narratives (and, I add, other narratives too) for explaining events as motivated actions.

But I want to develop the idea by differentiating between the two moves—the disruptive move from an equilibrium to a function-A situation and the ameliorative move from a function-A situation to a new equilibrium. In the case of a flood, the waters rise and then they recede. A factual narrative about a flood may tell us no more than that. But the St. Louis newscasts introduced into this narrative the sandbaggers. In doing so—in interpreting the disruptive move as the result of random forces (the flooding) and the ameliorative move as potentially the result of motivated action (by the sandbaggers)—the newscasts, I suggest, were following an extremely common pattern. Both in literary narratives and in narratives about events in our world, the ameliorative move is represented as the result of motivated action more often than the disruptive move is. We can speculate that the reason for this is that random forces are, in fact, more often disruptive than ameliorative, whereas motivated actions are (or so we hope) more often ameliorative than disruptive. A further reason, I suggest, is that we find it comforting to interpret motivated action as contributing to an ameliorative—but not to a disruptive—move.

Let me explain. Sandbagging is undertaken by men and women who assume that by their actions they may be able to control the

spreading water during a flood. As we have seen, the pivotal function-C decision links the subsequent intentional action (functions
C' through H) to the function-A situation that motivates it. By
including the sandbaggers in the narratives reported, the television
newscasts reminded viewers that the ravages of a flood can sometimes be contained by human action. For viewers of the newscasts,
the representation of the sandbaggers' activities is comforting
because it suggests that even randomly caused function-A situations are at least potentially responsive to human behavior. This is
the way that as a thematics, I am proposing, function C brings
comfort to viewers (readers, listeners): by encouraging belief that
intentional acts by human beings can improve the circumstances
of individuals, a community, our world.

Assuredly, human action that causes function-A situations has
some of the appeal of human action intended to resolve function-
A situations. Gerald Prince perceives that "the extent to which [a
narrative] fulfills a receiver's desire" depends, in part, on its being
"meaningful in terms of a human project and a humanized uni-
verse" (*Narratology,* 160). Numerous examples suggest that a
desire to believe in the efficacy of human intentional action—for
good or for bad—is shared by people of many cultures and times,
and various levels of sophistication. The title of this chapter, in
fact, is inspired by a phrase in a National Public Radio commentary: "the comfort of letting us think that somebody is in control."
According to the commentator, conspiracy theories are popular
because (in contrast to floods, fires, droughts, and accidents) they
posit human intentional actions as causes of what I call function-
A disruptive situations.[3] Although I am using the word *comfort* in
my argument to describe the effects of function C (and only function C), I find the ramifications of the commentator's argument
compelling. Conspiracy theories would be attractive because they
permit interpreting human intentional actions as causes of disruptive events. If disruptive events were thought to be caused by
human intentional action, they would seem easier to counteract
than if thought to be caused by random forces, the power of
which sometimes seems unlimited. A complementary example is
found in the conflicting accounts of a crime in the story from
which the film *Rashomon* is developed. All three main characters
each report having been the person who killed the samurai
Takehiko: the bandit, Takehiko's wife, and the dead man himself
(who speaks through a medium).[4] In this instance, all three characters choose to claim the criminal act as his or her own, rather

than to ascribe the power to carry out such an act to someone other than him- or herself. Even in the case of the flooding, although newscasts at the time ascribed the cause of the rising waters to an ungovernable random force (heavy rainfall, in conjunction with a rapidly melting snow cover), later accounts after the flooding had ended speculated about the role of the government agencies that determine the placement and the operation of dams, and of farmers who plant crops and build homes in areas known to be subject to flooding.

The science fiction and fantasy writer Ursula K. LeGuin proposes in a recent interview (in the context of a discussion of fictional wizards in novels made into films) that "[r]ather than being primarily about good and evil . . . a lot of fantasy is an exploration of what power is" (quoted by James Gorman, "Which Wizard Beats 'Em All?" B37). I suggest that narratives of many genres are often explorations of power: the power of intentional actions in relation to the power of random forces, and the power that causes a function-A disruption in relation to the power that a C-actant needs to resolve it. Not all function-A situations can believably be presented as the effects of human intentional acts. But as the newscasts about the flooding suggest, the introduction of a C-actant who undertakes action in response to a function-A situation is common in narratives and, I argue, a thematics that comforts viewers (listeners, readers). Perhaps one of the purposes of narratives—fictional narratives and accounts of events in our world that, like the newscasts about the sandbaggers, adopt patterns that include C-actants and their efforts—is to provide a site to explore the interplay between powerful forces and human intentional action, to reduce our fear of the world in which we live, and to give us the courage to undertake function-C decisions ourselves, even in situations in which we cannot be assured of success.

In addition to bringing comfort as a thematics, by encouraging belief in the efficacy of intentional action, function C also brings comfort, I propose, as a hermeneutic device. Representations of function C comfort viewers (listeners, readers) by guiding hermeneutic activity. Interviews with sandbaggers and pictures of sandbagging in the evening newscasts not only establish, as we have seen, that intentional acts to contain the flooding are ongoing. In addition, and perhaps as importantly, the pictures and interviews indicate to viewers that the many people stacking bags are in agreement with, and thus confirm, the television reporters' interpretation that the flooding is a disruptive situation to be alleviated. At the beginning of this chapter I described function C as the pivotal event that creates the causal link between the motivating situation (function A) and the intentional action it motivates (functions C' through H), and I noted that that pivotal position is the basis of both forms of comfort I propose that function C brings. As we saw, that link between intentional action and the situation that motivates it underlies the thematics that intentional action is potentially effective. Similarly, that link enables an indication of a function-C decision to incite hermeneutic interest in identifying the function-A situation to which it is a response, and the C-actant's actions (functions C' through H) that it motivates.

During the process of interpreting events (in the world or in narratives), the coming-into-being of intent at function C is often the keystone element that permits us to construct a causal sequence. Even in situations in which information becomes available to us in chronological sequence, we often cannot immediately identify an event as a function-A disruption, largely because what constitutes a function-A disruption depends, in our world or fictional worlds, on who is interpreting it, and in addition, in narratives, on how a representation is guiding readers (listeners, viewers) to interpret it. Thus a function-C decision to attempt to fix a given situation establishes that situation retrospectively as one that needs to be fixed. In chronological accounts, if a function-C decision is revealed at the time it is made, it will also incite prospective speculation about the means and the outcome of the intentional action we are led to expect. The function-C decision that the word *sandbaggers* denotes, guides attention both to the flooding and to the activity of sandbagging and its outcome.

In more complex narratives, readers may not know which in a series of potentially disruptive events will be sufficient to motivate a potential C-actant to decide to act (a drought curtails the corn harvest, a fungus contaminates the remaining stored grain, and then the bull becomes ill and dies) until a C-actant takes action (the farmer applies for a full-time job in the local grocery store). Similarly, we may interpret a situation as a restored equilibrium (the neighborhood park is suddenly very clean), and then consider whose activities brought about that result (who are the C-actants who picked up the litter and mowed?), and what aspect of the park's previous state led the C-actants to decide to undertake the task (e.g., what, for them, was the motivating function-A situation?). As pivotal as function C is to interpretations of causal relations among events and situations, often the coming-into-being of intent that it marks is nowhere stated in so many words and can only be surmised. Whichever events we attempt to interpret first—those that in the end we will interpret as function C, as function A, or as functions C' through H—our interpretation of one of these sites complements and furthers our interpretations of the other two. Information about what someone is doing guides our attention to whether we can ascertain from those actions an intent. Information about intent guides our attention both to the action to be undertaken and to the function-A situation to be corrected. Information about a function-A situation that needs to be corrected guides our attention to whether someone is intending to correct it. When a function-C decision is revealed, in our world or in a narrative, we find it comforting because we can use it as a lodestar in relation to which we can locate our position in the ongoing causal logic.

In *Reading for the Plot,* Peter Brooks proposes that the desire for the ending that carries readers of narratives "forward, onward, through the text" (37) is a passion for meaning that can be satisfied only retrospectively, with the knowledge that the ending brings: "those shaping ends . . . that promise to bestow meaning and significance on the beginning and the middle" (19). Surely Brooks is correct, as I argue elsewhere (see chapters 3, 5, and 6), that endings inspire reinterpretations of events previously revealed. But function C, I suggest, provides meaning that is not dependent on the ending. As the newscasts about the sandbaggers indicate, a function-C decision (both as a thematics and as a hermeneutic device) gives meaning to the ongoing action that is not contingent on the success of the intentional action the decision inspires. Moreover, when extended or repeated, function-C decisions offer, I propose—presumably because of the thematic and hermeneutic comforts they bring—among the most satisfying ways of filling middles.

Thus far in this chapter I have made no distinction between the representation of a narrative (the words or images we perceive) and the fabula (the chronological account we assemble from explicit and implicit information in a representation). In analyzing the role of the C-actant this distinction is necessary, in part because the C-actant's function-C decision that establishes intent may be directly revealed in the representation or indirectly revealed by the action that the C-actant undertakes (functions C' through H). If we learn that potential flood victims are attempting to acquire sand and bags, we will probably interpret their action as indicating that they have made the function-C decision to sandbag—that

they have become C-actants. The comfort that function C brings
as a thematics requires that a representation reveal or at least
imply that a function-C decision has been made. The comfort that
function C brings as a hermeneutic device depends on when—as
well as whether—a representation reveals or implies that a function-C decision has been made. To serve as a lodestar to guide
interpretations, function C has to be understood to have occurred
while readers (viewers, listeners) are still in the process of discovering where they are in the ongoing action.

Further, the relative duration of the events interpreted by a
given function (function H, for instance, or function A, or function C) varies tremendously from narrative to narrative, sometimes influenced by genre. In detective fiction, for example, generally the detective's function-C decision to investigate takes place
during the first chapter, the function-A crime is summarized as
part of the exposition, and most of the pages of the novel are
devoted to the detective's function-H activity designed to uncover
information about the crime. A typical detective novel, in other
words, has an extended function H. In the newscasts about the
sandbaggers, pictures of sandbaggers sandbagging represented
function-H activity and pictures of neatly sandbagged perimeters,
and broken sandbagged walls represented respectively (tentatively) successful and (clearly) unsuccessful outcomes (functions I and
I_{neg}). Interviews with sandbaggers, however, tended to extend
function C. These interviews lingered over elements of the decision-making, asking people's reasons for undertaking sandbagging
and encouraging people to describe the circumstances that
allowed them to be available day after day during weekdays to
engage in sandbagging.

In analyzing the duration of function C, I am considering that
the process of decision-making (in my terms, function C) begins
when a potential C-actant interprets a situation as a function-A
situation to be alleviated, or hears a function-B request to alleviate a situation that the requester considers a function-A situation
to be alleviated, and continues until a C-actant, having decided to
act, begins to act (function C'). I emphasize again: in our world
these interpretations are made by people, and in fictional worlds
by fictional characters. In response to narratives, readers (listeners, viewers) make their own interpretations (guided, of course, by
the representation) about when characters in fictional worlds or
people in our world interpret situations as needing to be alleviated and decide to attempt to alleviate them. The duration of func-

tion C can be measured in a fabula by the time (minutes, weeks) that it takes a C-actant to reach a decision, and in a representation by the number of pages (for readers) or minutes (for viewers or listeners) devoted to the function-C decision-making process.

If function C brings comfort, both as a thematics and as a hermeneutic device, as I am proposing the newscasts about the sandbaggers indicate, then representations that emphasize function C by extending or repeating it may give particular satisfaction. To examine in detail how function C is emphasized in several exemplary representations, and to consider the possibility of a correlation between a narrative's very successful reception and an emphasis in its representation on function C, I look first at two plays, *Hamlet* by William Shakespeare and *Phaedra* (*Phèdre*) by Jean Racine, and then a novella, *Daisy Miller* by Henry James. The two plays are equally famous in their respective traditions—*Phaedra* holds the same position in the francophone canon as *Hamlet* does in English-speaking parts of the world—and both have been found eminently successful by audiences over the centuries. During James's lifetime, *Daisy Miller* was the most popular of his narratives—in James's words, "the ultimately most prosperous child of my invention" (*Daisy Miller*, 18: vi). While still read, it is not viewed at present as James's crowning accomplishment. I analyze interpretations of the novella at four historical periods, looking for correlations between the importance of function C in an interpretation and the reception of the novella at the times of the various interpretations.

∎

Phaedra was given its first performance on January 1, 1676, approximately seventy-five years after *Hamlet,* which we cannot date as precisely. A similarity in the shape of the two plays has previously drawn attention. William Kerrigan comments that "[t]he peculiar structure of the revenge plot, in which a determining crime has taken place before the opening of the play, makes *Hamlet* itself seem like the conclusion of a tragedy already under way" (*Hamlet's Perfection,* 124). In "Racinian Spaces," Thomas Pavel notes that "[o]f the several sub-genres of English Renaissance drama, only [the revenge tragedy, exemplified by *Hamlet*] typically opens 'late.'" Except for that sub-genre, Pavel theorizes, Elizabethan and Jacobean "tragedy has not yet managed to free itself from the strangle-hold of the narrative genres," whereas as early as the 1630s, in French classical tragedy, "there is a noticeable effort to remove everything epic, everything that can be narrated as well as enacted, from the stage." For Pavel, who points to *Phaedra* as an example, it is "precisely at the juncture when the excess of silent—pre-tragic—suffering crystallizes into language that the tragedy proper begins" (120–21).[5]

The continuing emphasis in both plays on the event or events that protagonists and playgoers interpret as function C is arguably one of the reasons that both plays seem to begin "late." In both *Hamlet* and *Phaedra,* the events that represent function C are extended over nearly five acts. Although the two plays are often at function C, the patterns that keep or bring them there are different. I will argue that Phaedra's function-C decisions lead to action—action that worsens her situation, thus requiring further function-C decisions—whereas Hamlet's situation worsens while he remains at or near function C.

Hamlet's indecisiveness, as it is often called, is perhaps the most commonly recognized feature of the play. In Act 1, in the interchange between Hamlet and the dead king's Ghost, the Ghost demands revenge. As soon as the Ghost reveals that the old king has been murdered, and even before he identifies the murderer, Hamlet immediately indicates that he has already made a function-C decision to undertake the revenge that the Ghost demands:

> Haste me to know't, that I, with wings as swift
> As meditation or the thoughts of love,
> May sweep to my revenge. (1.5.29–31)[6]

Again at the end of their interchange, after the Ghost names the murderer, describes how he was poisoned, and departs saying "Remember me" (1.5.91), Hamlet confirms that he considers the C-actant promise he has made to the Ghost a vow:

> Now to my word.
> It is 'Adieu, adieu, remember me.'
> I have sworn't. (1.5.110–12)

At this point in the play, most playgoers will interpret the function of the primary events that have been revealed like this:

A   old king murdered by his brother Claudius
B   old king's Ghost speaks to Hamlet, demands revenge
C   Hamlet vows to avenge his father's murder

The events that bring this sequence to a conclusion do not occur until the last scene of the play, and only after Hamlet becomes aware that his mother, Laertes, and he himself have been fatally poisoned as a result of a plot that Claudius has approved and helped plan. At that point Hamlet wounds the King with the poisoned sword and forces him to drink from the poisoned cup (function H), and thus avenges his father's murder (function I).

This is a familiar reading of the play. In my terms, the play extends the representation of events that Hamlet and playgoers interpret as function C from the last scene of Act 1 to the last scene of Act 5. I am saying that the play projects—as Hamlet's interpretation of where he is in an ongoing action—that he stays at function C, or at least that he is never very far from function C, throughout nearly the entire play. I argue moreover that playgoers tend to interpret the function of events as Hamlet does: for act after act he remains at function C. Given this interpretation, I want to look at how Shakespeare so successfully extends function C throughout nearly the entire play. My theory is that by establishing so clearly for Hamlet and for playgoers that the action is remaining at the pivotal position that function C marks, the play can and does freely accumulate additional events that Hamlet and we interpret as creating the function-A situation. Thus the ongoing function C holds playgoers' fascinated attention because we see it in relation to an ever-expanding set of function-A events. Since a function-C decision is made in response to a function-A situation, if the function-A situation changes, then the function-C decision to be made must also at least subtly change.

Already in Act 1, before Hamlet meets the Ghost, he is unhappy (and we know he is unhappy) about the death of his father, the immediate remarriage of his mother, and (we learn later) his not having been chosen as his father's successor as king. The information that his father was murdered, which he hears from the Ghost, provides one more entry in the accumulating set of events disrupting Hamlet's life, although it is the first of these events that requires (or is presented as requiring) that Hamlet take action in response. By the end of Act 1, it may seem (and it is often interpreted) that Hamlet's pretending to be mad is his initial action (function C') toward carrying out the Ghost's demand for revenge.

A_1 death of Hamlet's father
A_2 Hamlet's mother's remarriage, so soon
A_3 Claudius—not Hamlet—becomes the next king

A_4 Hamlet's father murdered by Claudius
B   Ghost demands revenge
C   Hamlet vows to avenge his father's death
C'   Hamlet pretends to be mad

In Act 2, the function-A disruptions in Hamlet's life continue to accumulate. First (function A_5), following her brother's advice and her father's orders (in scenes that playgoers hear in Act 1), Ophelia denies Hamlet access to her presence. Whatever Hamlet's intentions in regard to Ophelia (if in fact he has analyzed his intentions), he must surely find this change in their relationship an additional desta-bilizing element in his situation. Second (function a_6), and even more central to the progress of the action, Hamlet begins to doubt whether he can give the same credence to the Ghost's message as he would to words spoken by his father. As a result, Hamlet's intellectual focus shifts from considering how to avenge his father, at the end of Act 1, to something closer to a detective's form of ratiocination, made famous by Poe more than two centuries later, by the end of Act 2. Hamlet's speech at the conclusion of Act 2 expresses a function-C decision, but it is a different decision from the one that the Ghost and playgoers think he has made in Act 1, and he makes it in response to an expanded set of function-A events:

> If [Claudius] do blench [in response to the play Hamlet
>   arranges],
> I know my course. The spirit that I have seen
> May be a devil, and the devil hath power
> T'assume a pleasing shape, yea, and perhaps
> Out of my weakness and my melancholy,
> As he is very potent with such spirits,
> Abuses me to damn me. I'll have grounds
> More relative than this. The play's the thing
> Wherein I'll catch the conscience of the King. (2.2.593–601)

At the end of Act 2, Hamlet's situation (as I interpret it) looks to him like this:

A_1 death of Hamlet's father
A_2 Hamlet's mother's remarriage, so soon
A_3 Claudius—not Hamlet—becomes the next king
A_4 Hamlet's father murdered by Claudius (according to the
     Ghost)

A_5 Ophelia denies Hamlet access to her presence
a_6 Hamlet recognizes that the Ghost may be a devil, using deception to urge Hamlet to sinful action
C   Hamlet decides to determine for himself whether Claudius is guilty

In Act 3, Claudius's response to the play confirms for Hamlet his guilt (a_6 is resolved). But Hamlet's situation is once more disrupted and his action postponed when he recognizes that he must kill Claudius unshriven (function a_7; otherwise, Hamlet assumes, he would be sending Claudius directly to heaven, whereas Hamlet's father's sudden murder, according to the Ghost, by not allowing him time for confession, has required him to endure purgatory [3.3.76–79]). At this point just past the middle of the play, Hamlet acts, but his action goes awry.

A_1 death of Hamlet's father
A_2 Hamlet's mother's remarriage, so soon
A_3 Claudius—not Hamlet—becomes the next king
A_4 Hamlet's father murdered by Claudius
A_5 Ophelia denies Hamlet access to her presence
a_6 Hamlet recognizes that the Ghost may be a devil, using deception to urge Hamlet to sinful action
a_7 Hamlet recognizes that revenge requires that Claudius be killed unshriven
B   Ghost demands revenge
C   Hamlet decides to kill Claudius unshriven
H   Hamlet stabs man spying from behind curtain
I_{neg} dead man is Polonius, not Claudius

Shortly thereafter the Ghost appears again to Hamlet, in Hamlet's words "to whet [his] almost blunted purpose" (3.4.111), and Polonius's death confirms that Hamlet will have to leave for England, with Rosencrantz and Guildenstern.[7] This is how I interpret Hamlet's situation at the end of Act 3:

A_1 death of Hamlet's father
A_2 Hamlet's mother's remarriage, so soon
A_3 Claudius—not Hamlet—becomes the next king
A_4 Hamlet's father murdered by Claudius
A_5 Ophelia denies Hamlet access to her presence
a_6 Hamlet recognizes that the Ghost may be a devil, using

deception to urge Hamlet to sinful action
a_7 Hamlet recognizes that revenge requires that Claudius be killed unshriven
A_8 Hamlet must leave for England
B_1 Ghost demands revenge
B_2 Ghost returns to whet Hamlet's purpose

During Act 4, playgoers (in 4.3) and Hamlet (before writing the letter Horatio receives in 4.6) learn that Claudius has sent Hamlet to England to have him killed there (function A_9). By the end of Act 4, Ophelia is dead (function A_{10}). For playgoers, during Hamlet's absence from the court (and from the stage) during most of Act 4, the twin poles of action apparently available to him are played out by Ophelia (who goes mad) and Laertes (who conspires with Claudius to avenge his father's murder). By the end of Act 4, Claudius and Laertes are firmly committed to their plan of action to kill Hamlet.[8] But even as late as Act 5, Scene 2, Hamlet is still trying to bring himself to a firm function-C decision to kill Claudius, this time by reciting to Horatio a litany of what I call function-A events:

> Does it not, think thee, stand me now upon—
> He that hath kill'd my King [function A_4] and whor'd my
>   mother [function A_2],
> Popp'd in between th'election and my hopes [function A_3],
> Thrown out his angle for my proper life [function A_9]
> And with such coz'nage—is't not perfect conscience
> To quit him with this arm? [5.2.63–68]

With by now (by my count) ten function-A disruptive events now accumulated, four of which he lists himself, Hamlet still continues to question whether he should act. By the time that Hamlet kills Claudius, later in the scene, he makes his function-C decision to act in response to a set of function-A events that includes two new events (A_{11} and A_{12}).

A_1 death of Hamlet's father
A_2 Hamlet's mother's remarriage, so soon
A_3 Claudius—not Hamlet—becomes the next king
A_4 Hamlet's father murdered by Claudius
A_5 Ophelia denies Hamlet access to her presence
a_6 Hamlet recognizes that the Ghost may be a devil, using

deception to urge Hamlet to sinful action

a_7 Hamlet recognizes that revenge requires that Claudius be killed unshriven

A_8 Hamlet must leave for England

A_9 Claudius has sent Hamlet to England to have him killed

A_{10} Ophelia is dead

A_{11} Hamlet's mother is poisoned and dies

A_{12} Hamlet is poisoned and dying

B   Ghost demands revenge

B_2 Ghost returns to whet Hamlet's purpose

C   Hamlet decides to kill Claudius

F   Hamlet still has sufficient strength to kill Claudius, but not for long

H   Hamlet stabs Claudius and forces him to drink poison

I   Claudius dies unshriven

EQ Hamlet's father's murder is avenged

As I interpret the function of the events, three changes occur between Hamlet's still-indecisive speech to Horatio near the beginning of Act 5, Scene 2, and the moment when Hamlet kills Claudius at the end of Act 5, Scene 2: (1) There are two additional function-A events (functions A_{11} and A_{12}). The accumulated weight of disruptive events is perhaps sufficient to bring Hamlet to action. (2) Hamlet's mother has been killed. This event not only allows Hamlet to kill Claudius to avenge her death, but frees Hamlet to kill Claudius without earning her disapproval. (3) Hamlet himself is near death. Since Hamlet has known for some time that Claudius wants him dead (function A_9), Claudius's obvious animosity does not alter the situation. What is changed (and greatly curtailed) by Hamlet's being about to die is how much time he has left in which he can expect to retain the physical strength he will need (function F) to be able to kill Claudius. Hamlet himself draws attention to the function-F "strength, and means" he needs, in a speech in Act 4 in which he offers an interpretation of his position in the ongoing action that resembles a function analysis:

> I do not know
> Why yet I live to say this thing's to do [function H has not
>   been accomplished],
> Sith I have cause [function A], and will [function C], and
>   strength, and means [function F]
> To do't. [4.4.43–46]

The purpose of my analysis is not to argue that one or another of the three changes I identify brings Hamlet to action, nor, for that matter, that the possibilities are limited to these three. The very number of function-A events that are relatively easily identified helps to explain, and perhaps even to corroborate, the many different interpretations the play has attracted. My purpose in this context is, first, to draw attention to the greatly extended duration of the period in which Hamlet and playgoers interpret his position in the ongoing action as at or near function C; and, second, to demonstrate the degree to which the five acts are filled by an accumulating number of events—an additive increase in the set of events—that Hamlet and playgoers interpret as function A or function a: more and more disruptive events occur as the play progresses, of which few are resolved until the last scene.

In *Hamlet*, then, as a hermeneutic device, function C comforts almost unremittingly. Hamlet's inaction and his repeated commentary (in soliloquies and to Horatio) about his inaction serve as the lodestar that guides playgoers to recognize that Hamlet remains at or near function C nearly throughout. In this respect—as a hermeneutic device—function C brings comfort almost exactly as it does in the newscasts about the sandbaggers.

As a thematics, however, function C comforts in *Hamlet* less simply and less obviously than in the newscasts about the sandbaggers—as one would expect, since the newscasts and the play are of course not comparable aesthetically. (I look at them together because the simpler illuminates the more complex.) In the newscasts, the sandbaggers' function-C decision is immediate and immediately put into action, and comforts by suggesting throughout the period of the flooding that intentional acts may be effective. The play holds playgoers' interest through five acts that remain at or near function C, as a function analysis indicates, by the increasing tension between the expanding function-A situation and Hamlet's function-C (in)decision in response. That is, while the additive accumulation of function-A events makes the need for action increasingly apparent, Hamlet's continuing inaction as the play progresses makes it seem increasingly a possibility that he will not be able to decide to act. By forcing playgoers to confront the issue of whether the function-C decision will occur, the mounting tension between function A and function C holds playgoers' attention on function C for act after act. This emphasis on the need for a function-C decision, in combination with the postponement of the decision until the final scene, intensifies, I suggest, the thematic comfort that function C brings: even Hamlet ultimately can bring himself to carry out intentional action to resolve a disruptive situation.

In this most successful and perhaps most satisfying play written in English, nearly the entire play is given over for playgoers to question whether the protagonist will act to alleviate a situation that is increasingly obviously disruptive. In my terms, by so clearly indicating that Hamlet remains at or near function C for nearly five acts, the play provides hermeneutic comfort throughout and in doing so focuses playgoers' attention on the withholding of thematic comfort until the final minutes. In the end, after five acts of indecision, Hamlet acts. When he stabs Claudius with the envenomed sword and forces him to drink the poisoned potion, playgoers understand—from his actions, not from anything he says—that Hamlet has now made a function-C decision and that the play has now moved beyond function C. Whatever individual playgoers' feelings about the mass slaughter on the stage, Hamlet's interpretation of the function of events, which has guided us throughout, here too leads playgoers to interpret the effect of his actions as he does. His final speech, which is a request to Horatio to report what has happened, suggests that he considers the outcome as (at least relatively) successful; he *wants* his story told. For playgoers, the effect of this pattern is that the long-awaited, intensified thematic comfort that function C brings is followed within minutes (even seconds) by the satisfaction of seeing intentional action brought to a successful conclusion. The extension of function C and near juxtaposition of function C and function I in part explains, I suggest, the enormous success of the play over the centuries.

■

Racine's *Phaedra* has long been understood to be a meditation on the relation between human and random forces. A function analysis brings new clarity to demonstrating the interplay in the drama of the effects of chance and of Phaedra's own intentional acts. In *Phaedra* as in *Hamlet,* playgoers are led to assume in Act 1 that an event is about to occur that does not take place until the end of the play. When Phaedra first comes on stage in Act 1, she is emerging from indoors to see the sun one last time. She has previously decided to die; she is dying. At the very end of Act 5, she dies.

Phaedra's initial words when she enters express a function-C decision: "No further. Here, Oenone, Let us stay" (1.3.153).[9]

Because Oenone, Phaedra's attendant and former nurse, has reported just a few lines previously that Phaedra is "dying from a hidden malady" (1.2.146), Phaedra's expressed decision not to walk further is easily heard as a metaphor for her decision not to live longer. That function-C decision—Phaedra's decision to die— plays the pivotal role that function-C customarily does in guiding hermeneutic activity. Like Oenone, playgoers who recognize that Phaedra has decided to die will focus their attention both on whether Phaedra will die (function I) and on what has happened to make her want to die (function A).

Oenone soon succeeds in getting Phaedra to tell her (and us) why she has decided to die. Shortly after her new husband, Theseus, brought her to Athens, Phaedra explains, she met Theseus' son (from a previous marriage) Hippolytus. Phaedra describes the effect:

> As I beheld, I reddened, I turned pale.
> A tempest raged in my distracted mind.
> My eyes no longer saw. I could not speak.
> I felt my body freezing, burning; knew
> Venus was on me with her dreaded flames,
> The fatal torments of a race she loathes. (1.3.273–78)

To whatever combination of divine intervention and the blind chance of passion Racine's sophisticated seventeenth-century audience (and playgoers today) ascribe the power that Phaedra refers to as "Venus," the grip of passion under which Phaedra suffers is presented in the play as the same kind of awful and awe-inspiring function-A event as the rising of the flood waters during the floods in the Midwest.[10] As I read the play and as the play is often interpreted, Phaedra is no more responsible for the onset of her passion than the sandbaggers are for the rising of the flood waters.[11] Phaedra has struggled against her passion, moreover, she tells Oenone and us, in every way she knows, including planning to die without speaking of it:

> Dying, I could have kept my name unstained,
> And my dark passion from the light of day. (1.3.309–10)

Given this information, playgoers can reconstruct retrospectively Phaedra's interpretation of the situation at the moment when the play begins.

A_1 Phaedra's incestuous passion for Hippolytus
C_1 Phaedra decides to die to protect her and her ancestors' honor
C' Phaedra stops eating

Still in Act 1, however, the news arrives that Theseus is dead. Oenone argues that the news makes Phaedra's love for Hippolytus no longer incestuous, and that in fact the news requires that Phaedra live to protect her son's chances of inheriting his father's political power. At the end of Act 1, Phaedra responds: "Your counsels have prevailed. / I'll live" (1.5.363–64), a statement I interpret as a new function-C decision, which she immediately puts into action. In Act 2, Phaedra sends for Hippolytus, and when he arrives she asks him initially to protect her son, then—apparently overcome by his presence—admits to him her passion for him. Thus in Act 3, when the report of Theseus' death proves inaccurate and Theseus returns, Phaedra immediately recognizes that by confessing her love to Hippolytus she has dishonored her husband and herself:

> My husband lives. Oenone, say no more.
> I have confessed a love that soils his name. (3.2.832–33)

At this point in the play, if Phaedra's son no longer needs her political guidance (function A_2), the initial function-A situation is as problematic as ever, and now Phaedra's own actions have brought about the very situation—Theseus' and her own dishonor—that she had hoped at the beginning of the play to avoid by dying.

A_1 Phaedra's incestuous passion for Hippolytus
C_1 Phaedra decides to die to protect her and her ancestors' honor
C' Phaedra stops eating
A_2 with Theseus dead, Phaedra's son needs her (and her incestuous passion perhaps seems to her less guilty)
C_2 Phaedra decides to live
C' Phaedra sends for Hippolytus
H_1 Phaedra asks Hippolytus to protect her son
H_2 Phaedra admits her love to Hippolytus
A_3 Theseus is alive, and Phaedra has dishonored herself and him

For the onset of Phaedra's function-A_1 passion I have argued that Phaedra is not responsible. For the function-A_3 situation, she holds

herself responsible. Nonetheless playgoers will recognize that
although Phaedra has acted rashly in admitting her love to
Hippolytus, the exceedingly unfortunate situation she is now in
has as its primary cause the inaccurate chance-driven rumor that
reached her about Theseus' death.

But worse is yet to come. In her shame, Phaedra permits Oenone
to carry out a plan that Oenone has devised: Oenone will falsely
accuse Hippolytus to Theseus of having forced himself upon
Phaedra, which at the beginning of Act 4 Oenone does (function
A_4).[12] Then when Phaedra, regretting this, goes to Theseus to
attempt to alleviate its effects, she learns from him that Hippolytus
loves Aricia—information that playgoers have had since the first
scene of the play but that for Phaedra reveals for the first time that
"Hippolytus can love but loves not me" (4.5.1203).[13] For Phaedra
this information leads her to break off her attempt to save
Hippolytus' life and to reevaluate her situation (function a_5).

A_1 Phaedra's incestuous passion for Hippolytus
C_1 Phaedra decides to die to protect her and her ancestors'
      honor
C' Phaedra stops eating, becomes ill
A_2 with Theseus dead, Phaedra's son needs her (and her
      incestuous passion perhaps seems to her less guilty)
C_2 Phaedra decides to live
C' Phaedra sends for Hippolytus
H_1 Phaedra asks Hippolytus to protect her son
H_2 Phaedra admits her love to Hippolytus
A_3 Theseus is alive, and Phaedra has dishonored herself and
      him
C_3 Phaedra decides to accept Oenone's offer to falsely accuse
      Hippolytus
C' Phaedra gives Oenone permission to accuse Hippolytus to
      Theseus
A_4 Oenone falsely accuses Hippolytus *with Phaedra's permis-
      sion*
C_4 Phaedra decides to defend Hippolytus
C' Phaedra asks Theseus to spare Hippolytus
a_5 Phaedra learns from Theseus that Hippolytus loves Aricia

At this point Phaedra turns on Oenone, punishing her for
tempting Phaedra to act in ways that have made Phaedra's situation worse now than at the beginning of the play:

Wretch! Thus it is that you have caused my doom.
You, when I fled from life, you called me back;
At your entreaties duty was forgot;
It was *you* made me see Hippolytus.
You meddling fool. Why did your impious lips,
Falsely accusing him, besmirch his life?
You may have killed him, if the gods have heard
A maddened father's sacrilegious wish.
I'll hear no more. Hence, loathsome monster, hence.
Go, leave me to my pitiable fate. (4.6.1309–18)

Oenone dies (she drowns herself; function A_6). Hippolytus dies
(function A_7). Phaedra takes poison and then speaks to Theseus to
clear Hippolytus' name before dying herself. In my analysis of the
function of the primary events in the play,[14] I indent in each
sequence function C and the actions it motivates, to draw attention to how often Phaedra's motivated actions cause subsequent
function-A situations, a topic that I will discuss in some detail
below.

A_1 Phaedra's incestuous passion for Hippolytus

    C_1 Phaedra decides to die to protect her and her
          ancestors' honor
    C'   Phaedra stops eating, becomes ill

A_2 with Theseus dead, Phaedra's son needs her (and her inces-
    tuous passion perhaps seems to her less guilty)

    C_2 Phaedra decides to live
    C'   Phaedra sends for Hippolytus
    H_1 Phaedra asks Hippolytus to protect her son
    H_2 Phaedra admits her love to Hippolytus
    H_3 Phaedra sends Oenone to tempt Hippolytus by
          offering political power

A_3 Theseus is alive, and Phaedra has dishonored herself and him

    C_3 Phaedra decides to accept Oenone's offer to
          falsely accuse Hippolytus
    C'   Phaedra gives Oenone permission to accuse
          Hippolytus to Theseus

A_4 Oenone falsely accuses Hippolytus *with Phaedra's permission*

        C_4 Phaedra decides to defend Hippolytus
        C'   Phaedra asks Theseus to spare Hippolytus

a_5 Phaedra learns from Theseus that Hippolytus loves Aricia

        C_5 Phaedra decides to punish Oenone for tempting
                her
        C', H Phaedra berates Oenone, sends her away

A_6 Oenone drowns herself
A_7 Hippolytus dies

        C_6 Phaedra decides to clear Hippolytus' name and
            then die
        C' Phaedra takes poison
        H Phaedra explains to Theseus that—and why—
            Oenone falsely accused Hippolytus
        I   Phaedra dies

Like *Hamlet, Phaedra* seems barely to move. Both plays introduce in Act 1 what playgoers initially hear as a firm function-C decision—Hamlet's to avenge his father, Phaedra's to die—and both postpone action to carry out that decision until the final scene of Act 5. Throughout the three middle acts and the larger part of Act 5, *Phaedra* like *Hamlet* is often at or near function C. In both plays too, function-A situations accumulate as the action progresses. But the patterns by which *Phaedra* and *Hamlet* emphasize function C and accumulate function-A events are not identical. I call attention to three ways they differ.

First, although function C is emphasized in both plays, in *Hamlet* it is extended (Hamlet makes one decision slowly) and in *Phaedra* it is repeated (Phaedra makes a number of decisions). In *Hamlet,* as we saw above, Hamlet seems to have made a function-C decision before the end of Act 1, but considers and reconsiders until the end of the last act how and whether to take action to carry out that one putative decision. Phaedra, in contrast, is constantly making decisions; I draw attention to six in the function analysis above. Moreover, Phaedra's function-C decisions all lead to action (each function C in the analysis above is followed by a function C'). And each of her actions worsens the situation in

which she finds herself. A function analysis supports the traditional reading of Racine's play: that perhaps we do not hold Phaedra
responsible for her love for Hippolytus, but we do hold her
responsible for her actions during the play that cause her dishon-
or. By dying at the beginning of the play as she had planned,
Phaedra could have preserved her honor and her ancestors' honor.
But instead, from the end of Act 1 to the final scene of Act 5,
Phaedra makes a series of function-C decisions that each motivate
action that makes it increasingly difficult and finally impossible for
her to escape dishonor. If we look at her function-C decisions that
I number from C_2 through C_5, she decides to live (function C_2),
which leads her to confess her love to Hippolytus. Because by this
confession she has dishonored herself and Theseus, when Theseus
returns she agrees to Oenone's plan (function C_3) and sends
Oenone to accuse Hippolytus. Because she has permitted
Hippolytus to be falsely accused, she decides to defend him to
Theseus (function C_4), but stops without doing so when she learns
from Theseus that Hippolytus loves Aricia. Forced to recognize at
last that under no circumstances could she have obtained
Hippolytus' love, Phaedra decides to punish Oenone (function C_5),
who drowns herself.

Second, although function-A events accumulate in both plays,
in *Hamlet*, none are the result of Hamlet's intentional acts. In
Phaedra, however, Phaedra's intentional acts contribute to or
cause all the disruptive function-A events that occur after the play
begins. Of the seven function-A events I identify, the first,
Phaedra's incestuous passion for Hippolytus, which is reported in
the first act but has occurred earlier, can be ascribed to Venus (in
the context of the play). The second (Phaedra's interpretation that
with Theseus dead, her son needs her political guidance) is an
effect of a combination of chance misinformation, Oenone's well-
intentioned but ultimately misguided pleading, and Phaedra's decision to listen to Oenone. For the third (Phaedra's having dishonored Theseus and herself by confessing her love to Hippolytus),
Phaedra holds herself fully responsible and is, but playgoers may
see her responsibility as somewhat mitigated by her having been
misinformed about Theseus' death. The remaining four function-
A events are all directly effects of Phaedra's intentional acts: the
false accusation of Hippolytus, the information that Hippolytus
loves Aricia, Oenone's death, Hippolytus' death.

Third, function-A events accumulate in both plays, but with different effect. In *Hamlet*, the accumulation is additive. As the play

progresses, the number of disruptive function-A situations increases. But the change is quantitative, not qualitative. The primary motivating situation (the murder of Hamlet's father) is not fundamentally altered—it remains neither more nor less horrifying—from the first act to the concluding scene, when it is finally avenged. In *Phaedra,* on the other hand, the accumulating function-A events make a qualitative change in the initial disruptive situation. In Act 1, Phaedra's death would have resolved her incestuous passion for Hippolytus, with her reputation intact and with damage to no one other than herself. By the end of the play, the acts that her passion has led her to engage in make her responsible for the deaths of Hippolytus and Oenone, for depriving Theseus and Aricia of son and prospective husband, and (most important to Phaedra) for her own irreparably damaged reputation. This intensification of the criminality of who she is and of the function-A situation she finds herself in at the end of the play is thus far beyond what her confession and death in the final scene can resolve.

As it is in *Hamlet,* the comfort that function C brings as a hermeneutic device is pervasive. Phaedra's repeated function-C decisions are as effective as Hamlet's extended decision in identifying for playgoers a lodestar in relation to which to gauge where they are in the ongoing action. As a thematics too, the repeated function-C decisions in *Phaedra* are as effective as the extended function C in *Hamlet* in holding playgoers' attention for act after act on the issue of the effectiveness of human intentional action. But just as the comfort that function C brings as a thematics is less easy in response to *Hamlet* than to the newscasts about the sandbaggers, the response that function C as a thematics brings in *Phaedra* is more complicated than in *Hamlet.*

In *Hamlet,* I argued, the thematic comfort that function C brings is in effect intensified by a representation that guides playgoers to expect it and then withholds it until the final scene. To the degree that we become unsure that Hamlet is capable of intentional action, it is all the more comforting to learn that he is. In *Phaedra,* while the repeated function-C decisions hold our attention to the issue of the effectiveness of intentional action, "comfort" is not a word one easily uses to describe our response. In *Phaedra,* intentional action is all too effective; each of Phaedra's decisions leads to action that intensifies the already painful situation we find her in at the beginning of the play.[15]

Yet even in *Phaedra,* as we watch Phaedra take her fate into her own decisive control, we find satisfaction in being shown just how effective intentional action can be, even when its effects are not what Phaedra, or playgoers, would wish. Often understood as a study of the effects of random power (Venus) and human intentional action (Phaedra's), the play is satisfying *because* Phaedra's tragedy is to such a degree of her own making. The respect we develop for Phaedra is not for her lineage, or the familial curse visited upon her, but for how hard she tries: her function-C decisions and the intentional actions to which they lead. And yes, even if *comfort* may seem far removed from *Phaedra,* I will use the word. Do we not find comfort in recognizing that Phaedra's terrible fate is not solely the result of blind chance but rather, in part—even largely—of her own making? And if we do, it is because of the comfort function C brings as a thematics: that human intentional action can be effective.

■

In the Preface to the volume in the New York Edition that includes *Daisy Miller,* Henry James reports that after Leslie Stephen published the novella in *The Cornhill Magazine* in 1878, it was "promptly pirated in Boston—a sweet tribute I hadn't yet received and was never again to know" (18: vi). The "tribute" from Boston must have seemed the sweeter because the Philadelphia publisher to whom James initially offered the novella rejected it, James writes:

> with an absence of comment that struck me at the time as rather grim—as, given the circumstances [James's previous publications in this publisher's magazine], requiring indeed some explanation: till a friend to whom I appealed for light, giving him the thing to read, declared it could only have passed with the Philadelphia critic for "an outrage on American girlhood." (18: v)

At the time of its publication and for several decades afterward, *Daisy Miller* remained both more popular and more controversial than any other of James's novels and stories.

Daisy Miller is the narrative that Tamar Yacobi selects to exemplify the quantity and the variety of the data that affect readers' decisions about who is the focus of interest (the protagonist) in a narrative. In a detailed analysis of the process by which readers determine the identity of the protagonist, Yacobi first summarizes the six textual indicators of the protagonist that Meir Sternberg describes, then adds to his list six contextual indicators: in her words, the "centralizing force [of the contextual indicators] derives less from the intratextual signals encountered and the patterns made of them *in* the reading than from the models and expectations of interest that we bring *to* the reading" ("Hero or Heroine?" 10; her emphasis). Then turning to the published record of readers' responses to *Daisy Miller*—the reviews and commentaries from the early decades, and twentieth-century critical accounts—Yacobi reports "a sharp division on [the identity of the protagonist, Daisy or Winterbourne] among readers, and what is more, a systematic division along historical lines: between contemporaries and moderns." Yacobi's analysis of the documents shows that in the early decades "the girl—her character, morality, fate—caught the imagination and dominated the response of the reading public," while Winterbourne's "elevation to the role of protagonist came as late as the 1960's" (13, 14).[16]

Yacobi's historicizing account of interpretations of the identity of the protagonist in *Daisy Miller*, in conjunction with James's emphasis on the popularity of the novella during the early period in which, as Yacobi discerns, Daisy is seen as the protagonist, leads me to return to the recorded readers' responses to look for a correlation between the novella's reception at a given historical period and the importance of function C in the interpretations of that period. Also supporting this undertaking is my own interpretation that (as fascinating as James's novella is) neither Daisy nor Winterbourne is a very satisfactory protagonist, largely because neither, in my reading, makes the function-C decision that would establish her or him as a C-actant. But I will move chronologically, looking first at the immediate response, next at William Dean Howells's commentary written at the turn of the century, then at Wayne Booth's analysis sixty years later, and lastly at my own.

As Yacobi points out, in the decades following the publication of the novella readers' identification of Daisy as the central character "cut across all oppositions in attitude and judgment . . . [T]he focus on the heroine united her attackers and her defenders, those who viewed her as a type and those who saw a caricature, the Philadelphia editor who [James's friend suggests] rejected the story as 'an outrage on American girlhood' and the champions of decorum who celebrated it as a lesson to that girlhood" (13–14). Some aspects of the controversy that surrounded the novella at the time of its publication are not relevant to my project of formulating a function analysis that represents James's contemporaries' interpretations of the novella: chauvinist defenses of American girls, or arguments about whether James intended Daisy as a faithful portrait of a typical American girl or an exaggerated representation designed to teach his compatriots proper behavior. I look instead for indications of contemporary interpretations of why Daisy behaves as she does.

For its first generation of readers, *Daisy Miller* drew attention to the difference in the behavior that was expected of young unmarried women in Europe and in the United States. The primary difference, as I understand the materials I have read, is in the customs regarding chaperonage. In England and on the Continent, at the time, marriageable young women were chaperoned at home when they received visits from young men and always when they went out. According to an editorial in *The New York Times* that was written the year after *Daisy Miller* was published, chaperones were required in the highest circles in New York, but not in many cities even nearby:

> Again, as to social customs, ask a young lady in highest grade of life in New York whether it is considered the correct thing to go to a theatre alone with a young man, and she will exclaim at such an idea; yet there are cities not many hours distant where her cousins, who occupy an equally good social position, do this with perfect propriety. (June 4, 1879, in William T. Stafford, *James's Daisy Miller*, 123–24)

In other words, in Schenectady where Daisy has grown up, "going about" unchaperoned is acceptable behavior. For that matter, various published voices suggest that the freer social customs practiced in places like Schenectady are appropriate for American women abroad. A writer identified as "J. P. T." asks in a commentary published in 1878: "As to young ladies who have already taken a place in society at home, why should they not travel abroad as freely as young men, whether for study, pleasure, or 'general culture'?" (*Nation* 36, 356; quoted by Elizabeth F. Hoxie, "Mrs. Grundy Adopts Daisy Miller," 126). Even the social arbiter Mrs. John Sherwood wrote in 1884 that "Independent American girls may still choose to travel without a chaperon, but they must be prepared to fight a well-founded prejudice if they do" (*Manners and Social Usages* [New York, 1884], 26, quoted by Hoxie, 129).

Leslie Fiedler, revisiting from a much later period James's contemporaries' response, refers to Daisy's "resolve" when he asks, somewhat rhetorically, what made American girls in 1878 "indignant at and resentful of poor Daisy, with her unspeakable little brother, her shocked American admirer and her naïve resolve to consort with Italians just as she had with her 'gentlemen friends' in Schenectady" (*Love and Death in the American Novel*, 311). Guided by Fiedler, I suggest that James's contemporaries are reading Daisy's behavior as that of a C-actant who has resolved to behave in Europe exactly as she has behaved at home. If one looks for textual evidence to support this interpretation, one can find some. Daisy tells Winterbourne that she introduces her gentlemen friends to her mother, her mother's timidity notwithstanding, because if she didn't, "'I shouldn't think I was natural'" (31). She comments that "'[p]eople have different ideas'" of propriety, comparing Mrs. Walker's "'wanting me to get into her carriage and drop poor Mr. Giovanelli, and under the pretext that it was proper,'" to her own view that "'[i]t would have been most unkind; he had been talking about that walk for ten days'" (70). She tells Winterbourne, "'The young ladies of this country [Italy] have a dreadfully pokey time of it, by what I can discover; I don't see why I should change my habits for *such* stupids'" (70; James's emphasis). The same logic can be interpreted as motivating her arrival after her mother's at Mrs. Walker's party (she sent her mother ahead, she explains to Mrs. Walker, because she "'wanted to make Mr. Giovanelli practice some things before he came . . . and I want you to ask him to sing'" [69]) and her trip to the Roman Colosseum ("'I was bound to see the Colosseum by moonlight—I wouldn't have wanted to go home without *that*'" [88; James's emphasis], she tells Winterbourne).

A function analysis might look like this:[17]

EQ   Daisy lives happily in Schenectady

A_1 Daisy is brought to an unfamiliar environment, where she does not know how young women are expected to behave

C_1 Daisy resolves to behave as she would at home: she decides to go to Chillon alone with Winterbourne

H_1 Daisy goes to Chillon alone with Winterbourne

I_{neg1} Mrs. Costello refuses to meet Daisy

$I_{neg1} = A_2$ Daisy loses the guidance Mrs. Costello could have given her

$\qquad$ C_2 Daisy resolves to behave as she would at home: she decides to walk in public alone with Giovanelli; she decides to go to Mrs. Walker's party alone with Giovanelli

$\qquad$ H_2 Daisy walks in public alone with Giovanelli; she goes to Mrs. Walker's party alone with Giovanelli

$\qquad$ I_{neg2} Mrs. Walker excludes Daisy from her guest list

$I_{neg2} = A_3$ Daisy loses the guidance Mrs. Walker could have given her

$\qquad$ C_3 Daisy resolves to behave as she would at home: she decides to visit the Colosseum alone with Giovanelli at night

$\qquad$ H_3 Daisy goes to the Colosseum with Giovanelli alone at night

$\qquad$ I_{neg3} Winterbourne decides he need no longer respect her; she is exposed to Roman fever

$I_{neg3} = A_4$ Daisy loses Winterbourne's respect and dies of the Roman fever

I draw attention to the similarity between this function analysis and the one earlier in this chapter that represents Racine's *Phaedra*. Both include repeated function-C decisions. In both, the protagonist's decisions motivate intentional acts that make her situation worse. Although neither is responsible for the initial function-A situation she finds herself in, both bring about as the result of their function-C decisions a qualitative change that increases the difficulty of the initial disruptive situation. For readers today, Daisy's stubborn insistence on going about unchaperoned does not carry the semiotic value it apparently did at the time the novella was published; as a result, we easily miss the signs that I am proposing that readers of the period interpreted as function-C decisions. For readers who understood the semiotics of chaperonage, Daisy's function-C decisions would presumably have brought the comforts that function-C brings both as a hermeneutic device (providing the lodestar that locates where one is in an ongoing sequence) and as a thematics (the comfort of believing in the efficacy of human intentional action, even in situations in which the effects happen to be unwelcome).

The function analysis above with its repeated function-C decisions, I am proposing, represents interpretations at the time of the novella's greatest popularity. Moreover, this analysis represents equally well the interpretations at the time of Daisy's defenders and of Daisy's accusers: those who see her as choosing to behave abroad as she does at home and thereby retaining her naturalness and her identity, and those who see her as choosing to behave abroad as she does at home and thereby foolishly damaging her reputation and unnecessarily restricting the society she moves in. A function analysis represents interpretations of causal relations; judgments about the appropriateness of a character's intentional acts are a separate issue. As judgments, approval and disapproval of a given behavior both require the assumption that the behavior has been chosen. I am suggesting that among the first generation of readers, at the period of the novella's greatest popularity, readers who defended Daisy and readers who disapproved of her behavior all typically interpreted Daisy's behavior as that of a C-actant who repeatedly made and acted upon decisions about how to behave.

For William Dean Howells, who just over twenty years after *Daisy Miller* was published wrote a study to which I turn, James's novella offered so accurate a portrait of the American girl at a specific historical moment that the portrait had the effect of altering the species portrayed: "[James] recognized and portrayed the innocently adventuring, unconsciously periculant American maiden, who hastened to efface herself almost as soon as she saw herself in that still flattering if a little mocking mirror, so that between two sojourns in Europe, a decade apart, she had time to fade from the vision of the friendly spectator" (*Heroines of Fiction*, 2: 166). Howells is a defender, both of Daisy and of *Daisy Miller* ("[i]t is pathetic to remember how 'Daisy Miller' was received, or rather rejected, as an attack on American girlhood" [2: 169]). But the defense he offers consists of an after-the-fact ("in the retrospect") description—a static portrait—of a girl who has died, rather than a sequential representation of discrete events leading to a death. The effect is to remove from the character her resolve—her function-C decision-making, whether judged for good or for ill—that the first generation of readers seems to have found in the novella and to have found fascinating. I draw attention particularly to Howells's expressed interest in the psychology over the incidents, and to his use of the verb tenses to indicate an ongoing state (Daisy "goes about Europe" and "knows" and "is") until she "is dead" (of "the blows" and the Roman fever):

> Such drama as arises in the simple circumstances precipitates itself in a few spare incidents which, in the retrospect, dwindle to nothing before the superior interest of the psychology. A girl of the later eighteen-seventies, sent with such a mother as hers to Europe by a father who remains making money in Schenectady, after no more experience of the world than she had got in her native town, and at a number of New York dinners among people of like tradition; uncultivated but not rude, reckless but not bold, inexpugnably ignorant of the conventionally right, and spiritedly resentful of control by criterions that offend her own sense of things, she goes about Europe doing exactly what she would do at home, from an innocence as guileless as that which shaped her conduct in her native town. She knows no harm and she means none; she loves life, and talking, and singing, and dancing, and "attentions," but she is no flirt, and she is essentially and infinitely far from worse. Her whole career, as the reader is acquainted with it, is seen through the privity of the young Europeanized American who meets her at Vevey and follows her to Rome in a fascination which they have for each other, but which is never explicitly a passion. This side of the affair is of course managed with the fine adroitness of Mr. James's mastery; from the first moment the sense of their potential love is a delicate pleasure for the reader, till at the last it is a delicate pang, when the girl has run her wild gantlet and is dead not only of the Roman fever but of the blows dealt her in her course. (2: 170–71)

To emphasize the iterative aspect of Howells's description (in contrast to the discrete events reported in narrative accounts), I compare Howells's account to a similar account by James—not *Daisy Miller*, but rather James's report of the germ from which he developed the novella, an incident mentioned by a friend:

> some simple and uninformed American lady of the previous winter, whose young daughter, a child of nature and of freedom, accompanying her from hotel to hotel, had "picked

up" by the wayside, with the best conscience in the world, a good-looking Roman, of vague identity, astonished at his luck, yet . . . all innocently, all serenely exhibited and introduced: this at least till the occurrence of some small social check, some interrupting incident. (Preface, 18: v)

James uses different tenses (the young woman's activities "had" gone on until an event interrupted them), but both accounts report by summarizing a state of affairs that continues over a period of time, followed by a disruptive event. According to the germ James reports,

> EQ an American girl goes about Rome with a good-looking Roman
> A   some interrupting incident occurs

Or, according to Howells's account of the completed novella,

> EQ Daisy goes about Europe
> A   Daisy dies of the Roman fever and "the blows dealt her in her course"

In both cases—James's report of the germ, Howells's report of the completed novella—the events of the American girl's life are presented as part of the exposition: as prior chronologically to "that point in time which marks the beginning of the *fictive present*" in the representation (Meir Sternberg, *Expositional Modes*, 21). James, of course, begins with such an account and makes from it *Daisy Miller*. But Howells reduces *Daisy Miller* to this account *in order to defend Daisy*.

By describing Daisy's activities as "going about Europe," Howells offers an interpretation of the character that includes no indication that she is engaging in any form of function-C decision-making. In fact, elsewhere in the same essay, Howells refers to the "witless purposelessness" that Daisy illustrates ("where else [other than James's novella, can one] find the witless purposelessness . . . in much of a girl's behavior more sufficiently yet more sparingly suggestive" [2: 173]). According to Howells's interpretation of Daisy as I understand it, Daisy should not be considered an affront to American girlhood because what she does when she "goes about" is purposeless—that is, that her actions are not guided by function-C decision-making. Perhaps too she seems to him too "witless" to recognize a function-A disruptive situation or to formulate a decision in response to it. As I read Howells's commentary, his defense of Daisy consists of absolving her of her "sins" by presenting her as incapable of distinguishing and deciding between appropriate and inappropriate behavior. As outrageous as a defense in these terms seems today, Howells's interpretation of Daisy also leaves her less interesting—even in 1901, when his study was published—than in earlier interpretations that credited Daisy with decision-making ability. In addition, by 1901, the "topical interest" (Yacobi's term; "Hero or Heroine?" 17) in Daisy as a type had long since waned with the disappearance of the type, which Howells reports. In conjunction with changing social conditions, Howells's often-cited commentary not only presages but perhaps influenced declining interest in the character and the novella for a number of decades to come.

In *The Rhetoric of Fiction* (1961), Wayne Booth famously reinterprets *Daisy Miller,* renewing interest in the novella by guiding readers to turn their attention to the focalizer Winterbourne, rather than to the object on whom Winterbourne focuses, Daisy. Describing Daisy as "really, as James said, a 'scant' object" (283), Booth concludes:

> the drama of Winterbourne's chilly misunderstanding of her true nature is really more important in the finished tale than Daisy's own actions. Seen through his eyes she can hardly become emotionally important to us, though of course we must recognize that she is worth much more than he suspects. His slow caution and ready suspicions are admirably suited to make us aware of the pathos of Daisy, without giving our awareness too much emotional force. (283)

Continuing, Booth points to a scene in the novella that explains how the "drama" that he envisions ("the drama of Winterbourne's chilly misunderstanding") concludes:

> When Winterbourne discovers [Daisy] alone with her Italian at night in the Colosseum, his "final horror is mitigated by a final relief." "It was as if a sudden clearance had taken place in the ambiguity of the poor girl's appearances and the whole riddle of her contradictions had grown easy to read.   ·
> She was a young lady about the *shades* of whose perversity a foolish puzzled gentleman need no longer trouble his head or his heart." (Booth, 283–84, quoting *Daisy Miller,* 86)

The answer to the riddle that Winterbourne is relieved in this
scene to have discovered is "wrong," Booth says, and implicates
Winterbourne because of his "faulty vision [as] a necessary cause
in the overt action" (284).

As I understand Booth's interpretation, Winterbourne is the C-
actant.

EQ	Winterbourne is making one of his frequent visits to his aunt
A_1	Winterbourne meets Daisy and is puzzled and fascinated
C	Winterbourne decides to try to understand Daisy
C'	Winterbourne takes Daisy to Chillon
E	Winterbourne looks for guidance in interpreting Daisy from Mrs. Costello, Mrs. Walker, Daisy's mother and brother, and Daisy herself
F_{neg}	Winterbourne fails to acquire the information he needs
G	Winterbourne arrives at the Colosseum at midnight
H	Winterbourne sees Daisy there, decides that that "once questionable quantity *had* no shades—it was a mere black little blot" (*Daisy Miller,* 86); he tells her it doesn't matter to him whether she's engaged
I_{neg}	Winterbourne's interpretation is wrong
$I_{neg} = A_2$	Winterbourne's misunderstanding of her behavior contributes to Daisy's death
EQ	with Daisy dead, there is no more information to study; Winterbourne returns to Geneva

Booth's interpretation reestablishes in the novella (in my terms) a
C-actant—although a different one than the readers in James's
lifetime found. Interestingly, his interpretation coincides with a
new popularity for the novella, which many of us have read and
taught, under Booth's influence, as an example of James's use of a
reflector-character.

Writing near the end of the twentieth century, Kenneth Graham
discerns a linguistic parallelism between Winterbourne's comment to
Daisy during their final meeting and her response to him. The resultant emphasis on Daisy's words guides Graham's interpretation:

> Winterbourne's laughing words are harshly contemptuous:
> "I believe that it makes very little difference whether you are

engaged or not!" Daisy's reply is a rhythmic and syntactic echo of Winterbourne's, the two forming an ironic, because fatally antithetic, couplet: "'I don't care,' said Daisy, in a little strange tone, 'whether I have Roman fever or not!'" The enforced grammatical echo makes the emotional point: without Winterbourne's jealous concern and affection she has no interest left in life. . . . Daisy's last line of direct dialogue is the narrative's one confession of love. In a tale about incommunication, and about the distance-beyond-words of one young woman's growing inner world of feeling, it comes to us appropriately through the indirections of silence and of richly associative imagery, quite counter to the surface brusqueness and briskness of language. (Graham, "*Daisy Miller:* Dynamics of an Enigma," 51, quoting *Daisy Miller,* 89)

Like Graham, I read the novella as exemplifying a thematics of incommunication or miscommunication in which Winterbourne does not receive a message or messages that Daisy may be attempting to communicate. About how (or when or whether) Daisy's feelings develop, I remain less sure than he. And I will suggest that Winterbourne is listening for—and not receiving—a message from Daisy long before her final words to him, which are emphasized by the lovely parallelism Graham so happily discerns.

From their first meeting, Winterbourne's interest in Daisy is intense. Initially he finds her "strikingly, admirably pretty" (8), and thinks "it was impossible to be prettier than that" (36). During their penultimate meeting "[i]t struck him . . . that Daisy had never showed to the eye for so utterly charming; but this had been his conviction on every occasion of their meeting" (81). He likes her too. During their trip to Chillon he tells her, "'I never was better pleased in my life'" (41). He admits to Mrs. Walker, "'I like her awfully, you know'" (65). He recognizes that he has shown "the zeal of an admirer [by stopping] on his way down to Rome . . . neither at Bologna nor at Florence, simply because of a certain sweet appeal to his fond fancy" (51). Even in the final section, when he assumes he is intruding on private moments between Daisy and Giovanelli, he "liked her the better for [the] innocent-looking indifference and [the] inexhaustible gaiety" (74) she displays whenever he joins the two of them. Moreover, the representation emphasizes Winterbourne's interest in Daisy by offering almost no indication of his perceptions or thoughts about anyone or anything else.

In addition to Winterbourne's interest in Daisy, the focalization permits readers to see, in the sequence in which Winterbourne acquires it, the information he learns about the young woman. The first three scenes, all of which occur on the day he meets Daisy, are instructive. First, Winterbourne learns from her brother that her father is in Schenectady (13). Second, Mrs. Costello's "declin[ing] the honour" (26) of permitting her nephew to introduce Daisy to her surely indicates to Winterbourne, who has been taught to understand his aunt's world, that not just she but all the matrons who are her social peers will refuse to serve for Daisy *in loco parentis*. Third, Daisy's mother, when Winterbourne first sees her, turns away in an attempt to avoid meeting him, and, Daisy explains, regularly does so when her daughter attempts to introduce to her mother her "gentlemen friends" (31)—behavior that Winterbourne recognizes is "a very different type of maternity from that of the vigilant matrons who massed themselves in the forefront of social intercourse in the dark old city at the other end of the lake" (35).

Moreover, already on that first day of his acquaintance with Daisy, Winterbourne recognizes in himself a desire to take care of her. When he is forced to tell her that Mrs. Costello refuses to meet her, he senses from her response that he has hurt her, and "wondered if she were seriously wounded and for a moment almost wished her sense of injury might be such as to make it becoming in him to attempt to reassure and comfort her" (29). According to the logic of the society in which he has been reared, Winterbourne must assume that an attractive young woman of marriageable age, which Daisy is, is in need of protection. In the first few hours of their acquaintance, Winterbourne has learned that neither mother nor father nor society itself is providing the protection she needs. Under these conditions, I suggest, he must assume that only a husband can protect her, and thus that she must need one. In my terms, Winterbourne interprets Daisy's circumstances as a function-a situation: the lack of a spouse.

a   Daisy is an attractive young woman of marriageable age, placed in an unfamiliar environment without the protection of father, mother, or society; she needs a husband

From this point on, as I interpret the function of the events, Winterbourne listens to Daisy with the expectation that she will make a function-B request—that she will indicate that she likes and trusts him—to which he seems to be willing to respond by performing function C: deciding to act to alleviate her situation by asking her to marry him.[18]

But Winterbourne never makes a function-C decision to marry Daisy, because he does not receive a function-B request until it is too late; she is already mortally ill. Conversations between the two characters occur, but very little communication takes place.[19] For me, Daisy's emotions and intentions are unknowable; I am less sure what messages she is sending than Winterbourne, at the end of the novella, is. But even her parting words to Winterbourne when she leaves the Colosseum, which are as strong a statement as she makes and which Graham interprets as "the narrative's one confession of love," Winterbourne does not hear as such. Winterbourne receives a function-B message from Daisy only when her mother conveys it, just a week before Daisy dies: "she wants you to realise she ain't engaged. I don't know why she makes so much of it, but she said to me three times 'Mind you tell Mr. Winterbourne'" (91). Winterbourne's conversation with Mrs. Costello at the very end of the novella informs readers that he receives this message as the function-B message for which he has been listening. But by then, the message has come too late to motivate action. A *negative function* represents a specified event that does not occur; Winterbourne does not decide to ask Daisy to marry him.

a   Daisy is an attractive young woman of marriageable age, placed in an unfamiliar environment without the protection of father, mother, or society; she needs a husband

B   Daisy conveys through her mother a message that Winterbourne hears as indicating that she "would have appreciated [his] esteem" (93)

C_{neg} because Daisy dies, Winterbourne cannot propose marriage to her

The move from function B to function C requires a completed communication—a message that is sent and received—which does not and (the novella may be read as suggesting) cannot occur across the social barriers that perhaps both characters attempt to cross. As I interpret the novella, Winterbourne listens throughout for a function-B request from Daisy, but cannot hear the message from her, even if she attempts to speak it. If she expresses her interest in him, he considers her a flirt and assumes she says the same things to other men. If she does not express her interest, he assumes she prefers someone else. The only message that Winterbourne hears is the one that is echoed by Daisy's mother. The very condition that has aroused Winterbourne's desire to take care of Daisy—her vulnerable social situation, with no one to protect her—leaves Winterbourne at such a loss to grasp the semiotics of the situation that he receives a message only when it arrives under the aegis of an appropriate sponsor.

As I interpret *Daisy Miller,* the logical sequence of action stops at function B. In narratives that move from function B to function C, a message is successfully transmitted. The addressee, having heard the full urgency of the message, agrees to help. Communication has occurred.[20] Because function B marks the sending of a message, a narrative that stops at function B necessarily includes a thematics of failed communication. In my reading, as interesting as the novella continues to be for theorists to analyze, it offers readers neither the comfort that function C brings as a thematics (no one's intentional acts ameliorate Daisy's situation) nor the comfort that function C brings as a hermeneutic device (without a clearly indicated function-C decision, it is difficult to be sure what any of the characters interpret as problems to be solved).

Given these four interpretations—all of which I offer as examples of credible readings in their time—the issue I find most compelling is why James's relatively traditional narrative can be the subject of so many, and such varied, interpretations.[21] In her analysis of the shift in interpretations of the protagonist, Yacobi points to the topical interest in the 1870s and 1880s in the behavior of young women from the United States traveling in Europe, and the interest that had developed by the 1960s in the psychological process of perceiving and analyzing illustrated by Winterbourne—in addition to the shift in interest among readers and critics from what happens in a narrative to how it is represented, which in the United States is most clearly marked by Wayne Booth's *The Rhetoric of Fiction.* One might add to the changes in the readership that Yacobi discerns, an increased tolerance for ambiguity in the present day.

In addition, James's novella leaves open the identity of the C-actant to a degree that I think is unusual in Anglo-American and Continental narrative fiction of the period. As we saw in the first section of this chapter, a C-actant's function-C decision that establishes intent may be directly revealed by depictions of the decision-making process that precedes motivated action, or indirectly revealed by action that a C-actant undertakes which in the context suggests that it is motivated by a function-C decision. In the case of Daisy, the novella gives no access to her unspoken thoughts so no decision-making is directly revealed; if she makes decisions we cannot see her making them. As for actions that indirectly reveal decision-making, Daisy's actions are so minimal—she goes to parties, takes walks, visits monuments—that twentieth- and (early-) twenty-first-century readers will probably not interpret them as motivated by a function-C decision. As we saw earlier, however, James's contemporaries, who were trained to expect and look for a chaperon whenever a young woman appeared, apparently did interpret Daisy's actions as motivated: as the effect of a choice she had made.

As for Winterbourne, we see his mind in action, but we do not see a directly revealed C-actant decision. In fact, Winterbourne's reported thoughts are almost entirely devoted to analyzing Daisy and include very little self-analysis. The closest he comes to analyzing his motives, I suggest, is when he thinks of himself as having traveled to Rome with "the zeal of an admirer" (I am reading the passage as free indirect discourse: the signifiers for the most part—including "zeal" and "admirer"—reflecting the character's vocabulary, although reported in syntax formulated by the narrator). But even this thought, in the context in which it is offered, is subjugated to an analysis of Daisy; Winterbourne is "a trifle disconcerted . . . by her inadequate measure of [his] zeal" (50–51). Similarly, as far as Winterbourne's actions are concerned, we cannot read his trip to Rome as indirectly revealing a C-actant decision to pursue Daisy since he has planned a trip to Rome during the winter to visit his aunt. Nor do any of his other actions necessarily indicate a C-actant's pursuit. While we know that Winterbourne finds Daisy interesting, because he says so and because he talks and thinks about her often, we are given insufficient information to determine whether he finds her merely an appealing distraction or whether he has made a C-actant decision to attempt to win her affection.

In other words, what I have described as the comfort function C brings as a hermeneutic device is largely unavailable to readers of *Daisy Miller*, except perhaps to the first generation of readers. As function analysis demonstrates (for instance, in the analyses above that represent interpretations of *Daisy Miller*), without the hermeneutic guidance provided by a directly revealed function-C decision, or an indirectly revealed but readily inferred function-C decision, readers' interpretations of where they are in a logical sequence—of where the characters are in a logical sequence at the time in their lives that is represented—can vary to an astonishing degree. The variation in interpretations of the function of events in *Daisy Miller* attests to the degree to which relatively clear indications of a C-actant, whether direct or indirect, can center and support interpretations of the logical relations among events in a sequence. Moreover, as the interpretations of *Daisy Miller* that I have analyzed exemplify, when readers' interpretations of where they are in a logical sequence shift, so do the thematics of the narrative being interpreted: naïveté abroad, the innocence of "American girlhood," a search for truth, miscommunication.

In the analysis above of how *Daisy Miller* was read in relation to its reception, the periods of the novella's popularity seem to coincide with interpretations in which first Daisy, for the first generation of readers, and later Winterbourne, beginning in the 1960s, are interpreted as C-actants. Both interpretations would seem to offer (to have offered) both the hermeneutic comfort of knowing where one is in an ongoing situation and the thematic comfort of being permitted to believe that intentional acts can sometimes effectively change situations. These two interpretations of *Daisy Miller,* in conjunction with *Hamlet, Phaedra,* and the St. Louis newscasts during the flooding in the Midwest in 1993, suggest—but offer far too small a sample to prove—a correlation between an emphasized function-C decision, whether repeated or extended, and a strongly positive reception. The other two interpretations of *Daisy Miller* suggest, by default as it were, the value for readers of a directly revealed or readily inferable function-C decision, whether or not it is emphasized by being repeated or extended. As we have seen, a function-C decision as a hermeneutic device guides interpretations of where one is in an ongoing logical sequence—and thereby shapes interpretations of a narrative's thematic focus. Representations of function C, when emphasized, guide recognition that the decision-making process is the central thematics of a narrative. In complementary fashion, representations of function C that are not emphasized but that serve to establish where one is in an ongoing logical sequence also play an important role—perhaps an even more important role than the selection of the events portrayed, I suggest—in guiding interpretations of the thematic focus of the narrative.

As we have seen in this chapter, by explicitly or implicitly indicating when a function-C decision is occurring, narratives satisfy our desire to know where we are in a represented sequence and to understand what message we are receiving. In chapter 5, I look at narratives that deny us these forms of hermeneutic and thematic comfort, and I draw attention to our similar lack of these forms of comfort when we interpret events in our world that we perceive directly, without the guidance of a narrative. In narratives about our world, the comforts that function C brings are often deceptive comforts. The real-world danger, to which I turn in the concluding chapters, is that we may not recognize the extent to which narratives are shaping our interpretations and bringing us comfort where comfort is not to be had.

CHAPTER 5

LINGERING AT FUNCTIONS D, E, AND F:

James's *The Ambassadors* and Kafka's "Before the Law"

Life, including life for those who live it as characters in a narrative, is more difficult to interpret than narratives are for readers. In chapter 4 I investigate, as one aspect of the importance of indications of function C, their value as a hermeneutic device—a lodestar—to guide interpretations of where one is in a logical sequence. In a narrative, as we saw, a function-C decision must sometimes be surmised from its consequences, but is sometimes reported by a narrator with knowledge of a character's thoughts. For people in our world and for characters in fictional worlds, however, no one but a C-actant herself can know what decisions she has made, unless or until she reveals them through speech or action. Another reason that life is more difficult to interpret than narratives is that the beginning and the conclusion of a narrative sequence are more difficult to discern when the sequence is not packaged between the covers of a book.

A narrative sequence—the movement from an equilibrium (EQ), through a period of imbalance (in my terms a function-A situation), to another equilibrium (EQ)—is a pattern as useful for interpreting events in our world as for interpreting events in narratives. But for events in our world, it is difficult to obtain a sufficiently broad temporal perspective to be able to gauge with any accuracy where an individual sequence begins and ends. Narratives, on the other hand, whether they include one sequence or more than one sequence, generally begin at one of two positions in a sequence—at an initial equilibrium or at a disruptive moment near the onset of a period of imbalance—and conclude at or near the end of a sequence when equilibrium has been regained or seems about to be regained. Experienced readers (listeners, viewers) of narratives grow accustomed to this pattern and tend to rely on it, although generally not consciously, to locate where they are when they initially begin to read (listen, view). In certain modern novels and stories, however, the representation—and sometimes the fabula too—begins at a later point in the sequence and does not reach a concluding equilibrium. These narratives include in the representation only a part of the path from equilibrium to imbalance to equilibrium; they contain even less than one complete narrative sequence. Interpreting the function of events in representations that trace so short a path is sometimes nearly as difficult as interpreting the function of events in our world—where we are left to determine which events to include in a sequence without the guidance of novelist, playwright, or historian.

In Henry James's *The Ambassadors* (published in 1903) and Franz Kafka's "Vor dem Gesetz" ("Before the Law"; published in 1919), the initial event in the representation is the arrival of the protagonist at a destination to which he has traveled. For both James's Strether and Kafka's man from the country, the arrival with which the narrative begins marks the completion of a journey motivated by a prior disruptive event: both protagonists have already traveled to the one place where it may be possible to alleviate a troublesome situation that the earlier disruptive event has caused. These narratives contain less than one complete narrative sequence; they begin long after the onset of imbalance and linger along the narrative path, extending the few functions they contain to fill an entire text.

For readers, an incomplete narrative sequence creates false clues that initially lead us astray as we attempt to determine the function of the narrated events. The effects of this structural "red herring" are supported by the disjuncture, in these and other narratives, including many by James and Kafka, between the narrative voice that speaks and the focalizer that perceives and conceives.[1] Like the protagonists who misread the function of their acts, readers who are permitted to see only through the protagonists' focalization misread the function of events. Misled by the book covers, or by the paratextual signs that indicate the beginning of a story, readers who expect the opening section of a narrative to coincide with a period of equilibrium or the moment of its disruption often interpret an event initially as an expression of one function, and then later reinterpret the same event as an expression of a different function. Readers of these narratives by Kafka and James repeatedly reinterpret the function of events as they read, continuing to shift their interpretations even in response to the events with which the two narratives conclude. After analyzing these interpretations and reinterpretations, first in James's novel and then in Kafka's story, in the final section of this chapter I consider the relation between the incomplete sequence and a Modernist epistemological doubt that, like the protagonists, readers of these two narratives experience.

■

Because Strether, in the opening pages of *The Ambassadors,* is so obviously enjoying the first days after his arrival in Europe, readers who know from experience that narratives tend to begin either at a period of equilibrium (EQ) just before it is disrupted, or at a moment of disruption that marks the onset of imbalance (function A or function a), initially interpret the opening scene as an equilibrium and expect a disruptive function-A event to occur. James's first sentence both responds to and defers this expectation: "Strether's first question, when he reached the hotel, was about his friend; yet on learning that Waymarsh was apparently not to arrive till evening he was not wholly disconcerted" (James, 21: 3). Because Strether is not "disconcerted," we understand that Waymarsh's delay is not the function-A event we anticipate.

(James: fabula 1)

EQ Strether's joy during his first days in Europe
A   not Waymarsh's delay, but some other disruptive event

So we read on to find a disruptive event, only to discover that one has already occurred and that Strether has come to Europe, at Mrs. Newsome's request, to rectify it: to remove her son Chad from the arms of a foreign woman and send him back to Woollett to the bride his mother has chosen.

In discovering that Strether has come to Europe to bring Chad home and that Chad's liaison is the function-A situation that has disrupted the equilibrium in Woollett, we are engaging in the process of constructing the novel's fabula, the chronological account that readers organize in response to the representation that we read. The initial events of the fabula of *The Ambassadors* include the details that the representation slowly reveals about Strether's life during the period of presumed equilibrium in Woollett that the news of Chad's liaison disrupts. The initial event in the novel's representation is Strether's request for information about whether Waymarsh has arrived at the hotel in Chester: the event that the first sentence addresses. Because functions name interpretations of the causes and consequences of events in the sequence in which the events are perceived, the vocabulary of functions enables discussing and comparing interpretations of events in the developing fabulas one constructs during the process of reading, and between a complete fabula and its representation.

Once we have established Chad's liaison as a function-A event in the fabula that is being revealed, we can interpret the events it motivates that precede Strether's question about Waymarsh, the first event in the representation. We probably interpret Mrs. Newsome's request to Strether to bring Chad back as function B. Strether's decision (function C) to attempt to alleviate the disruptive situation by retrieving Chad marks the moment of his assumption of the C-actant role. As his first act (function C'), he sets sail for Europe. This reading is supported, even indicated, by the vocabulary choices James's characters make. Strether tells Waymarsh, "'I've come . . . on [Mrs. Newsome's] business'" (21: 32). Maria Gostrey summarizes Strether's situation: "'You've accepted the mission of separating [Mr. Chad] from the wicked woman'" (21: 54).

Once we have read far enough to discern and to interpret these events that in fabula precede Strether's arrival in Europe, we will need to reinterpret the initial event in the representation. With the information we now have, we can no longer interpret Strether's first days in Europe as an unbroken equilibrium; we can consider the opening events as, at best, a period of temporary relaxation prior to the resumption of an extended, ongoing effort. Thus the function of the opening scene shifts, for readers, from opening equilibrium to momentary stasis immediately prior to primary action. If we interpret Strether's arrival in Europe as function G, we are indicating that we assume that Strether is the C-actant, the agent for change, and that he has arrived at the locus of his primary endeavor (function H), which is about to begin. (Brackets indicate interpretations of events that precede chronologically the initial event in the representation.)

(James: fabula 2)

[EQ]   equilibrium in Woollett
[A]   Chad's liaison becomes known in Woollett
[B]   Mrs. Newsome asks Strether to bring Chad back to Woollett

[C]   Strether decides to attempt to bring Chad back
[C']   Strether sails to Europe
G   Strether arrives in Europe

If we understand Strether's arrival in Europe as function G, however, as we read on we will be forced to reinterpret the initial scene once again, this time as a result of what we learn about the relationship that develops between Strether and Maria Gostrey, during the time they spend together while they are still in England. At whatever point in our reading we recognize the degree of importance Strether attaches to Maria Gostrey's offer to assist him—her promise, at the conclusion of their last meeting before both of them travel to Paris, that he will succeed in his mission and that "to that end I'm yours" (21: 75)—this information guides us in interpreting her promise as function F, an event that empowers Strether in his further action. If her promise is function F, then function G—Strether's arrival at the locus of his primary action—is expressed by his arrival in Paris. In this context we interpret the initial scene in the representation for the third time, shifting our interpretation from (1) opening equilibrium to (2) function G to (3) a quiet moment that precedes the events of function D. (Again, brackets indicate interpretations of events that precede chronologically the initial event in the representation.)

(James: fabula 3)

[EQ]   equilibrium in Woollett
[A]   Chad's liaison becomes known in Woollett
[B]   Mrs. Newsome asks Strether to bring Chad back to
       Woollett
[C]   Strether decides to attempt to bring Chad back
[C']   Strether sails to Europe
D   Strether is tested by Maria Gostrey, who introduces
       herself to him to discover whether she likes him as
       much as she thinks she will
E   Strether responds to Europe and to Maria Gostrey
F   Maria Gostrey's offer of help empowers Strether
G   Strether arrives in Paris
H   Strether's primary actions to return Chad to Woollett

By interpreting Maria Gostrey's promise of assistance as function F, a preliminary event that empowers Strether in his primary endeavor to convince Chad to return to Woollett, we are distinguishing between preliminary and primary actions. Functions D-E-F represent preliminary events that empower the C-actant to accomplish a later and more important goal. Function H represents the primary actions to alleviate a motivating function A. By interpreting Strether's efforts to return Chad to Woollett as function H, we are saying that we consider Strether's actions in France as the primary endeavor of the narrative sequence.

Although the moment in the process of reading at which different readers interpret and reinterpret events as functions undoubtedly varies to some extent from reader to reader, most readers, I suggest, as they read Book Third (the sixth and seventh chapters of the novel) if not earlier, will reach an interpretation of the functions of the primary events in the fabula that is in accordance with the function analysis represented above—an interpretation that is unlikely to change until one reaches the concluding chapter 36. Certainly, as we read on, we become aware that the information we are given concerns Strether's thoughts more often than his actions. Moreover, the focalization permits us to watch Strether's growing approval of the changes he perceives in Chad, and to see that he attributes those changes to the beneficial influence of Mme. de Vionnet. As a result, any reader must wonder whether Strether will continue to attempt to carry out his function-C mission of returning Chad to Woollett, and even whether Strether will be able to complete the mission if he chooses to do so. In other words, as we read on, we become increasingly aware of the question of whether Strether will succeed (function I) or fail (function I_{neg}). But in part because of our attention to this issue, readers who are as satisfied with the interpretation represented above (fabula 3) as I think most are, will continue to interpret the events that are revealed as those of Strether's primary endeavor (function H), even until they reach the final pages.

The novel's conclusion, however, forces readers to reconsider their earlier interpretations of events as functions, this time in light of their consequences. Even the initial question of success or failure is no easy matter to resolve. With Chad still in France we cannot label Strether's efforts a success (function I). Nor, as we listen to Strether as he appeals to Chad "by all you hold sacred" (22: 311) not to abandon his liaison with Mme. de Vionnet, can we label Chad's continued presence in France as Strether's failure (function I_{neg}) to accomplish his goal. The difficulty in interpreting the problematic ending of this novel, however, exceeds the mere inability to determine success or failure. I cite the decisive words in the final conversation between Strether and Maria Gostrey. Strether has understood that what she is offering "was as the offer of exquisite service, of lightened care, for the rest of his days":

> "I know. I know. But all the same I must go." He had got it at last. "To be right."
>
> "To be right?"
>
> She had echoed it in vague deprecation, but he felt it already clear for her. "That, you see, is my only logic. Not, out of the whole affair, to have got anything for myself."
>
> She thought. "But, with your wonderful impressions, you'll have got a great deal."
>
> "A great deal"—he agreed. "But nothing like *you*. It's you who would make me wrong! (22: 325–26; James's emphasis)

According to the logic of this passage as I read it, both characters agree that Strether has gained, with his "wonderful impressions," much from his experiences, while Strether feels that to accept Maria Gostrey's offer would be to behave in a way that would "make [him] wrong." In terms of a function analysis, this passage confirms that the change that has occurred is not in Chad's situation but in Strether himself. We reinterpret the events in Paris as a series of tests for Strether (function D), to which he responds admirably (function E), and thereby acquires extraordinary powers of perception (function F).[2] If we accept Strether's logic, we understand the novel's concluding scene as he does: that since he has not accomplished a primary action (function H), he can accept neither the reward for success (function I) that Maria Gostrey offers, nor the equilibrium (EQ) that remaining with her would establish.

Readers who interpret the concluding scene according to Strether's logic will reinterpret the primary events of the novel as a whole, after they finish their reading, according to this sequence of functions:

(James: the complete fabula)

EQ   equilibrium in Woollett
[A]   Chad's liaison becomes known in Woollett
[B]   Mrs. Newsome asks Strether to bring Chad back to Woollett

[C]   Strether decides to attempt to bring Chad back
[C']   Strether sails to Europe
D   Strether is tested by his experiences in Europe
E   Strether has "wonderful impressions"
F   Strether's empowerment consists of becoming a more
        complete human being who has learned to under-
        stand complex situations

According to the interpretation this sequence of functions represents, the single narrative sequence of the novel's fabula is incomplete. It stops at function F; Strether is preparing to leave Paris,
and the equilibrium in Woollett is not restored. A complete
sequence would require a set of events to fill several additional
functions: for example, arriving somewhere (function G), Strether
undertakes a primary endeavor (function H), succeeds or fails
(function I or I_{neg}), and lives happily or dies (EQ). James's suppression of the events to fill these functions creates an ending that represents a Modern view of a protagonist's chances for success.
Strether neither wins nor loses, neither lives happily nor dies. Life
goes on, and consolation consists in recognizing one's personal
growth (function F).

   In the representation, moreover, the initial event is Strether's
arrival in Europe, an event that occurs after the bracketed events
that in fabula fill functions A, B, C, and C'. The path of the representation is cut off at both ends. By designing the novel's representation so that its initial event occurs after the event that fills function C', and by suppressing all further events after those that
express function F, James constructs a representation that effectively traces only three functions. It lingers, for hundreds of pages,
at functions D, E, and F.

(James: representation)

D   Strether is tested by his experiences in Europe
E   Strether has "wonderful impressions"
F   Strether's empowerment consists of becoming a more com-
    plete human being who has learned to understand com-
    plex situations

   The postponement in the representation of the events that fill
functions A to C', which are revealed only gradually as the representation progresses, creates the shifting interpretations of the function

of the opening event that I have traced.[3] The suppression in both the fabula and the representation of events to complete the sequence is responsible for our failing to recognize until the final chapter that the set of events in Paris is not the primary endeavor of a function H, but, instead, the subordinate preparatory events of functions D-E-F that are designed to empower a protagonist to accomplish a later, more important endeavor that can be interpreted as a function H. Inherent to the cutting off of events at the beginning and the end of a representation is the creation of false clues. Readers misinterpret the function of events because they are accustomed to relying on the position of an event in a sequence as an indication of its function. Since readers bring these expectations to their reading, a representation that begins after a function-A disruption and does not include a function-C decision (which, as I argue in chapter 4, provides hermeneutic comfort) leads us astray—even if the events that express function A and function C are revealed, as they are in *The Ambassadors,* in the course of the novel.

The shifts in interpretation that the representation's incomplete narrative sequence demands of readers are supported by the separation between narrative voice and focalization. A first-person narration raises epistemological questions that an anonymous third-person narration does not. Readers know from experience that when first-person narrators speak, the information they convey cannot exceed what one mind can know and can rarely if ever escape the (dis)coloration of subjectivity. A third-person narration raises doubts such as these more subtly, if at all.[4] For the voice to speak in the third person, I suggest, encourages readers to trust the information it conveys, even when that information is subjectively colored, as it is in *The Ambassadors* where the focalization is restricted to Strether's perceptions and conceptions. It is at least in part because we trust Strether more than we would if he spoke to us directly in the first person, I suggest, that we are willing to adopt his interpretation of the function of his acts, again and again, as our guide in interpreting his behavior.

The degree to which we give credence to Strether's focalization can be illustrated by a comparison of our interpretations, as readers, to Maria Gostrey's interpretations. Because Maria Gostrey is a character, she is on Strether's ontological level, and can hear him speak but cannot hear the narrator. She is Strether's narratee, whereas readers share the situation of the novel's narratee, who hears Strether through the filter of the narrator's voice. Yet Maria Gostrey's interpretation of the function of the events of Strether's

life is identical to our own: "'You've accepted the mission of separating him from the wicked woman'" (21: 54). Her words reveal
her interpretation of the events of function A ("wicked woman"),
function B ("accepted," which requires a prior request), and function C (both "accepted" and "mission"). We interpret the events
that precede the first event in the representation as we do because
Strether sees himself (and Maria Gostrey sees him seeing himself)
as Mrs. Newsome's knight who will do her bidding and retrieve
Chad.[5] We (mis)read the events in Paris as Strether's primary
action to retrieve Chad and return him to his mother (function H),
because that is the way Strether interprets his actions at the time
they occur. Only when Strether reinterprets the function of his
actions retrospectively, in the last chapter, from a primary action
(function H) to a preliminary period of growth (functions D-E-F),
do we also retrospectively shift our interpretation of the events
that have already occurred.

Successive reinterpretations of one's own behavior, and specifically the retrospective reinterpretation of what one has conceived
as a primary endeavor (function H) as, instead, a merely subordinate experience (function F), resonant in psychic impressions but
utterly ineffectual in altering the external world, are typical of the
ironic reflections, in the literature of Modernism, of protagonists
and poetic personas on their own ineffectiveness. For readers too,
a Modernist indecisiveness in interpreting the function of events is
not only portrayed in the protagonist's self-reflections, in *The
Ambassadors* and similar works, but played out, as we too shift
our interpretations of the functions of events in response to the
results of the protagonist's own soul-searching. A representation
that lingers at functions D, E, and F is an ideal structure to portray
the character who continually grows, but never projects that
growth into accomplishment.

It is the fabula, however, that is the primary source of the interpretative dilemma that the novel poses when it is contemplated in
its entirety, after the reading process is completed. The novel's
refusal of conventional closure can be described, in my terms, as
the effect of the suppression in fabula of the functions and the
events to fill them that a complete sequence requires: the primary
endeavor of function H, its success or failure (function I or I_{neg})
and an ensuing equilibrium (EQ). The suppression of the events to
fill these functions is naturalized by the focalization, which withholds all information that Strether does not know—including, of
course, everything that happens after the novel's concluding scene.

But not only are the concluding events suppressed; the concluding functions are also suppressed. Had James written that most conventional of endings, that Strether lived happily ever after (or, for that matter, that Strether regretted that day's decision for the rest of his life), the effect would have been to provide the interpretation without the event: an *empty function* that interprets an unspecified event or events. Specifically, a "happily ever after" ending, which is not unusual in novels and occurs frequently in fairy tales, indicates that a protagonist reaches some successful situation (function I), which is followed by an unbroken equilibrium (EQ). A function analysis draws attention to the radical suppression, at the conclusion of *The Ambassadors,* of *both* the functions to complete a sequence and the events to fill them. The primary interpretative dilemma the conclusion raises, I suggest, is that for the period after Strether's final conversation with Maria Gostrey, neither events nor functions are reported: neither the events, which could ground speculation about their function (their consequences), nor the functions, against which one could gauge speculation about Strether's subsequent actions. Without textual support on either plane—the event or the function that interprets it—any interpretation of Strether's future behavior can be no more than one hypothesis among other equally possible hypotheses.

Although, from the perspective of a function analysis, Strether's future behavior is closed to interpretation, his situation at the conclusion of the novel, on the other hand, is established in the final conversation between Strether and Maria Gostrey, in which sufficient information is given to permit readers to determine the position Strether has reached in the sequence of functions that constitutes a complete narrative sequence.[6]

My claim is that readers who reinterpret the events of the novel in light of their consequences will agree that sending Chad back to Woollett is Strether's original goal, but that Strether does little to accomplish it (function H does not occur), and that as a result of his experiences Strether grows immeasurably (there is no doubt that function F occurs). In her brilliant analysis of ambiguity in James, Shlomith Rimmon-Kenan defines *narrative ambiguity* as a structural pattern in which "we can discern two mutually exclusive *fabulas* in the same *sju et* [representation]" (*The Concept of Ambiguity,* 50). In the specific narratives by James dating from 1888 to 1901 in which she traces the phenomenon, the events of one representation reveal two different fabulas. For such a procedure to be possible, it is necessary for some of the events the two fabulas share to express one function in one fabula and another function in the other fabula. In this novel James uses other procedures to undermine the narrative sequence; *The Ambassadors* is not an example of narrative ambiguity.[7] For the reader who has completed the novel and perceives it in its entirety, the functions of the revealed events of the fabula are not ambiguous. During the process of reading, however, the cutting off of the representation at both ends, the incomplete sequence of the fabula, and the restricted focalization permit the reader to experience an almost dizzying sequence of interpretations and reinterpretations of events as functions.

■

Although Kafka's "Before the Law" ("Vor dem Gesetz") is very short, the story is complete; it was published during Kafka's lifetime in the collection *Ein Landarzt*.[8] The similarities in structural pattern and concomitant character type between this story and *The Ambassadors* illuminate epistemological issues that arise as a result of differences in the ontological status of the events that in the two fabulas precede and follow the events that the representations delineate. Like *The Ambassadors*, "Before the Law" depicts as its first event the arrival of the protagonist at the locus of the ensuing action. Like *The Ambassadors*, the story's representation traces only a small portion of a complete narrative sequence.

The story's first sentence describes a static scene that precedes the arrival of the protagonist: "Before the Law stands a doorkeeper" (148).[9] Like James's opening scene, Kafka's first sentence suggests an opening equilibrium that is about to be disrupted.

(Kafka: fabula 1)

EQ a doorkeeper standing before the Law
A   some disruptive event that is about to occur

But the equilibrium is very short and does not extend beyond the arrival of the man from the country, which is reported in the second sentence. As soon as the man arrives, "prays for admittance to the Law" (148), and hears the doorkeeper refuse his request, we shift our interpretation. Just as we do as we read the opening pages of *The Ambassadors*, we construct a prior sequence according to which some previous disruptive event (function A) has motivated the man from the country (the C-actant) to decide (function C) to attempt to alleviate the disruption, as a result of which he has set out (function C') to travel to the site of the Law, where he has now arrived. If we interpret the first event in the representation, the man's arrival, as function G, we are indicating that we assume that the man is the C-actant and that he has reached the site of his primary endeavor. According to this reading we shift our interpretation of the first event, just as we do as we read the beginning of *The Ambassadors,* from a moment of equilibrium that is about to be broken (fabula 1) to the motivated arrival of function G (fabula 2). (Brackets indicate interpretations of events that precede chronologically the initial event in the representation.)

(Kafka: fabula 2)

[EQ] equilibrium, in the country
[A]   motivating disruptive event
[C]   the man decides to attempt to alleviate the function-A situation by addressing the Law
[C'] the man sets out on his journey to the site of the Law
G   the man arrives at the site of the Law

But as we read on, we shift our interpretation of the opening scene again, as we do when we decide that Maria Gostrey is testing Strether prior to empowering him for his future endeavor by offering her assistance. In "Before the Law," when the doorkeeper describes a succession of increasingly powerful doorkeepers beyond the gate that he guards, we reconsider our interpretation of the initial event in the representation and reinterpret the present situation as the first stage of a number of preliminary testings. We see the doorkeeper's behavior as function D, a test to which the protagonist must respond successfully (function E) in order to be empowered to pass through the gate (function F)—the set of events expressing functions D-E-F to be repeated successively when each doorkeeper is encountered, until the protagonist succeeds in reaching the Law (function G), the site of the primary action (function H). (Again, brackets indicate interpretations of events that precede chronologically the initial event in the representation.)

(Kafka: fabula 3)

[EQ]   equilibrium, in the country
[A]   motivating disruptive event

[C]   the man decides to attempt to alleviate the function-
             A situation
[C']   the man sets out on his journey to the site of the
             Law
$(D-E-F)_n$ successive doorkeepers test the man and empower
             him to pass through their gates
G   the man arrives at the site of the Law
H   the man's primary action to alleviate the function-A
             situation

If the doorkeeper's behavior is a test (function D), then the protagonist's arrival marks a moment before the onset of function D. Our three successive interpretations of the opening scene of Kafka's story and James's novel are identical: (1) equilibrium, (2) function G, (3) a moment that precedes the events of function D. Moreover, in Kafka's story as in James's novel, a third-person voice speaks throughout, while the focalization—until the final sentence—is restricted to the perceptions and conceptions of the protagonist, whose interpretation of what he perceives guides readers' interpretations of the function of events.

A text in which the voice is in the third-person cannot immediately indicate that focalization is restricted to a single character unless it blatantly announces that it will follow a specific character's vision. When the focalization of a single character is narrated by a third-person voice, readers can know at most, as they begin to read, that what the voice tells includes at least one character's perceptions and conceptions. Only as one continues to read is it possible to begin to establish that a narrative's focalization is restricted to a single character's perceptions and conceptions. Whereas James announces in the first sentence, which reports that Strether was not "disconcerted," that aspects of Strether's mind are to be revealed, "Vor dem Gesetz," in this respect, is more subtle. Only when we return to the first sentence, after we have discovered that no scene is depicted that is not in the protagonist's purview, do we realize that the representation opens when the man from the country approaches the gates to the Law; the opening scene depicts the protagonist's initial perception of the doorkeeper who stands before the Law.

In Kafka's story, a change in the quality of the language emphasizes and draws attention to the restricted focalization. A cluster of visually descriptive nouns and adjectives enters the language at the moment the man must make a crucial decision. When the doorkeeper, who has already prohibited entrance, suggests that the man might test the prohibition, the visual imagery of the text reveals that the man carefully inspects the doorkeeper, to acquire all the information about his situation that he can, before he decides how to respond.

> [A]s he now takes a closer look at the doorkeeper in his fur
> coat, with his big sharp nose and long, thin, black Tartar
> beard, he decides that it is better to wait until he gets per-
> mission to enter. (148)

The narrative voice describes what the protagonist sees when he looks closely at the doorkeeper to determine his chances of being able to pass through the gate. Because readers are permitted to perceive the doorkeeper as the man perceives him, we realize that the man's decision to wait indicates that the man has decided that the doorkeeper is too large and powerful to challenge directly, and that as a result the man has chosen an alternative method to reach his goal.

Like Strether, Kafka's protagonist interprets and reinterprets his situation, and readers adjust their interpretations in response to the man's shifting interpretations, as they do to Strether's. The attention the man fixes on the one doorkeeper he can see draws readers' attention away from the other doorkeepers whom the doorkeeper describes. The man's behavior suggests that he per-ceives this doorkeeper as his only impediment to the Law: he waits for years; he uses up all of his belongings to give the doorkeeper bribes. Finally, "[h]e forgets the other doorkeepers, and this first one seems to him the sole obstacle preventing access to the Law" (149). Readers shift their interpretation in accordance with the interpretation the man has reached.

(Kafka: fabula 4)

[EQ]   equilibrium, in the country
[A]   motivating disruptive event
[C]   the man decides to attempt to alleviate the function-A
       situation
[C']   the man sets out on his journey to the site of the Law
D   the doorkeeper tests the man
E   the man responds by waiting
F   the doorkeeper empowers the man to pass

G   the man arrives at the site of the Law
H   the man's primary action to alleviate the function-A situation

But the man's interpretation changes again, and once more readers change their interpretation in response. After focusing his attention for so long on his contest with the doorkeeper, the man finally looks for assistance wherever it might be found:

> [S]ince in his yearlong contemplation of the doorkeeper he has come to know even the fleas in his fur collar, he begs the fleas as well to help him and to change the doorkeeper's mind. (149)

For the man to turn to the fleas as a source of potential empowerment, I suggest, is an indication of a shift in the man's interpretation of his contest with the doorkeeper. Whereas the doorkeeper's prohibition has seemed to him a preliminary test (function D) to which he must successfully respond in order to be permitted to undertake his primary endeavor (function H), now the contest with the doorkeeper has acquired such importance in his eyes that he perceives it as his primary concern (function H). It is this reinterpretation that makes possible the man's turning to some source of empowerment other than the doorkeeper—even the fleas—to aid him in his contest with the doorkeeper. In his new interpretation, begging the fleas for assistance in changing the doorkeeper's mind is comparable in its function to, in his previous interpretation, waiting for the doorkeeper to permit entrance to the Law; both actions express function E. Readers shift their interpretation (at least momentarily) in accordance with the man's new interpretation.

(Kafka: fabula 5)

[EQ]   equilibrium, in the country
[A]   motivating disruptive event
[C]   the man decides to attempt to alleviate the function-A situation
[C']   the man sets out on his journey to the site of the Law
E   the man begs the fleas for assistance
F   the fleas intercede with the doorkeeper
H   the contest with the doorkeeper is the primary action

In the final sentence of the story, however, a shift in the focalization from the man to the doorkeeper creates a complication for readers who have adopted the protagonist's interpretation of the function of events as the model for their own interpretation. Indicated by the word *recognizes* ("*erkennt*"), the shift in focalization occurs at the moment when the doorkeeper perceives that the man is near death. The man has just asked the doorkeeper why no one else has requested admission during all the years he has spent waiting. The concluding sentence reads:

> The doorkeeper recognizes that the man has reached his end, and to let his failing senses catch the words roars in his ear: "No one else could ever be admitted here, since this gate was made only for you. I am now going to shut it." (149–50)

The doorkeeper's speech with which the text concludes is, as I read the story, the last thing the man perceives. Because the shift in focalization occurs before the man hears the doorkeeper's words, the man's interpretation of the doorkeeper's speech is not revealed. Thus the man's interpretation is unavailable to guide and support readers' reinterpretations of earlier events in light of the final scene.

Without the assistance of the protagonist, then, we accept the doorkeeper's affirmation that the locus of the story is the man's personal gate to the Law, rather than the Law itself, and we interpret the man's long waiting as function E, as the man himself interpreted it for many years after he made the crucial decision to wait (see "Kafka: fabula 4"). Now that we know the consequences of that decision, however, we can interpret it more definitively than we (or he) could at the time he made it. We may even surmise that the man's last question is an indication of his own awareness of those consequences, and that he hoped, as he reflected on his life, to mitigate his own failure by perceiving it in comparison to the failure of others. In any case, I propose, after reading the entire story we interpret the events of the fabula as a sequence that ends in what I call *negative functions:* functions that represent specified events that do not occur.

(Kafka: the complete fabula)

[EQ] equilibrium, in the country
[A]   motivating disruptive event

[C]   the man decides to attempt to alleviate the function-A sit-
        uation
[C'] the man sets out on his journey to the site of the Law
D   the doorkeeper tests the man
E   the man waits
F_{neg} the man receives no empowerment
G_{neg} the man does not reach the site of the Law
H_{neg} the man does not address the Law
I_{neg} the man does not alleviate the function-A situation

But although the information from the doorkeeper—for which
there is no equivalent in James's novel—permits us to conceive a
completed fabula, the duration of the representation is restricted to
the duration of the man's perceptions: from his first view of the
gate, to the moment when his perceptions fail as he dies, which is
the very moment that empowerment, were he to receive it, would
become useless. Throughout the representation, the doorkeeper
tests the man (function D), and the man's response (function E)
fails to win for him the power to approach the Law, and to permit
the story to move to function F. The representation lingers along a
segment of the narrative path that is even shorter than James's representation, which traces functions D-E-F. Kafka's representation
is reduced to function D and function E.

(Kafka: representation)

D   the doorkeeper tests the man
E   the man waits

■

The differences between James's novel and Kafka's story obviously extend far beyond the single additional function in *The
Ambassadors* that indicates that Strether—but not the man from
the country—develops his abilities as a result of the activities in
which he engages. What I would like to call the *texture* of the two
narratives is very different. The pages of James's novel are filled
with the details that color the primary events that do and do not
take place. In large part this is the material that Roland Barthes
describes in an early article as *integrational units* or *indices:* indexical information that refers "not to a . . . consequential act but to
a more or less diffuse concept which is nevertheless necessary to

the meaning of the story: psychological indices concerning the characters, data regarding their identity, notations of 'atmosphere' ("Introduction to the Structural Analysis of Narratives," 92).[10]

Kafka's story, as we saw, provides details of this sort only in the one sentence that tells that the man inspects the doorkeepers' appearance while deciding whether to test the latter's prohibition against entry. The absence otherwise of such details in this story, and for the most part throughout the corpus of Kafka's work, is one of the reasons that Kafka's stories and novels can be interpreted in as many different ways—religious, political, psychological, etc.—as we have seen them interpreted. The other reason is demonstrated by the function analysis of "Before the Law." The representation includes only the events that we interpret as a testing to permit entrance and the character's response: waiting. For events that precede chronologically the represented period of testing, we are given enough information to interpret the function but no specification at all about what the events are that express those functions. Literally for this segment of the story, and often throughout Kafka's corpus, his narratives are open to multiple readings because the events are unspecified and readers are given only the interpretation—the function. For the events that are chronologically subsequent to the man's function-E waiting, the only information provided is that they do not occur. Moreover, the represented event—a testing to permit entrance—is as generic an event as one can imagine. In fact, Jurij Lotman has proposed, in an article "The Origin of Plot," "[L]ooked at typologically, the initial situation is that a certain plot-space is divided by a single boundary into an internal and an external sphere, and a single character has the opportunity to cross that boundary" (167).[11]

As many disparate interpretations as have been proposed of the events that express the functions in Kafka's narratives, and as differently as Kafka's story and James's novels express the very few functions in the representations of both narratives analyzed in this chapter, a function analysis nonetheless reveals a similar pattern of causality in the two narratives. Both linger at functions D and E and, in James's novel, function F; the representations of both narratives trace only a small segment of a narrative sequence.

In a complete narrative sequence, a C-actant undertakes action that begins (function C'), continues (function H), and concludes (function I or function I_{neg}). For all the emphasis I have placed (and have argued that readers place) on a C-actant's decision to act (function C) and on the moment where thought leads to action (function C'), function H is a C-actant's primary action. Functions D-E-F, on the other hand, are expendable. In some traditional narratives, as we have seen, functions D-E-F are omitted. In other traditional narratives, in instances in which C-actants initially lack the strength or knowledge they need to accomplish function H, functions D-E-F trace the process of empowerment that prepares them for and precedes function H. Function H is primary; functions D-E-F are merely preparatory. In the schema of traditional narrative, functions D-E-F, without a further function H, are meaningless. The protagonists of *The Ambassadors* and "Before the Law" both fail to reach, much less to accomplish, function H. Both substitute preparatory behavior for primary action, permitting the primary goal to disintegrate while devoting their energies to the expendable.

Function analysis provides tools to analyze ways that narrative representations guide readers' (listeners', viewers') interpretations of the causal relations among reported events. Changes in the ways that representations guide interpretation of causal relations can be discerned over time, and in response to prevailing social and political as well as aesthetic priorities. A recurring pattern at a given historical period, as we saw in chapter 3, can sometimes guide understanding of the expectations and values of a time and place. Although no two narratives can fully represent a historical period, the protagonists of *The Ambassadors* and "Before the Law" do illustrate the behavior and perceptions of behavior of a typically Modernist character type that seems to arise in Anglo-American and Continental literature toward the end of the nineteenth century. Strether at least accomplishes function F. The stage of Modernism he typifies offers a discouraging view of the possibility of altering the outcome of events in the world, but retains as a lure the possibility of psychological and intellectual development. The man from the country, on the other hand, typifies a later stage of Modernism that offers an even more negative view of mankind's potential. Spending his years in waiting, at function E, he fails to reach function F. Even the consolation of personal growth is denied him.

Moreover, the experience of misinterpreting and reinterpreting the function of events to which readers of both narratives are subjected dramatizes an epistemological doubt that Brian McHale, in *Postmodernist Fiction,* perceives is a characteristic of Modernist narrative.[12] A function analysis of *The Ambassadors* and "Before the Law" illustrates several ways that representations of

Modernist narratives can create epistemological doubt. The representations of both narratives include the events of no more than two or three preparatory functions. But the procedure by which the two representations are cut off, at the beginning and at the end, are different in each of the four cases. For the segment of fabula that precedes the representation, the procedure we find in *The Ambassadors* is not unusual. James postpones the events that are chronologically prior to the initial event of his representation, but gradually reveals both the events and their consequences, which permits readers to assign functions to the events and to establish the segment of fabula that precedes Strether's arrival. For this segment, both the events and their functions are given.[13]

In Kafka's story, for the segment that precedes the representation, the events are never revealed, but their consequences are. Because a function is an interpretation of an event in light of its consequences, readers can determine the functions of events that are unspecified. By determining the functions, one can establish the segment of fabula that precedes the arrival of the man from the country as a set of empty functions—functions that are empty because the events to fill them are not expressed. Empty functions represent events that take place in the represented world, but that except for their consequences are suppressed in the representation.[14] For this segment, the events are suppressed, but their functions are given.[15]

Because James does not conclude *The Ambassadors* with the conventional "they lived happily ever after," or with any other indication of the effects of otherwise unrevealed events that would establish empty functions, the fabula of James's novel does not extend beyond the events that conclude the representation. After the conversation at the novel's end between Strether and Maria Gostrey, there are no further events in the represented world, just as there are no further events in the representation. James's fabula has no concluding segment; neither events nor functions are given.

In Kafka's story the sequence is completed. Equilibrium is reinstated, but only as a result of the man's death, which brings his efforts to a conclusion, rather than by an action that effectively alters the events of function A. Because of the shift in focalization in the final sentence, although the representation concludes at the moment of the man's last perception, the new focalizer who watches the man die can conduct the countdown to the moment of death, which the reader is permitted to know occurs. The primary structural difference in the conclusions of the two narratives is the shift in focalization in Kafka's story, but the consequences of that shift for the final segment of the story's fabula are profound. Because the man's death is revealed, readers are permitted to construct a set of negative functions, which represent actions that are not accomplished: specific events that do not occur, but for which the locus of their nonoccurrence—unlike the realm of the individual reader's imagination to which Strether's further actions are consigned—is the represented world of the story. The concluding segment of Kafka's fabula contains both events and functions: negative functions and specified events that do not occur. Negative functions interpret consequences that are unachieved; the events that express these functions are a motivated not-doing of an action that, were it to occur, would contradict the negative quality of the function that interprets it.[16] Were the man to enter the gate, for example, we would interpret the event as function F, rather than function F_{neg}.

Except for the opening segment of the fabula of *The Ambassadors*, the three other procedures by which the representations of these narratives are cut off at each end are innovative in the extreme. James's incomplete fabula, with its effective suppression of concluding functions as well as events, represents in its structure the problematics of epistemology that are recurrent in Modernist literature. The empty functions in the opening positions in Kafka's fabula—a common procedure for closing a fabula but not, as Kafka uses it, for representing the primary causal disruptive event—draw attention to epistemological issues as well, while the negative functions with which his fabula concludes are representative of a motivated cessation of action that is a specifically late-Modern phenomenon. For the protagonists of both narratives, as a function analysis shows, epistemological doubt is dramatized in the interpretations and reinterpretations of their own behavior that both find necessary. Readers too share the protagonists' interpretive shifts, in part because the focalization reveals the protagonists' epistemological quandaries, but also because the two representations linger at the preparatory functions, which undermines the book covers as a guide to interpreting the function of the reported events.

CHAPTER 6

SEQUENTIAL PERCEPTION:

James's *The Turn of the Screw* and Balzac's *Sarrasine*

Reproduced on the cover of this book is Josef Albers's painting *Homage to the Square: Aurora*. In the Preface I describe Albers's experiments which demonstrate that interpretations of pigment as color depend on the context in which the pigment is perceived: the color or colors next to which a given color is placed when viewed. Similarly, as we have seen, interpretations of the causes and consequences—the function—of a given event depend on the context in which the event is perceived: the events that chronologically precede and follow it in the set of sequential events in which it is encountered. In this chapter, to explore the effect of context, I look at two narratives in each of which some of the same events are perceived by certain characters, by other characters, and by readers—but not in the same sequence. In other words, these narratives offer a situation in which the same events are perceived and interpreted in contexts that vary. By comparing interpretations, we can analyze the effect of context.

Because narratives impart information sequentially (narratives are sequential representations), readers (viewers, listeners) learn about some events before they learn about other events. In other words, during the process of reading (viewing, listening to) a narrative, some information is always missing. As a result, inevitably, while we are reading (viewing, listening), we interpret the causes and consequences of events in a context in which some events— events that are chronologically prior, or subsequent, or both—are not yet known. When the set of events one knows about is incomplete, whether the missing information is temporarily deferred (not yet known) or permanently suppressed (not ever to be known), one's interpretation of the function of a known event may differ from what one's interpretation would be if the deferred or suppressed information were available.

Because we acquire information sequentially in life as in narratives, throughout our lives there is always some information yet to be obtained, as well as some information we will never obtain. Both life and narratives mete out information sequentially. Narratives, however, come to an end, and can be considered retrospectively in their entirety. Thus in analyzing narratives one can distinguish between temporarily deferred and permanently suppressed information; in analyzing narratives one can test whether the distinction between deferred and suppressed information is as significant as intuitively it probably seems to most people. In this chapter I look at the epistemological effects of sequential perception, in narratives but with reference to the corresponding situation in life, initially by distinguishing between deferred and suppressed information, and then by considering how closely related the effects of sequential perception are in our lives and in our response to narratives.

In life, the set of events one knows about at a given moment depends in large part on a perceiver's spatio-temporal position. One learns about events either through observing them, which requires one's presence at the time and place where they occur, or through channels of communication that are open at the time and place where one is. Channels of communication are diverse: conversations, e-mail, a sixteenth-century manuscript written by a Bolognese nun, a recently published book on the history of Hong Kong. Which channels are open for a given individual depends in part on who the individual is—her interests, her visual acuity, what languages she speaks, how tired she is at the end of a particular day. But as important as these and other aspects of individuality are, none overcomes the exigencies of time and place. One can read a centuries-old document, for example, only if the original or a copy of it survives into one's own time, and is placed within reading distance of one's eyes. To watch a broadcast of the day's network news requires being near a television set at the time of the broadcast or making prior arrangements for recording. This necessary correlation between the spatio-temporal position of a perceiver and the set of events that the perceiver can know holds, readers assume, not only for people in the world, but also for characters and for character narrators in realistic fictional narratives.

Because our spatio-temporal position determines to such a

degree which events we have information about at a given
moment, it is not at all uncommon that the sequence in which we
learn about events is different from the chronological sequence in
which the events occur. Because the effects of a perceiver's spatio-
temporal position on the information that is received apply to
characters in narratives and to character narrators, as well as to
people in our world, characters and character narrators are also
subject to instances in which information about events is temporarily or permanently missing. Moreover, for readers, the set of
events that one knows about at a given moment in the process of
reading depends not only on how much a narrator knows, but
also on how much a narrator tells. Character narrators, whose
information is restricted to what characters in their spatio-temporal position can know, and unrestricted narrators both have the
power to withhold information that they possess. In Meir
Sternberg's terms, narrators may be *omnicommunicative* or *suppressive* (*Expositional Modes and Temporal Ordering in Fiction*,
260ff).[1] Thus for readers, information may be deferred or suppressed in situations in which an unrestricted narrator or a character narrator does not reveal information, as well as in situations
in which a character narrator does not (yet) have the information.

As we have seen throughout this book, readers (listeners, viewers) interpret the function of events on the basis of the information that is available at that moment. Missing information matters because it can lead us to interpret the consequences and causes of events differently than we would if we were in possession of
the information—with results that in some situations are more
serious than in others. In narratological terms, missing information, whether the information is deferred or suppressed, creates
gaps—gaps in the representation and sometimes gaps in fabula.
Gaps, in fact, provide windows through which the differences
between a representation and its fabula are often easier to perceive than in other circumstances. By analyzing gaps in a representation in relation to gaps in the fabula that we construct in
response, we can explore how we process information that we
perceive sequentially.

My ideas about the effects of deferred and suppressed informa-
tion have developed under the influence of two important books
on gaps in narratives: Shlomith Rimmon-Kenan's *The Concept of
Ambiguity—The Example of James* (1977) and Meir Sternberg's
Expositional Modes and Temporal Ordering in Fiction (1978).[2]
Both theorists distinguish between temporary and permanent gaps

in information, and differentiate between the two types according to whether the gaps are located solely in the representation or also occur in the fabula (Rimmon-Kenan, 48; Sternberg, 51). Since a chronological fabula (according to the definition I am using) is made by readers (listeners, viewers) from information found in a representation, a fabula can contain only those events that a representation either explicitly states as having occurred, or provides information to permit a given reader at a given reading to deduce as having occurred.

In instances in which an event is suppressed (permanently missing) in a representation, there is a gap in the representation where the information might have been included, and a corresponding gap in the fabula at the location in the chronological sequence where the event would have occurred. A gap in fabula occurs whenever an event is permanently suppressed in a representation; if a representation gives no indication that an event has taken place, a reader will not include the event in the fabula she makes. In instances in which an event is deferred (temporarily missing), there are two gaps in the representation: one where the information would have been revealed if it were not deferred, and *another* where the information is later revealed ("a double chronological displacement—both when opened and filled in"; Sternberg, 241). But there is no gap in the fabula because finally, when the reader reaches the conclusion of the representation and places the last events revealed into the chronological fabula she is assembling, the previously missing piece is available to be included.

The idea that one can distinguish between temporary and permanent gaps through the presence or absence of a gap in fabula is grounded in the Formalist/early structuralist view of fabula as a material: a set of events from which a representation is made. Because fabula (in this view) is conceived as finite (a finite set of events), it can be assumed to be available as a totality for analysis. Both Sternberg and Rimmon-Kenan move beyond this position. In Rimmon-Kenan's analysis of James, to which I will return later in this chapter, she addresses the question of how a representation reveals one—and in the instances she studies more than one—fabula, thereby reversing the perspective from the Formalist view of fabula as a material to be shaped into a representation, to a view of a representation as revealing its fabula(s). Sternberg, as we have seen previously (particularly in chapter 3), considers the effects for readers of the placement in representations of (temporarily withheld) expositional material, thereby addressing the relations between a representation and a fabula from the perspective of the reader and also considering the effects of temporary gaps on the process of reading, as the set of events revealed to the reader gradually expands.[3]

Understanding fabula as a construct that readers (listeners, viewers) make opens the possibility of comparing how we create causal sequences in response to a narrative, to how we create causal sequences in response to events we learn about in our world. My interest in the epistemological effect of sequential representation extends beyond literary narratives to include all narratives—whether fictional or not—and also individual experiencing of the world. I assume that we experience the world, minute by minute and hour by hour, as if it were a narrative that we were reading (listening to, viewing), and that we interpret the events and situations that come to our attention by creating fabulas, which continue to develop and grow in response to new information. Theories about how historical events are understood, and how narratives that recount historical events affect interpretations of those events, influence my ideas about how narratives shape interpretations and about the process we engage in in interpreting events in the world.

From Hayden White's work I develop an image of the sequence of events in our world (annals, chronicles) as a ribbon or string from which the historian cuts a segment for representation. As White perceives, the historian's interpretation determines the placement of the cut. The placement of the cut guides readers' interpretations by determining which events will be reported and what their chronological position in the reported sequence will be. According to White: "The same event can serve as a different kind of element of many different historical stories . . . The death of the king may be a beginning, an ending, or simply a transitional event in three different stories" (*Metahistory*, 7).[4]

In my terms, the function of an event—in White's example, the death of the king—depends on exactly these determining factors: the set of events in the configuration in which the king's death is perceived, and the chronological position of the king's death in that configuration. Since White's example provides information only about the chronological position and not about the other events in the configuration, one can only speculate about the causes and the consequences of the king's death in each of the three positions, but the interpretive process White describes is the process by which we interpret the function of an event. At the beginning of a narrative, the death of the king may be perceived as a function-A event that disrupts the equilibrium of a long and peaceful reign, or merely as a change of circumstances that will perhaps encourage a neighboring king to invade (function A).[5] In the middle of a narrative, the transfer of power from one king to another may make little difference (the ongoing equilibrium or the ongoing function-A situation continues), or may provide an opportunity for a C-actant to make great changes for better or for worse. At the end of a narrative, the death of the king may confirm the wisdom of the plans for succession he has put into place (EQ, as the result of the king's C-actant activity), or mark the conclusion of a long battle for power, perhaps between the king and a prospective leader viewed by the historian as preferable (EQ, as the result of the new leader's C-actant activity).

In chapter 5 I argued that life is generally more difficult to interpret than narratives are because we are left to determine where we are in a narrative sequence without the guidance of novelist, playwright, or historian. In our own experiencing of the world, each of us takes on for ourselves the historian's task: to decide which segment of the ribbon of life to consider as a related set of events. The philosopher Louis O. Mink, in "History and Fiction as Modes of Comprehension," analyzes the ways we understand that events we perceive sequentially—in narratives and in life—are related. Mink defines *comprehension* as "an individual act of seeing-things-together" (553), or, more precisely, as a grasping "in a single act, or in a cumulative series of acts, the complicated relationships of parts which can be experienced only *seriatim*" (548). According to Mink, there are perhaps no more than three fundamental modes of comprehension. The one that is relevant to interpreting events in narratives and in the world is the *configurational mode* in which "a number of things may be comprehended . . . as elements in a single and concrete complex of relationships," for example, as "a particular configuration of events" (551).[6]

Mink's ideas about how we understand sequentially perceived events as elements in a configuration are similar to and have helped me formulate my ideas about functions. To grasp a number of events as a configuration requires, I point out, two complementary and closely related processes: understanding both that and how events are related. The historian's decision about which segment of the ribbon to examine reflects her understanding *that* the recounted events are related; the account the historian offers reflects her understanding of *how* the events are related.

Interpreting an event as a function requires making both decisions: *that* a set of events are related, and *how* a given event is
related to the other events in the set. By defining the function of
an event in relation to the configuration in which it is perceived, I
am indicating, as I have throughout this book, that the function of
events is contextual and depends on which events are included in
the configuration in relation to which it is interpreted. As we have
seen in example after example, whether we are comparing two or
more accounts of approximately the same events or comparing the
information that the beginning of a narrative gives us with the
information we have at a later stage in the process of perception,
interpretations of an event depend on the configuration in which
the event is perceived and may change if the configuration
expands (or decreases) in response to new information.

Mink also considers how understanding is affected by the temporal position of the perceiver in relation to the perceived event(s).
Suggesting that anticipation and retrospection are different forms
of cognition, Mink proposes that "the difference between following a story and *having followed* a story is more than the inciden-
tal difference between present experience and past experience"
(546).[7] Summarizing, Mink argues that "it is not following but
having followed which carries the force of understanding"
(545n9). Similarly, when we interpret the function of an event, to
be able to take into account its consequences we have to position
ourselves—at least imaginatively—at a point that permits retrospective viewing. We interpret the function of an event, in fact, as
if both the event and the configuration in which we perceive it
were completed actions. We interpret events retrospectively, as if
they had occurred, I am suggesting, because we interpret events in
the same manner—*as if* retrospectively, in relation to the configuration in which we perceive them—whether or not they have
occurred, and whether the place they have occurred or may occur
is our world, a narrative world, or our imaginings of what may or
may not occur at some future time.

To consider the effects for interpreting functions of the varying
configurations that deferred and suppressed information can create—effects that I assume apply in our world as well as in the narratives we read (listen to, view)—I take as examples two literary
narratives that offer the possibility of comparing interpretations
of the same events from different spatio-temporal positions and in
different sequences. The two narratives are *Sarrasine* (1830) by
Honoré de Balzac and *The Turn of the Screw* (1898) by Henry

James. Both works present a frame narrative in which another narrative is told. This structure offers an embedded set of events (the events of the contained story), which is perceived from three locations: by characters in the contained story, by characters in the containing story, and by readers. Perceivers at the three locations are looking at the same events. Not every event, however, can be perceived from every location; nor are events revealed in the same sequence to perceivers at each location. Thus we can test the effects of both suppressed and deferred information by comparing interpretations by perceivers who receive information at different locations.

The opening section in *The Turn of the Screw* provides an introductory frame that remains unclosed; there is no parallel scene at the end of the novella. But the section gives information, to James's readers as well as Douglas's listeners, that the governess's account of events at Bly does not contain, including information that the governess does not know at the time of the events that she describes. The framing scene offers its information through the double lens of two men whose interaction with each other indicates a mutual respect that reinforces, for readers, the authority of both as sources of trustworthy information. Specifically, a first-person narrator quotes and summarizes—and offers as factual data—prefatory remarks that his friend Douglas makes to the people to whom Douglas reads the manuscript that the governess entrusted to him decades previously, before she died.

The two men convince us, I think, at least as we begin to read, that they know how less sophisticated people, like the governess, think. She is twenty, the youngest daughter of a poor country parson, taking service for the first time. Her prospective employer, they tell us, "struck her, inevitably, as gallant and splendid, but what took her most of all and gave her the courage she afterward showed was that he put the whole thing to her as a favour, an obligation he should gratefully incur" (James, 153). The favor he asks is that she take complete charge of his deceased brother's orphaned children, and under no circumstances consult him.

Given this information, most readers probably interpret the governess's otherwise cryptic statement at the beginning of her manuscript about having "ris[en], in town, to meet his appeal" (158) initially in this way:

A   the children are a heavy burden to employer
B   employer asks governess to relieve this burden
C   governess decides "to meet his appeal"
C' governess sets out for Bly
G   governess arrives at Bly
H   governess takes charge of the children

According to this interpretation the governess is the C-actant who decides (function C) and then begins to act (function C') to alleviate her employer's function-A problem, which she is aware of because he asks her (function B) to relieve his burden.

Because Douglas has told his auditors, and thus readers know, that the governess will not see her employer again after she accepts the position, we may find somewhat pathetic her willingness to assist her employer in his desire so completely to shirk his responsibilities, particularly when she admits that she often thinks how charming it would be if he were to appear "at the turn of a path . . . and smile and approve. I did n't ask more than that—I only asked that he should *know*" (175; James's italics). The governess cannot know that he will never appear;[8] it is the possibility that he may that sustains her infatuation.

The governess's infatuation is the first premise of Edmund Wilson's influential early study of the novella. Perceptively noting that the scene in which the governess wishes that her employer might appear immediately precedes the scene in which she first sees a ghost, Wilson proposes a causal relation between the two scenes. If the governess is sexually repressed, Wilson suggests (after reminding us that she is the daughter of a country parson), then her infatuation may have led her to have "conjured up an image who wears the master's clothes but who (the Freudian 'censor' intervening) looks debased, 'like an actor,' she says" ("The Ambiguity of Henry James," 91). Peter Quint, in this view, is the governess's employer in neurotic disguise. The governess's situation, as Wilson describes it, can be represented by these functions:

A   father's occupation ensures daughter's sexual repression
a   governess is infatuated with employer (lower-case a, indicating that she sees as disruptive an otherwise unchanged world)
A   governess sees visions
B_{neg} governess is isolated at Bly, with neither white knights nor psychoanalysts nearby whom she can ask for help

Wilson's worldview is not unlike that of the two men in the introductory framing scene. Although from ontologically disparate worlds, all three are sophisticated, perceptive, experienced men of the world in the worlds they inhabit. The governess's view of her situation is very different from Wilson's, and the difference is in this instance not the result of a specific piece of information that one has and the other does not, but in the governess's very lack of experience. If she is sexually repressed, she is too naive to know it. If she needs an analyst, she is aware only that other people need her. According to her interpretation, immediately after the second time she sees Peter Quint, the children are in danger and she is their best available protector. The words she chooses indicate that interpretation: Peter Quint has come, she says, "not for me [but] for some one else" (184); she tells Mrs. Grose she will not leave the children to go to church because she is "afraid [for them] of *him*" (189, James's italics). These functions represent her interpretation:

A   Peter Quint has come for one or both children
C   governess will try to protect the children
C' governess stays with the children instead of going to church

In the same scene, moreover, the governess establishes with Mrs. Grose the relationship that from the governess's perspective seems to continue throughout the rest of the narrative. Just after she tells Mrs. Grose that she is afraid "of *him*," she "made out in [Mrs. Grose's face] the delayed dawn of an idea I myself had not given her . . . I thought instantly of this as something I could get from her" (189). Mrs. Grose begins to ask questions (function D), to which the governess responds (function E). By the end of the scene Mrs. Grose has identified the apparition as Peter Quint, and informed the governess that Peter Quint is dead (function F). In this instance Mrs. Grose provides new information that the governess does not have. In ensuing conversations Mrs. Grose sometimes offers nothing more specific than an opportunity for discussion, which permits the governess to say aloud what she has been thinking—but this too the governess seems to perceive as a form of assistance (function F) from Mrs. Grose.

To the governess at the time that the events are occurring at Bly, it seems to me, Mrs. Grose seems as trustworthy as Douglas seems to readers during a first reading. Both Mrs. Grose and Douglas seem credible for the same reason: just as Douglas knew the governess while she was alive, Mrs. Grose knew Peter Quint and Miss Jessel. Many readers, I think, will see the following sequence of functions as a representation of the governess's interpretation of the events at Bly at the time they occur, and perhaps even until the final scene:

A   ghosts threaten the children
C   governess decides to protect the children
C' governess stays with the children instead of going to church
D   Mrs. Grose asks questions
E   governess answers Mrs. Grose's questions
F   Mrs. Grose provides information and discussion that help the governess
H   governess acts repeatedly to protect the children

Unlike *The Ambassadors* (as we saw in chapter 5), *The Turn of the Screw* is one of the narratives by James that exemplifies *structural ambiguity*, the pattern that Shlomith Rimmon-Kenan identifies in which a representation reveals mutually exclusive fabulas. Specifically, in *The Turn of the Screw* she discerns: "Take the governess as a reliable interpreter of events, and you have one story. Take her as an unreliable neurotic fabricator of non-existent 'ghosts of the mind' and you are reading a diametrically opposed narrative" (*The Concept of Ambiguity*, 119).

For readers to be able to construct two fabulas from one representation, some of the scenes the representation includes will need to be open to being read as one event in one fabula and another event in the other fabula (the governess sees real ghosts; she fabricates 'ghosts of the mind'). Moreover, where structural ambiguity exists, one or more events must fill one function in one fabula and a different function in the other fabula. The scene near the end of *The Turn of the Screw* where the governess and Mrs. Grose find Flora near the lake, and then the governess sees Miss Jessel on the opposite bank, offers an example. The governess says to Flora, "'She's there, you little unhappy thing . . . and you know it as well as you know me!'" (279), to which Flora responds by denying that she sees anybody or anything. Addressing the governess, Flora continues, "'I think you're cruel. I don't like you!'" (281), and then asks Mrs. Grose to take her away from the governess. Finally the governess says to Flora, "'I've done my best, but I've lost you. Good-bye.'" (282).

Both the governess's and Flora's interpretations of what is

occurring are revealed. As we have previously understood, the governess sees herself as a C-actant who is trying to protect the children from the ghosts she thinks have invaded their lives. The governess interprets her behavior in this scene as her major effort to vanquish Miss Jessel (function H), which fails (function I_{neg}). Flora, on the other hand, interprets the governess's behavior in this scene as cruel (function A), and asks (function B) Mrs. Grose to protect her from the governess.

For readers, if we have decided that the governess sees ghosts that are there, then we interpret this scene as she does: as a function H that concludes in an unsuccessful I_{neg}. If we have decided that there are no ghosts, we can interpret this scene as Flora does: the governess's ill-founded behavior has created a function-A situation for Flora, who asks Mrs. Grose to assume the C-actant role. The very same behavior can be read as a function H moving to an unsuccessful I_{neg}, or as a function A moving to a function B. These are very different interpretations of the function of the governess's behavior in this scene.

As Rimmon-Kenan perceives, ambiguity in *The Turn of the Screw* is in part an effect of the first-person narration: without independent confirmation the reliability of a character narrator's perceptions and conceptions cannot be confirmed (*The Concept of Ambiguity*, 119). Second, in this novella as in the other narratives by James in which Rimmon-Kenan locates structural ambiguity, ambiguity arises, as she skillfully demonstrates, as the effect of an "equilibrium of singly directed clues [which support one hypothesis—e.g., there are ghosts, and contradict the alternative] and the presence of doubly directed clues [which simultaneously support both alternatives—e.g., the governess's behavior in the scene at the lake]" (101). In addition, the ambiguity of *The Turn of the Screw* can be seen, by readers and Douglas's listeners, as the result of permanently suppressed pieces of information that the introductory framing section has given us reason to assume will be revealed. The account the governess writes covers the period from her arrival at Bly to the death of Miles. The chronological fabula that readers construct, from information in the introductory section and in her account, extends from at least a couple of years before her arrival at Bly to many years thereafter. The framing section draws attention to the gaps in information in the periods both before and after the governess's stay at Bly.

The gap that follows the governess's account stretches from the moment when, in her words, Miles's "little heart, dispossessed, had stopped" (309), to approximately a decade later when Douglas, who is ten years younger than the governess (she is twenty when she goes to Bly), finds her at home when he "com[es] down the second summer" (149–50) from Trinity. In terms of scenic treatment, which we know mattered to James, the gap extends from a scene in which the governess is holding a probably dead boy, to a scene in which she is entrusted with the care of a living girl, Douglas's younger sister. In terms of interpreting the final scene of the manuscript, James's entire suppression of the events of the decade in question effectively presents Miles's death as an *uninterpreted event:* an event to which no function has been assigned.[9]

We do not know what Miles dies of, and the diagnosis is important because the manner of death might indicate cause. Nor do we know the effects, if there are any, of his death; the configuration of events in which to interpret this event is incomplete. Moreover, interpretations of the event by characters in the narrative world are withheld. The governess's manuscript stops without indication of how she interprets the final scene and her role in it. Nor are we given at that time or later any knowledgeable, authoritative view. We do not even know whether the person who entrusts Douglas's sister to the governess is cognizant of the events of ten years before. Perhaps no one other than Douglas, who is very young when he meets the governess and finds her "most charming" (149), is in possession even of her version of the events at Bly. Retrospectively, we probably trust him (and the frame narrator who quotes him) less than we did on first reading, because of his failure to address the question that his listeners must surely have asked: please explain what happens to Miles.

Because the event comes to us uninterpreted, it encourages interpretations. Peter G. Beidler, who summarizes the critical history of the narrative, cites more than a score (*Henry James: The Turn of the Screw*, 141–44), including these four recurring possibilities: (1) Miles is not dead, or (2) Miles is not dead, and ten years later is called Douglas. (Our minds have a tendency, I suggest, to perceive uninterpreted events as if they have not occurred.) (3) The governess succeeds in getting Miles to confess (if we interpret the governess as the C-actant, we see this as function I, a successful concluding event); Miles thus dies free from Peter Quint's control. (4) The governess suffocates Miles, or frightens him to death (if we interpret the governess as the C-actant, we see this as I_{neg}, an unsuccessful concluding event; the governess does not achieve her goal, and will have no further opportunities to try).

However one chooses to interpret this event, a knowledge of it instigates retrospective reinterpretations of previous events, probably including events at Bly that preceded the governess's arrival. During our reading of the governess's manuscript we see the events she sees from her spatio-temporal position. When we attempt to construct a chronological account of the events that occurred prior to her arrival, we become aware of how much information we do not have. We may also begin to think about how the events at Bly might appear to the children, from their spatio-temporal position. The children were sent to Bly, we remember, two years before the governess, and following the untimely death of their parents in India. The children would view their lives, I suggest, as one disruptive event after another.

A	loss of both parents
A	sent to a new place (Bly)
A	either (1) the disappearance and death of Miss Jessel and Peter Quint, if the two have had a supportive relationship with the children; or (2) being controlled and then haunted by Miss Jessel and Peter Quint
A	uncle has no patience for children; he disappears
A	new governess arrives; they are now in the care of an inexperienced twenty-year-old and the illiterate Mrs. Grose
A	Miles sent down from school (and no other arrangements for schooling are considered)
A	the new governess sees ghosts—e.g., either (1) the children are possessed and the governess cannot save them, or (2) the governess's mental disturbance leads her to see evil in her charges
B_{neg}	there is no one the children can ask for help
C, C'	the children court the governess's good will by their incredibly beautiful behavior
I_{neg} = A	as beautifully behaved as the children are, the governess continues to think they are possessed
A	little Miles dies or is murdered
A	little Flora is hysterical
A? C'?	Mrs. Grose carries off Flora—e.g., either (1) the final disruptive event [A], or (2) a last hope for Flora's survival [Mrs. Grose as C-actant, trying to save Flora]

Although the events that the children and the governess see
include many of the same events, the configuration of events in
relation to which they interpret specific events is not the same, in
part because the children's spatio-temporal position leads them to
interpret the events at Bly from the time they arrived, and with reference to their memories of why they were sent there. The governess on the other hand considers (and writes about) the events
at Bly from the time she arrived, and with reference to her memories of why she accepted her position there. The two interpretations are obviously very different, and illustrate the effect of dif-
fering configurations on interpretations of the function of an
event. When the configuration changes, interpretations shift.

Narratives guide readers to discern a particular configuration in
relation to which to interpret given events. Readers are led to
include in a configuration certain events and not others in ways
that are illuminated by analyzing the gaps in representations in
relationship to the gaps in the fabulas we construct in response.
The gaps with which we have been concerned in *The Turn of the
Screw* are for the most part permanent—gaps in fabula. There are
so many gaps in the fabula because the representation reveals only
a few events that precede or follow the governess's summer at Bly,
and those few events are spread over a long period of time. The
fabula extends for decades. This particular fabula can nonetheless
be conceived as one line. We can see this fabula as a single line
because we are given enough information that we can arrange in
chronological sequence, reasonably accurately, every event we
learn about—from the arrival of the children at Bly to the frame
narrator's transcribing the governess's manuscript.

Within this chronological line, the governess's manuscript
traces only a short segment, no more than a few months. This
compression of duration in the governess's text guides readers to
assemble as a configuration the events that are available to the
governess to assemble as a configuration; thus the governess and
readers (at least on first reading) tend to interpret events in relation to the same configuration.

In *Sarrasine*, on the other hand, the gaps with which we will
primarily be concerned, both in the framing narrative and the contained narrative, are temporary. The contained narrative, to which
we will return, illustrates a gap-producing pattern of relations

between the representation and the fabula that we did not see in *The Turn of the Screw.* The framing narrative, however, creates a temporary gap in much the same way that James's novella creates a permanent gap, through a representation that traces only a segment of a single chronological line.

As Roland Barthes has discerned, the framing narrative of *Sarrasine* exemplifies the narrative contract. The bargain in this instance is between the narrator (of both the framing narrative and the contained narrative)[10] and his companion, Mme de Rochefide. The narrator will tell a story (the contained narrative, about Sarrasine and la Zambinella), and in return, his companion indicates, she will permit him a night of love. In Barthes's words: "Here, the [contained] narrative is exchanged for a body (a contract of prostitution); elsewhere it can purchase life itself (in *The Thousand and One Nights,* one story of Scheherazade equals one day of continued life); . . . in these exemplary fictions . . . one narrates in order to obtain by exchanging" (*S/Z,* 89).[11]

A contract indicates that both parties to a transaction want to exchange something for something; both parties are motivated by a desire (function a) to possess something. But a contract can be reached only when the two parties want different things—different things that the other happens to possess. For both parties the motivation is a function-a desire, but the object that is desired by each party is necessarily different. In *Sarrasine,* readers are ultimately given enough information to be able to recognize both characters' motivating desires. But although Mme de Rochefide's desire is chronologically subsequent to the narrator's desire, we learn about her desire first, because of the sequence in which the representation reveals information.

As we begin to read the narrative, on a first reading, we discover initially Mme de Rochefide's motivation. The narrator's companion is fascinated by the painting she sees at the party to which the narrator has taken her: an Adonis, who, she says, is "too beautiful for a man" (Balzac, 232, *114).[12] When the narrator tells her that the portrait "was copied from the statue of a woman" (232, *117), she asks whom it depicts, adding impetuously, "I want to know" (232, *119). He responds: "I believe [*je crois*] that this Adonis is a . . . a relative of Mme de Lanty" (232, *120). Readers interpret these statements, I suggest, according to the following functions:

a   companion wants to know the identity of the model for
      the Adonis

B   companion asks narrator who the model is
C   narrator decides to tell her
C'   narrator begins to reveal information[13]

These functions that I think represent readers' initial interpretations probably also represent the narrator's companion's interpretation. Her interpretations of the further events that conclude the
framing narrative are probably these:

G   narrator arrives the next evening and is shown to the
     "small, elegant salon" (234, *148) where she receives
     him
H   narrator tells story
I_{neg} companion finds story unsatisfactory, tells narrator to
     leave

Readers, however, if they continue to think about the fabula of
the framing narrative, may remember that the party takes place in
a house that is familiar to the narrator but that his companion is
visiting for the first time, and, if so, they may then consider that
although the representation begins at the party, the fabula must
contain an earlier event, in which the narrator invites the woman
he brings: a woman he describes when he first mentions her in the
story as "one of the most ravishing women in Paris" (228, *59). I
suggest that the following functions represent the interpretation of
the other party to the bargain, the narrator:

a   narrator's desire for Mme de Rochefide
C   narrator decides to try to win Mme de Rochefide
C'   narrator invites Mme de Rochefide to a party
D   his companion is fascinated by the Adonis
E   narrator tells her the portrait was copied from the statue
     of a woman
F   his companion's interest empowers the narrator to trade
     the story she wants for a night with her
G   narrator goes to the small salon where she receives him
H   narrator tells story
I_{neg} narrator's story does not please; she tells him to leave

If we compare the interpretations I ascribe to the two characters,
we see that the functions assigned to events are in some cases different. For example, Mme de Rochefide's request for information

about the identity of the model for the Adonis is interpreted (I suggest) by her as function B and by the narrator as function F.

The differences in the two characters' interpretations are the result of differences in the configuration in relation to which each is interpreting perceived events. For readers, the companion's interpretation is the one we are apt to perceive first, because the representation introduces us initially to her configuration. Although the narrator's desire (for Mme de Rochefide) chronologically precedes Mme de Rochefide's desire (for a story), we are slower to recognize the narrator's motivation, for several reasons.

First, the information that the narrator considers Mme de Rochefide "ravishing" and that it is he who has brought her to the ball is deferred in the representation until well after the reader's curiosity about the de Lanty household is firmly aroused. Second, the two pieces of information about Mme de Rochefide are revealed (and she herself first appears) at the same point in the representation that the ancient decrepit figure whom the narrator's story claims is la Zambinella is first seen. In fact, the first sign of Mme de Rochefide in the representation is her "stifled laugh" (227, *54) in response to the ancient figure—in comparison to whom we are thereby guided to see her initially as a subordinate character, as primarily a lens through which to show readers just how horrifying the old creature looks to her unaccustomed, young eyes.[14] Third, the narrator's desire for Mme de Rochefide (his function-a motivation, as I interpret it) is never explicitly stated in the representation, although the reader can deduce as a probability that if he finds her "ravishing" and has invited her to the ball, he has invited her *because* he finds her ravishing.

Nonetheless, like the events in *The Turn of the Screw,* the events of the framing narrative of *Sarrasine* can be conceived as a single chronological line. Although we can interpret the events according to two motivated sequences, Mme de Rochefide's and the narrator's, we can nonetheless arrange all the events we learn about in the framing narrative reasonably accurately in chronological sequence. In *Sarrasine,* in the framing narrative, the representation guides readers to interpret the situation initially as the companion does, by revealing the events of her configuration first. Readers are slower to understand the narrator's interpretation because information about the events that the narrator probably interprets as his motivating function a, his C-actant's decision, and his initial C' action is in part deferred in the representation and in part left for readers to deduce and never explicitly stated. As a result, I suggest, at least on first reading, we listen to the story he tells (the contained narrative) and consider its effect with our attention more directly focused on Mme de Rochefide's desire than on the narrator's.

In the contained narrative, the information that is deferred—that la Zambinella is not a woman but a castrato—is so central that the temporary withholding of the information motivates the primary action as well as interpretations by readers and the narrator's companion. The young French sculptor Sarrasine, sent to Rome to study, naively enters an opera house in the Papal States, where he perceives in the prima donna an ideal beauty; she seems "more than a woman, this was a masterpiece" (238, *227). Naiveté, I suggest, is one type of restricted configuration. Sarrasine does not know that la Zambinella is a castrato, nor that in the Papal States no women are permitted on the stage. Thus he interprets her as the woman to whom he will devote his life.

a	Sarrasine falls in love with la Zambinella
C	Sarrasine decides to win her love ("To be loved by her, or die" [ibid., 238; *240])
C'	Sarrasine accepts an invitation to meet her ("I'll be there" [ibid., 241; *289])
G	Sarrasine arrives at the mansion where the performers are assembled
H	Sarrasine tries to win her love
$I_{neg} = A$	he cannot succeed: she is a castrato; this knowledge motivates a new sequence
C, C', H	Sarrasine tries to destroy the statue for which she was the model and to kill la Zambinella
I_{neg}	Sarrasine is killed by la Zambinella's protector's henchmen

Only near the end of the narrator's story, when Sarrasine finally learns that the woman he loves is a castrato, is la Zambinella's condition—and her interpretation of her existence—simultaneously revealed to Sarrasine, readers, and the narrator's companion. Prince Chigi tells Sarrasine: "I am the one, monsieur, who gave Zambinella his voice. I paid for everything that scamp ever had, even his singing teacher. Well, he has so little gratitude for the service I rendered him that he has never consented to set foot in my house" (250, *470). In what Barthes calls this "whole little anterior novel" (S/Z, 186), we see revealed a set of prior events and are permitted to glimpse la Zambinella's interpretation of the life-altering event of his childhood.

A   Prince Chigi's "gift" of la Zambinella's voice—i.e., the prince pays for surgery to castrate a boy soprano; the boy (la Zambinella) is far from grateful

B_{neg} the surgery cannot be reversed; there is nothing for which to ask; there can be no resolution

From the perspective of la Zambinella, all later events are interpreted in relation to a configuration that includes his castration. The configuration in relation to which Sarrasine interprets events does not include information about la Zambinella's castration until just before the end of the story and a few hours before Sarrasine's death. The difference in the information each has available explains their different interpretations of ongoing events; their different interpretations motivate their actions, with grave results.

The information about la Zambinella's castration can be kept for so long from Sarrasine because of his naiveté. The information is kept from readers (and from the narrator's companion) by the perspective—the spatio-temporal position—that the narrator adopts to tell his story. The narrator tells the story through Sarrasine's focalization; Sarrasine's perceptions and conceptions are reported in the narrator's words.[15]

The temporary withholding of information from the reader and the narrator's companion is the effect in this instance of a relation between the representation and the fabula that *The Turn of the Screw* does not illustrate. In the contained narrative of *Sarrasine,* the events that are revealed cannot be conceived as a single chronological line. We cannot arrange all the events we learn about in an accurate chronological sequence. For the years in which Sarrasine is growing up in France and la Zambinella is growing up in Italy, we have some information about specific events in both characters' lives, but no information about the temporal correlations between the events of one life and the events of the other life. We do not know, for example, whether la Zambinella was castrated before or after the Good Friday when Sarrasine carved an impious Christ; we cannot determine where to intercalate the events of one character's life into the chronological sequence of the other character's life.

In situations such as this, I suggest, we conceive two parallel lines: two young people in two different places undergo apprenticeships that lead to mastery in their different art forms. I see these as separate lines, which become conjoined and can be thought of as one line only after the two characters meet, during the period when they interact. In chapter 1, I described the patterns that Todorov discerned in which multiple narrative sequences could be represented. A different telling of Sarrasine's and la Zambinella's stories might alternate between the two lines (scenes from la Zambinella's childhood and apprenticeship alternating with scenes from Sarrasine's childhood and apprenticeship); or could embed the story of Sarrasine's childhood and training within la Zambinella's story (perhaps at the point when Sarrasine's presence in the audience begins to be noticed); or could embed the story of la Zambinella's childhood and training within Sarrasine's story much earlier than Balzac's telling does (perhaps at the moment when Sarrasine first sees la Zambinella perform or first meets la Zambinella). But in *Sarrasine* the entire line that traces the events of la Zambinella's life prior to the moment that Sarrasine hears her sing is withheld until much later (and even when reported is merely summarized). As we have seen, this pattern gives readers no clue that crucial information is missing. When the information a representation reveals leads readers to construct a fabula that includes more than one chronological line, that entire line can be temporarily deferred, even without anyone's suspecting at the time that information is being withheld.[16]

We have now seen the two available patterns in which gaps can occur in the fabulas we construct as we read, whether the information to fill the gaps is temporarily or permanently missing. A tentative fabula that contains gaps is either a single line with missing segments (e.g., *The Turn of the Screw*, the framing narrative of *Sarrasine*), or two or more parallel lines, with at least one entire line missing (e.g., the contained narrative in *Sarrasine*). Either pattern reveals certain events and withholds others, and thereby guides narrator's audiences, including readers, to include certain events and omit others in the configuration they are assembling.

As we know, narratives impart information sequentially and are perceived sequentially. Readers (listeners, viewers) interpret events as they are revealed in relation to the configuration they have assembled at that stage in the process of perception. The sequence in which events are revealed in a representation guides the contents of the configuration that perceivers establish. As function analysis demonstrates, the power of the configuration to govern interpretation can be immense. Because of the effects of sequential perception on the configuration one establishes, and of the configuration on interpretation, any sequentially perceived representation of sequential events—*any narrative*—(necessarily, unavoidably) shapes interpretations of the events it represents.

Sternberg proposes that in literary narratives both the suppression of information and its subsequent disclosure "have to be quasi-mimetically accounted for, so as to avoid the reader's indignation at being 'cheated' (this motivation of the temporal ordering usually taking the form of shifts in point of view, notably shifts from indirect or external to direct or internal presentation" ("Temporal Ordering, Modes of Expositional Distribution, and Three Models of Rhetorical Control," 308).[17] Similarly, Menakhem Perry perceives (as we saw in chapter 3) that "[e]xamples of 'distorting the order of the *fabula*' . . . are usually cases where the text does conform to a 'natural'-chronological sequence [such as] the 'natural' sequence of an 'external' occurrence; the 'natural' sequence of a character's consciousness; the sequence within a block of information transmitted from one character to another, etc." ("Literary Dynamics," 39–40).

Both theorists are analyzing narratives that are *narrated* (told, as opposed to shown). In both theorists' examples, nonchronological narration is naturalized through focalization: the writer's selection of whose perceptions and conceptions readers will be permitted to know. In *The Turn of the Screw,* as we have seen, gaps are the effect of the interplay between two focalizations: the governess's detailed account of a few months' events and the frame narrator's much more general grasp of a few temporal signposts spread over a period of decades. In *Sarrasine,* the narrator's focalization at the time the events are occurring (in the framing narrative) and the restriction to Sarrasine's focalization (in the contained narrative) similarly explain gaps. Focalizers' perceptions are limited by their spatio-temporal position in the narrative world, and by personal characteristics that guide them to attend more closely to some events than to others.

Whether focalization is restricted to one or another character, or a narrator occasionally reveals one or another character's perceptions and conceptions, or a narrator's own perceptions and conceptions are the only ones revealed, the information that is available to a reader (listener, viewer) as she progresses through a narrated narrative depends on whose perceptions and conceptions are revealed from moment to moment. From the first pages of this book I have been claiming that events are functionally polyvalent, and that the function of an event depends on the configuration in which it is perceived and its position in that configuration. In this chapter I emphasize the effect of sequential narration and its complement, sequential perception. I am arguing that representations shape interpretations according to this causally linked sequence: (1) in narrated narratives, focalization controls which events are revealed and in what sequence in the representation;[18] (2) in all narratives (whether narrated or staged), the sequence in which the representation reveals events guides the formation of a configuration; (3) in all narratives, the configuration shapes interpretations.

■

At the beginning of this chapter I discussed the effect of the spatio-temporal position of an individual in our world on the information available to that individual. The quasi-mimetic nature of the sources of information in narrated narratives that Sternberg discerns ("Temporal Ordering," 308) ensures that a reader's sources of information about events in a narrative world and an individual's sources of information about events in our world are not dissimilar. Where focalization, in narrated narratives, controls which events are revealed and in what sequence, in our lives our spatio-temporal position controls what we can know and when we can know it. Where, in narratives, the sequence in which the representation reveals events guides the formation of a configuration, in our lives the sequence of experiencing guides the formation of a configuration. Where, in narratives, the configuration shapes interpretations, in our lives too, the configuration shapes interpretations.

Individuals in our world, characters in narratives, and readers (listeners, viewers) of narratives establish configurations from available sequentially perceived information and interpret the function of events in relation to those configurations. Gaps matter because, as we have seen, the absence of information in a configuration affects interpretations of known events. But the distinction between permanent and temporary gaps applies only to fiction, not to life and not, I now argue, to narratives that report events in our world. As I noted in chapter 1, Marie-Laure Ryan discerns and explains that fictional texts each refer to a world of their own, and cannot be validated externally because other texts do not share their reference world. Because there are no sources of information other than the novel, story, fictional film, etc., about the events in a fictional narrative, the gaps that have not been filled in by the end are permanent gaps.[19]

Nonfiction texts, on the other hand, Ryan perceives, "offer versions of the same reality" and can be validated by information in other texts that refer to the same reality: "The reader evaluates the truth value of the [nonfiction] text by comparing its assertions to another source of knowledge relating to the same reference world" ("Postmodernism and the Doctrine of Panfictionality," 166). In other words, if we adopt Ryan's perspective, as I do, an account of historical events can be complemented by other accounts of the same events. Moreover, events in our world do not come to a stop. Hayden White writes about the impossibility "of 'concluding' an account of *real* events; for we cannot say, surely, that any sequence of real events actually comes to an end, that reality itself disappears, that events *of the order of the real* have ceased to happen" ("The Value of Narrativity in the Representation of Reality," 26; his emphasis).

Since permanent gaps can be differentiated from temporary gaps only with reference to a point beyond which no further information can become available, all gaps in narratives about our world are temporary gaps—gaps that theoretically can be filled by other accounts of the same events (seen from other perspectives) and by accounts of later events. For individuals in our world too, all gaps are temporary gaps. Throughout the duration of consciousness there is always the possibility of obtaining additional information about events we already know about and of acquiring information about other events that have occurred and that continue to occur as time goes on. As we think about the effect of sequential perception in historical narratives and in our lives, the issue, then, is whether the effect of temporary gaps is (merely) temporary or whether temporary gaps have effects that endure. I argue that temporary gaps have permanent effects and that through analysis of our response to gaps in fiction we can perceive those effects.

It is easy enough to see that, for individuals in our world and for characters in narrative worlds (although less often for readers, particularly readers of fictional narratives), interpretations motivate actions, and actions change the configurations in relation to which further interpretations will be made. For the character Sarrasine, for example, the distinction between deferred and suppressed information is irrelevant. The gap in Sarrasine's information about castrati is temporary. But because there is this gap in his configuration when he meets la Zambinella, he falls in love with the semblance of a woman and adopts as his aesthetic touchstone for female beauty a being who is not female. The subsequent disclosure of the previously deferred information does not and cannot rectify the situation that Sarrasine's previous ignorance has brought about. In our world too (and too often), configurations of events motivate actions that new information cannot undo.

From the perspective of readers, let us consider the case that White makes—that the historian's selection of a segment of the historical record for representation unavoidably shapes readers' attitudes toward represented events. White's argument is supported by my concept of the configuration and its effect. An account (any account) represents some events and not others, and thereby guides the configuration that readers establish and in relation to which they interpret the function of the represented events. Nonetheless, as we have seen, after we have read one historian's account we can turn to another's. When we do so, do our interpretations of the causes and effects—the functions—of reported events suddenly change in response to the configuration that the second historian presents us? An open-minded reader, of course, attempts to pay attention to a well-reasoned presentation. But often, I am arguing, even as we add events that the second historian reports to the fabula we previously constructed, our interpretation of the function of events does not change. We continue to interpret the causes and effects of events just as we did in response to the configuration presented by the first historian.

Let us consider how this can be the case. Previous studies that suggest that temporary gaps in fictional narratives have a permanent effect approach the topic from several perspectives. For readers of fiction, it is well understood that temporary gaps color the experiencing of a narrative. Suspense, for instance, has been shown to be the result of temporary gaps that arouse desire and withhold satisfaction during the process of reading. Many of the emotions that readers feel in response to characters in fictional narratives endure even after the configuration of events that aroused those emotions expands to include information about how events in progress turn out.

Menakhem Perry traces an effect of the opening pages on readers' decisions about how to read the rest of the text: "The first stage of the text-continuum . . . creates a perceptual set—the reader is predisposed to perceive certain elements and it induces a disposition to continue making connections similar to the ones he has made at the beginning of the text. What was constructed from the text as the reading began affects the kind of attention paid to subsequent items and the weight attached to them" ("Literary Dynamics," 50). As I read this passage, Perry is describing a process in which one of the ways that readers respond to the first pages of a narrative they are beginning to read is by adopting a set of principles according to which to determine what kinds of information, and how much information, to include in the configurations they are starting to establish. I think that the principle of selection that Perry discerns is important to explaining how readers, as well as listeners and viewers, establish configurations.[20]

Both Perry (53ff.) and Sternberg (*Expositional Modes and Temporal Ordering in Fiction*, 93ff.) have summarized and analyzed studies reported by psychologists who designed experiments to determine the effect on interpretations of the sequence in which information is perceived. These studies document the *primacy effect:* our tendency to accept as valid the information we are initially given, even when that information is contradicted later in the same message.[21] During the process of moving through a narrative, we interpret events as functions. If the primacy effect influences readers (listeners, viewers) of narratives, and I concur with Sternberg and Perry that it often does, then, I propose, our initial interpretation of the function of an event may endure even after the configuration we have assembled no longer supports that interpretation.[22]

We have seen that, as we move through a narrative, initially we interpret the function of a given event in relation to the configuration of events we know about at the moment that the event is revealed to us. Then when the configuration expands to include information we continue to receive, we may reinterpret the function of the given event. Finally, when we reach the end of the narrative and construct a complete configuration—a final fabula—ideally we will interpret the function of the given event once again, this time in relation to all the information we have amassed.

But sometimes, I suggest, as a result of sequential perception, events simultaneously carry two or more conflicting interpretations as functions: the function we initially assign in relation to an incomplete configuration (or incomplete configurations), and the function that the position in a completed fabula implies. Sometimes, even, we interpret an event according to the function that seems appropriate in an incomplete configuration and then retain that interpretation after we become fully cognizant of a larger configuration, in response to which we would immediately interpret the event as a different function if only we recognized the need to reinterpret. In both cases, I am arguing, the primacy effect guides us to retain our first interpretation of the function of an event after we possess the information to recognize that that interpretation is inaccurate. Also in both cases, I assume, we fail to recognize that our thought processes are illogical.

One way to explore the enduring effect of the configuration in relation to which we interpret the function of an event is to consider the sequence in which we forget the narratives we have read (listened to, viewed). I suggest that readers of this chapter join me in thinking about a novel or a film read or viewed several months or years ago, so that we can compare our present conception of it with our conception of it during the first days after reading or viewing it. Our grasp of fabula is most thorough and detailed during the period just after one finishes reading or viewing, and the influence of the completed fabula on readers' and viewers' interpretations of events as functions is thus at its strongest at that time.

The character Pierre Menard, in Jorge Luis Borges's story that bears his name, proposes that a reader's recollection of a book read long ago, which through the passage of time is "simplified by forgetfulness and indifference, can well equal the imprecise and prior image of a book not yet written" ("Pierre Menard, Author of the *Quixote*," 41). The "imprecise . . . image" that readers are eventually left with is often, I suggest, a function: an interpretation of a few (perhaps only vaguely remembered) events, often attached to a character as an interpretation—perhaps expressed in the form of a judgment—of that character's actions. In instances in which a reader or viewer interprets an event in the completed fabula as a different function than she interpreted it in a previously revealed, incomplete configuration, we can consider which interpretation endures after the passage of time.

In my own experience, whenever I think of *The Turn of the Screw* (and if some months have passed since I last read it), I immediately envision the governess as innocent and vulnerable, and as valiantly devoting her youthful energies to C-actant activity that addresses existing problems: the children's uncle's "burden," the children's needs. This view of the governess, which is always the first thing about the novella that I remember, is in stark contrast to my considered opinion, if I am pressed to decide, which is that the governess's behavior causes a dangerous function-A disturbance: she seriously damages one child and is responsible for the death of the other. I would not permit this governess to care for a young person for whom I was responsible. Now my view of the governess as ardently devoted to saving her charges is in accord with my initial interpretation of the function of her behavior and is thus reinforced by the primacy effect, whereas my negative judgment of the effects of her actions is supported—to the degree that any judgment of a narrative characterized by structural ambiguity can be supported—by the fabula(s) I have constructed when I reach the end of the novella.

Similarly, when I find in an article on *Sarrasine* the question of why the narrator would go home and write up this particular adventure,[23] I realize that this excellent question is not one that I have ever thought to ask. As we have seen in the section above on *Sarrasine,* the object of Mme de Rochefide's function-a desire (for information about the painting) is clearly stated in the representation well before readers are given sufficient information to deduce the narrator's function-a desire (for Mme de Rochefide). Thus the representation guides readers to be more aware of and more interested in the fulfillment of her desire than his. For this reason, I suggest, I read the narrator's story of Sarrasine as a function-H fulfillment of *her* desire (in addition to reading it as a wonderfully told story). Then, when I read the concluding pages, my attention is taken by Mme de Rochefide's (in my reading) very ungracious response to the narrator's attempt to please her: her self-pity, her too slight tolerance for intellectual discomfort, her abrupt dismissal of the narrator.

But I had not thought about why the narrator would choose to tell a story in which he fails to win the woman he desires, and fails moreover because the story he tells her does not please her. This gap in my thinking occurs even though I have constructed a fabula according to which the narrator tells Mme de Rochefide a story as *his* function-H attempt to win her. But although I have conceived and can describe two different causal sequences (one motivated by her desire, the other by his), the primacy effect, apparently, without my having been aware of it, has led me to respond to the narrator's story according to the interpretation I initially gave it: as a function-H effort to satisfy Mme de Rochefide's desire.

Since my attention is caught up by her response to the story, I fail to consider how the narrator feels in response to his function-I_{neg} failure to please her.

Situations in which a first interpretation of an event as a function is in contradiction to the function of an event in a completed fabula are by no means limited to narratives in which the sequence of the representation diverges from the chronological sequence of fabula. As we have seen, all sequential representations reveal information piece by piece. Interpretations are made in relation to available information, and the information available to readers (listeners, viewers) during the process of reading (listening to, viewing) a narrative is necessarily less than the information they will have acquired when they reach the concluding moments.

The sequential representation in narratives mirrors the sequential experiencing of life. According to the definition made famous by Stendhal, a novel is a mirror that is carried along a path.[24] In the nineteenth century, this definition drew the attention of critics and theorists who emphasized the word *mirror*, claiming that the Realist novel, in its details and in the kinds of characters and situations represented, served or should serve as a mirror of life. But let us instead shift the emphasis to the verb *carried*. I am arguing that narratives mirror life in that both mete out events sequentially; in response to both, we perceive events sequentially. This means that the shaping of interpretations of causality, which, as we have seen, is an effect in narratives of sequential representation, must be assumed to occur, and to the same degree, as an effect of sequential experiencing in life.

Life, moreover, in contrast to narratives, which conclude, offers continually varying configurations of events in relation to which we interpret, reinterpret, or—in response to the primacy effect— fail to reinterpret given events. Prejudice, for instance, can be analyzed in relation to the primacy effect: as a clinging to initial interpretations of the function of events in one or another of our entrenched stereotyping "master-narratives"[25]—a prior interpretation that seems to block our ability to interpret real actions we have the opportunity to see played out by people whose race, gender, sexual preference, or religion is other than our own. What psychoanalysis hopes to accomplish, I suggest, can be seen as an effort to overcome the primacy effect: to change the function of a previously interpreted event or events by encouraging a reinterpretation in relation to the expanded configuration available to an adult patient and analyst.[26]

Like the color of the pigments in Albers's paintings, the function of events in narratives and in life is contextual. As Albers demonstrates, the color that we see when we look at a given pigment depends on the pigment adjacent to it. Similarly, the function we assign an event depends on the configuration of other events in which we perceive it. Whether a first interpretation of the color of a pigment affects subsequent interpretations, for instance, when one sees a familiar painting against a changed background or in a different light, I will not claim to be able to determine. But in response both to narratives and to life, I have argued in this chapter, the primacy effect sometimes leads us to interpret the function of events once—in response to the configuration in which they are presented initially in a narrative or are presented initially in our lives by our family, cultural circumstances, or education—and then to fail to reinterpret in relation to an expanded configuration.

The degree to which sequential perception shapes interpretations of causality in response to both narratives and life—and, arguably, even guides us through the primacy effect to retain illogical first interpretations—leads me to turn now to examples from what I think of as the narrative borderlands. Thus far in this book the examples I have chosen for analysis are narratives. I consider them narratives in that, in Roland Barthes's terms, they are, like *Sarrasine,* "incompletely plural" or "moderately plural (i.e., merely polysemous)" (*S/Z*, 6), and, in my terms, because they conform to my definition: they are sequential representations of sequential events. In chapters 7 and 8, to attempt to gauge how extensive the effects of narratives on interpretations of causality are—where these effects begin and end—I consider separately, to the extent possible, the effects of sequential events and of sequential representation. In other words, in chapter 8, I investigate ways that information can be represented sequentially without determining readers' interpretations of causality, and, in chapter 7, I look at how much—or rather, how little—information about sequential events we require to shape our interpretation of the function of an event.

To do this, in chapter 7 I look at representations of an isolated moment: both the lyric poem and the discrete image. The freedom to construct fabulas—and even to interpret the function—that a moment cut from the temporal continuum often offers demonstrates, by the contrast it presents to narratives, how significantly a narrative shapes interpretations by placing a given moment in one, and only one, sequence. Nonetheless, we will see both how readily language (the medium both of the lyric and of captions to visual representations) specifies a prior or subsequent event or situation and that that is often enough to determine the function.

The Turn of the Screw, as we have seen, is ambiguous; in Rimmon-Kenan's terms readers can construct in response to it two fabulas. Yet in my terms James's novella is a narrative. Whether we regard the governess's confrontation with ghosts as real or imagined, we can arrange in chronological sequence all the represented events including her (perhaps imagined) confrontations with ghosts. In chapter 8 I look at so-called novels that are quasi-narratives, or semblances of narratives: sequential representations in response to which attentive readers cannot construct a chronological sequence—a fabula—either because alternative sequences are equally likely or because it is impossible to distinguish which events occur in the characters' world and which in other worlds (for instance, the world of a novel that a character is reading, of a painting someone narrativizes, of a character's dreams), or to decide which elements of the narration are accurate representations of the characters' world and which are hypotheses, lies, or other counterfactual accounts.[27]

CHAPTER 7

NARRATIVE BORDERLANDS I:

The Lyric, the Image, and the Isolated Moment as Temporal Hinge

A function, in the vocabulary of this book, represents an event that changes a prevailing situation—an event that has consequences. Accordingly, to interpret the function of an event, one must either know something about its consequences or causes or rely, at least tentatively, on less factual data as a basis on which to speculate about the event's consequences or causes. While a narrative, by definition, represents a sequence of events or a situation and an event that changes it, both the lyric poem and the discrete image represent an isolated moment: a snapshot, whether of a moment in a process or in a stasis. For this reason, the lyric and the image offer a site to explore how perceivers interpret the function of an event that attracts our attention when information about prior or subsequent events or situations is not, or not yet, available. An understanding of the process we engage in in interpreting the function of an isolated moment is pertinent to understanding how we interpret events in our world as well as in narratives. As we saw in chapter 6, our initial interpretation of many of the events we learn about, both in narratives and in the world, are necessarily made before we have sufficient information to construct a complete fabula. As a result, our initial interpretations are often wrong, and moreover, as I argued in chapter 6, may linger even after we have constructed a fabula that contradicts them.

I have claimed throughout this book that we interpret anything that happens that attracts our attention (in our world), or that is brought to our attention (through a visual or verbal representation of our world or of a fictional world), by interpreting the function of the event and constructing a sequential fabula or fabulas that include the event. As we have seen, interpreting functions and constructing fabulas are complementary activities; each influences the other. A fabula that we construct guides our interpretation of the function of the events and situations that that fabula includes. But also, our interpretation of the function of events and situations guides our construction of a fabula that includes those events and situations.

In this chapter I analyze more closely how we interpret the function of an event that we perceive as an isolated moment cut from a context of prior and subsequent events. Specifically, I consider what kinds of information we use and how much information we require to establish the function of an isolated moment. To do this, I look at the process of interpreting functions in modes of expression that I see as situated at the borderlands of narratives: the lyric, the image, and, in chapter 8, novels written since the middle of the twentieth century that include images or verbal accounts of images, and are not narratives because they offer readers not one fabula but multiple and contradictory sequences of events, leaving readers unable to determine in what sequence and at what ontological level the reported events occur.[1] In response to all three of these genres on the borderlands of narrative—the lyric, the image, and novels that are not narratives—I suggest, readers and viewers attempt to interpret the function of represented events, just as they do in response to narratives, but often with more varied responses.

In the context of my discussion in chapter 1 of what a narrative is, I drew attention to the difference in emphasis in otherwise similar definitions by Meir Sternberg and Gerald Prince. Considered in relation to the lyric and the image, both theorists' ideas draw attention to situations in which the lyric and the image communicate somewhat like narratives. Sternberg sees as narrative's defining characteristic the interplay between its two temporal sequences, the sequence of the representation, which we perceive incrementally, and the chronological sequence, or fabula, that readers (listeners, viewers) construct in response to a representation ("How Narrativity Makes a Difference," 117). We perceive both the lyric and the image incrementally: the lyric in the sequence in which the words mete out information, the image in a sequence less precisely controlled by the artist or photographer. But what both communicate is not a sequence but a moment. A lyric, by definition, represents someone's thoughts or feelings at a given time. The type of image with which I am concerned in this chapter is a discrete representation (in any medium—painting, photograph, statue, etc.) of one isolated moment.[2] Since both the lyric and the image offer a representation of only one point in time, neither mode can actuate the full interplay between two temporal sequences that narratives offer.

But the choice of the moment that is represented in the lyric or in the image, like the choice of the sequence in which events are represented in a narrative, guides viewers' and readers' interpretations. In a narrative, as we have seen throughout this book, the position of a represented scene (as the initial scene, for instance, or a scene that is placed after its consequences have already been revealed) can focus attention on the represented event in relation to specific prior or subsequent events. Similarly, the image and the lyric focus our interpretive forces on the represented moment rather than some other moment. Moreover, as I show in this chapter, the lyric and the image sometimes focus our attention on the represented moment in relation to a prior or subsequent event. In situations in which we can construct even a fragmentary fabula in response to a lyric or an image, the position of the depicted event or situation in the set of events in which we perceive it guides our interpretation of the function of the depicted event or situation, just as it does in a narrative. To emphasize this power that the represented isolated moment sometimes possesses to focus interpretations of the depicted moment in relation to prior or subsequent moments, we can think of a lyric or an image that possesses this characteristic as a "compressed representation" or "compressed discourse."[3]

Prince, who defines a narrative as a representation of at least two events, or of a state and an event that alters it, sees as narrative's most distinctive feature that it represents a situation that from a given time to a later time undergoes change (*Dictionary of Narratology*, 58–59). His definition draws attention to the effect in a narrative of even a single event: that it can change the situation that previously obtained. A lyric represents an isolated moment. But language, which is the medium of the lyric, has the power to present precise information about a prior event that has caused a represented situation or a future event that, were it to occur, would resolve the difficulties of a represented moment. Because of the power of language, lyrics can—and often do—represent an isolated moment in relation to an earlier or a subsequent moment. Determining the function of an event does not require establishing a complete fabula. Often, information about even a single prior or subsequent event or situation is sufficient to establish the function of a represented moment. The lyric, as we shall see, often provides exactly this information.

A visual representation too can convey information about events that are prior or subsequent to the depicted moment—through a depiction of a moment in an easily recognized set of actions, one of the familiar action schemata,[4] or through iconography, which guides viewers to identify the depiction as an illustration of a moment in a known story. In these instances viewers interpret the function of the represented scene according to its position in a sequence of events, just as readers (listeners, viewers) of narratives interpret a given scene in relation to the fabula they have constructed.

Iconography offers one example of what Roland Barthes calls indices or indexical material. As we noted in chapter 5, Barthes distinguishes between two main classes of information in narratives: information about happenings (he calls these *functions,* but his use of the term is different from mine) and indexical information, or indices. As examples of indexical material Barthes lists notations of atmosphere, psychological data about characters, and "informants" that identify characters or places, or that locate characters or places in time and space ("Introduction to the Structural Analysis of Narratives," 93–96). Given Barthes's description of indexical material in narratives told in words, indices in the visual arts would seem to include, in addition to the depicted elements that iconography teaches us to read as indicating a specific scene in a known story, elements that guide interpreters but with less specificity: such things as a dark sky, sun reflecting on calm waters, rich brocades or jewels, cows grazing, an arid landscape, forceful brushstrokes, a palette restricted to muted colors.[5]

In instances in which viewers do not recognize a depicted scene as a moment in a known story or in a familiar action sequence, I suggest that indexical elements guide viewers' interpretations of the function of the depicted scene. I have argued in another context ("Implications of Narrative in Painting and Photography") that as long as the depicted scene includes some indication of a human or anthropomorphic being, viewers will often use indexical material to construct enough of a fabula to assign a function at least tentatively to the depicted scene, or to interpret the function of the depicted scene sufficiently to construct at least a tentative fragmentary fabula.[6] Whenever we encounter events and situations outside a context of other events, we necessarily rely on indexical information to interpret functions and to construct fabulas—whether the event or situation we are encountering is in our world, or is represented in an image or a lyric, or in a narrative as an initial scene or in a scene that is introduced without information about its relation to other events. But, as we shall see, indexical information is a less precise guide to determining the function of a represented or observed moment than information about prior or subsequent events or situations is.

Both types of information that we use to interpret functions and construct fabulas—indexical information and information about a prior or subsequent event or situation—can be communicated both by the lyric and by the image. But the differences in the way that the lyric and the image convey these types of information are instructive. Lyrics, because their medium is language, can and often do directly state the persona's interpretation of indexical information and even of the function of the represented moment, and can and often do specify temporal relations between the represented moment and some other moment, which is often sufficient information to establish the function of the represented moment. The image, in contrast, is more often open to divergent interpretations of the function of the represented moment—particularly in circumstances in which viewers rely only on indexical information because information about prior or subsequent events or situations is unavailable.

In these circumstances, viewing an image is not unlike witnessing an event in our world. When we must rely on indexical information, when information about prior or subsequent events is unavailable, and when no one's words guide our interpretations, the scene we are viewing, depicted or real, can often be interpreted as an expression of one of several different functions. This characteristic that the image shares with events we witness in our world—that the function of the viewed scene is often open to divergent interpretations—can explain at least in part, I suggest, a striking phenomenon in the fiction of the last half-century: the number of novels that include visual representations and anecdotes that are interpretations of visual representations. My theory is that by incorporating visual material and interpretations of visual material, novelists have found a way to make the experience of reading novels more like the experience of living in our world.

Because the lyric and the image both represent an isolated moment and both can offer indexical information and information about temporal relations, in order to differentiate between them I examine in the next section specific lyric poems, to show how precisely the lyric sometimes shapes interpretations both of the function of the isolated moment and even of a fabula in which the isolated moment occurs. Then in the following section I return to a discussion of the image. In chapter 8 I consider what the presence of images and descriptions of images in novels can show us about how we read images and how we read events in our world, and how our reading of images and events is related to constructing, as well as reading, narratives.

■

A lyric can be understood as an expression of the persona's interpretation of the represented moment in relation to whatever configuration of events and situations is of concern to her or him at that moment—in other words, as an expression of the persona's interpretation of the function of the represented moment. The words the persona speaks—the words of the poem—convey the persona's interpretation of the function of the represented moment and at the same time guide readers to interpret the function of the represented moment in accordance with the persona's interpretation. In fact, the information that a lyric provides is often exactly the information that a reader needs in order to be able to interpret the function of a situation or an event.

At least theoretically, lyrics can express any of the interpretive sites that functions name. If the significance of the moment, from the perspective of the persona, does not depend on an earlier event that has brought about the represented moment, or a subsequent event that would alter the represented moment, then the persona—and readers—usually interpret the represented moment as an equilibrium. Lyrics that are philosophical meditations often fall into this category. Other lyrics too express an equilibrium through indexical material and provide no information about a prior, ongoing, or subsequent event. Often, however, the persona describes the represented moment as the result of something that has happened, or as potentially altering a future situation or being altered by a future event. In response to lyrics that refer even to just one event, readers may construct a fragmentary fabula that includes the event and a situation that it has altered or could alter.

A fabula that includes one event and its effect often provides enough information to establish the function of the represented moment. When that is the case, readers' interpretations of functions are often reinforced by indexical material, and indexical material may inspire readers to construct extended fabulas that include additional events. Even in these imagined fabulas (assuming readers who are attentive to the information the lyric provides), the represented moment will express the same function it does in the lyric, and the chronological sequence will be unidirectional: the event will precede the situation it alters.

The four poems that I have chosen as examples of some of the ways that lyrics express functions were written prior to the twentieth century (so that gaps in information will not be perceived as Modern or Postmodern inventions) and in English (to avoid the added layer of interpretation in a translation). They all represent an isolated moment. In each, I consider how the poem indicates the persona's interpretation and guides readers' interpretations of the function of the represented moment. Specifically, I look at how much (and how little) information about events and their consequences these poems provide, to guide us in constructing a fabula or possible fabulas that include the represented moment.

William Butler Yeats's "The Lake Isle of Innisfree" reports one event—the persona's decision to go to Innisfree—which readers generally interpret as function C. I cite the first and third of the poem's three stanzas:

> I shall arise and go now, and go to Innisfree,
> And a small cabin build there, of clay and wattles made:
> Nine bean-rows will I have there, a hive for the honeybee,
> And live alone in the bee-loud glade. . . .
>
> I will arise and go now, for always night and day
> I hear lake water lapping with low sounds by the shore;
> While I stand on the roadway, or on the pavements grey,
> I hear it in the deep heart's core. (Lines 1–4, 9–12; in
> Williams, 413–14)

At the moment that the poem represents, the persona of Yeats's poem is declaring himself a C-actant. He is announcing his decision (function C) to go to Innisfree. The move from decision (function C, the moment represented in the poem) to intentional action (function C') has not yet occurred; the persona tells us he is going to "arise and go" but has not yet done so.

In chapter 4 I suggested that function C brings comfort both as a thematics and as a hermeneutic device. As a hermeneutic device, function C serves as a lodestar, first because it is easily recognized, even when removed from a context of prior or subsequent events, and second because it guides us to locate our position in the ongoing causal logic. Once we have recognized that a function-C decision is occurring, we can use the C-actant's decision to help us determine, on the one hand, the function-A or -a event that has created a situation that the C-actant hopes to ameliorate, and, on the other hand, the function-I resolution the C-actant hopes to achieve. In a full-scale narrative, the persona's repeatedly stated decision to go to Innisfree would guide readers to expect to be told both why he wants to "arise and go" from his present situation and whether he reaches Innisfree and is pleased to be there.

But just as, in narratives, the interplay between the two temporal sequences can guide readers' (listeners', viewers') attention to some, rather than other, events, lyrics too can focus our interpretive forces, as I suggested in the introduction to this chapter, on the represented moment rather than some other moment and on the represented moment in relation to one, rather than another, prior or subsequent event or situation. In a poem that represents a function-C decision, for example, the persona's attention can be directed to the decision-making process itself (function C), to the motivating function-A or -a disruption, to the action to be undertaken (functions C', H), or to the results of that action (function I) or the resultant equilibrium (EQ). Readers, at least initially, are guided by the persona and direct their attention to the interpretive site or sites that the persona is contemplating. In Yeats's poem the resultant equilibrium, life in Innisfree as the persona conceives it, is the subject of nearly every line. In this way readers are guided to think about the persona's decision in relation to the outcome he expects: the life in Innisfree that he imagines living.

With our attention focused on life in Innisfree, we use indexical information, first, I suggest, to understand why the persona wants to go there. From the indexical information that the poem provides (and without reference to extratextual information) we can determine that the persona conceives the place as removed from society and offering pleasures (the sounds of the water and the bees, but also potentially honey) as well as the necessities of life (shelter, water, a garden). Second, some readers will consider whether the persona will in fact go to Innisfree. As a thematics, function C provides indexical information. As I argue in chapter 4, function C comforts as a thematics by encouraging belief in the efficacy of a C-actant's motivated action. The repetition in the poem of the persona's decision, coupled with his obvious satisfaction with the place to which he says he will go, will lead some readers to construct a fabula in which the persona reaches Innisfree and lives there peacefully.

Third, some readers may then recognize that the persona's focus on going to Innisfree and living there distracts his attention, as well as ours, from his reasons for making the trip. Although the words of the poem tell us that the persona has decided to go somewhere, rather than to leave something, the poem includes indexical information (the grey pavements, for instance) that suggests that leaving may also be part of his motivation. In choosing to go to Innisfree where he will "live alone," he may be escaping an urban environment—or so we may speculate. We may even consider that he may be leaving someone who has been important to him and with whom his relationship is, or has become, a source of pain.

Yeats's poem reports the occurrence of only one event, the persona's decision to "arise and go." But when we interpret an event as the pivotal function-C decision, we are saying that we see it as a response to a function-A or -a event and as intended to restore an equilibrium. The persona describes what he envisions as a restored equilibrium, but not what the disruption is that motivates his decision. As we saw in chapter 5, some narratives never reveal a given event but do reveal its consequences. Since functions represent the consequences of an event, readers can interpret the function of unspecified events. An interpretation of an unspecified event is an *empty function*—a function that is empty because the event to fill it is unexpressed. In Yeats's poem, the disruptive situation that motivates the persona's function-C decision is an empty function. On the other hand, because we do not know whether the events occur that the persona's decision motivates, we interpret those events as either positive or *negative functions*: positive functions to represent events that occur, negative functions to represent specified events that do not occur.

Most readers of the poem will construct a function analysis that looks like this:

[A or a]   motivating event or situation (an empty function, bracketed because it precedes chronologically the represented moment)

C   persona decides to go to Innisfree

C' or C'$_{neg}$ persona does or does not set out

H or H$_{neg}$ persona does or does not travel to Innisfree
I or I$_{neg}$ persona does or does not reach Innisfree
EQ?   if persona reaches Innisfree, his desire to go there
             is satisfied

When information about an event and the changes it can bring is available, as it is in Yeats's poem, we rely on that information, I suggest, to interpret the function of the event and thus its position in a causal schema: a function analysis. But where information is lacking about events that express given functions in the schema we are constructing—for instance, in Yeats's poem, the function-A or -a event that motivates the persona's decision to leave—we use indexical material, as we saw above, to guide us in filling in the gaps to which a function analysis draws attention. Because indexical material by its very nature is somewhat amorphous, we must expect great variation from perceiver to perceiver in the events they select to fill in these gaps.

Readers who choose to construct a fabula that includes events in addition to the persona's decision will select varied events or situations to express the motivating function-A situation, and will envision a concluding situation in which the persona is happily ensconced on Innisfree, or there but less happy than he expects to be, or unable to get there. Individual readers may construct several fabulas, even fabulas that contradict each other. In all the fabulas that (attentive) readers construct, however, the persona's decision will express function C, and the chronological sequence will be unidirectional: the motivating function-A or -a event will be followed by the persona's decision, which will be followed by his successful or unsuccessful journey to Innisfree.

Robert Browning's "Home-Thoughts from Abroad" is similar in thematics to Yeats's "The Lake Isle of Innisfree." Both depict pastoral scenes that the persona longs to experience. But whereas the represented moment in Yeats's poem shows the persona expressing a function-C decision to go to a pastoral situation, the persona in Browning's poem is nostalgic for a pastoral situation previously experienced. I cite the opening and the concluding lines:

> Oh, to be in England
> Now that April's there,
> And whoever wakes in England
> Sees, some morning, unaware,

That the lowest boughs and the brush-wood sheaf
Round the elm-tree bole are in tiny leaf . . .

And though the fields look rough with hoary dew,
All will be gay when noontide wakes anew
The buttercups, the little children's dower,
—Far brighter than this gaudy melon-flower! (Lines 1–6,
17–20; in Williams, 257)

The persona's desire to be elsewhere is a typical expression of a function-a situation. Where he is, is by no means dreadful; he is after all holding a flower. But his situation is not to his present taste; like the prince in "The Pea Test" who one day decides that he wants a bride (see chapter 2), the persona of Browning's poem wants to be somewhere other than where he is. He wants to be "there," in England in springtime.[7]

Whereas Yeats's persona, as we saw, is represented at the moment of announcing his decision to go to the place where he wants to be, but not yet putting that decision into action, Browning's persona is represented as expressing his desire to be elsewhere but not (or not yet) deciding to go there. In Yeats's poem, as we saw, the persona is located at function C, and his attention—and thus readers' attention—is focused on the place he wants to go to (the potential function-I resolution). In Browning's poem the persona is recognizing that there is a pleasure he lacks (function a) and focusing on a prior situation: springtime in England as he has previously experienced it. That England is his home is information provided by the title. Given this much information, most readers, I suggest, will construct a fabula that includes, in addition to the present and prior situations, an event that causes the change from the earlier situation to the present one. (Brackets indicate interpretations of events that precede chronologically the represented situation.)

[EQ] persona experiences spring in England
[A]   persona departs from England
a   persona is nostalgic for England

The familiarity with the gradual progress of spring in England that the persona exhibits is indexical information. It confirms what the title specifically states, that England is the persona's home and that he has lived there. The indexical material thus supports, but is not necessary to, the construction of the fragmentary fabula sketched above. In Browning's poem as well as in Yeats's poem, indexical material provides a source of interest. It helps readers understand why the personas want what they want, and, as a result, guides readers to identify aspects of the personas' personalities. In this way indexical material can support readers' speculations about why, for instance, Browning's persona left England to travel to a place where the flowers seem to him gaudy, whether he is going to make a C-actant decision to return to England, or, as we saw, whether Yeats's persona will reach Innisfree.

But a lyric, because the medium is language, can specify that an event has occurred, is occurring, or may occur. Even one event brings change; it causes consequences. Because functions represent events that change a prevailing situation, information in a lyric about a previous or potential change indicates the function of the represented moment. In Yeats's poem, as we saw, the represented function-C event, because function C is pivotal, is sufficient to ground a unidirectional sequence. In lyrics like Browning's, indications of change allow readers to interpret the function of the represented moment and, by doing so, to establish the position of the represented moment in a sequence that is both causal and unidirectional. Indexical material cannot alter the sequence. Browning's persona was once in England and now is not in England; Yeats's persona now wants to go to Innisfree and later will or will not do so.

We saw that readers of Yeats's poem may construct a number of different fabulas, even contradictory fabulas, but that all those fabulas will include the persona's decision and in all those fabulas the persona's decision will express function C. Similarly, readers of Browning's poem may choose to imagine extended fabulas, and all these fabulas will include the represented moment—the persona's longing for England—and the represented moment will express the same function as it does in the poem: a motivating function-a situation. For instance, Browning's persona longs for England and decides to return there; Browning's persona longs for the landscape of his youth but never returns to England. As varied as the imagined events may be, readers who are attentive to the information provided in the poem will include the represented moment in the fabulas they construct, and place it in the same position in a causal sequence in which it appears in the poem. In other words, the represented moment will express the same function in the fabulas readers construct that it does in the poem. Just as information about prior or subsequent events or situations guides interpretations of the function of a given event or situation, once the function of an event or situation is established, that interpretation guides speculation about prior or subsequent events. In this way, even a single represented situation or event, as long as information about change indicates its function, both suggests possible fabulas and restricts the variety of fabulas that readers can construct.

In Christina Rossetti's "A Birthday," as in Browning's poem, information about a prior event establishes the function of the represented moment. But where Browning's poem includes information about the prior situation in the title and the opening line, in Rossetti's poem the event is revealed only at the end of the stanza, probably guiding many readers to rethink their initial interpretation of the function of the represented moment. I cite the first of two stanzas that both conclude "my love is come to me":

> My heart is like a singing bird
> Whose nest is in a watered shoot:
> My heart is like an apple-tree
> Whose boughs are bent with thickset fruit;
> My heart is like a rainbow shell
> That paddles on a halcyon sea;
> My heart is gladder than all these
> Because my love is come to me. (lines 1–8; in Williams, 317)

As I read Rossetti's poem, the joy of the opening lines is indexical information that suggests that the represented moment is an equilibrium. But the one event that is revealed at the end of the stanza—the beloved's return—guides readers to interpret the represented moment as the successful resolution of a function-a situation. In other words, whereas for the first seven lines we interpret the situation as an ongoing, more-or-less permanent equilibrium with neither beginning nor end, the eighth line informs us that the represented moment is instead an *achieved* equilibrium: an equilibrium that is the effect of a prior event (the beloved's return) and finite in duration (it began when the beloved returned). For most readers, information about the beloved's return gives meaning to the persona's happiness. In my terms, information about the one event is sufficient to allow readers to envision the represented moment in a causal chain and construct a fabula. (Brackets indicate interpretations of the initial situation and the subsequent events that precede the represented moment.)

[a]   beloved is away
[C]   beloved decides to return (the beloved as C-actant—since the poem gives no indication that the persona is a C-actant or that anyone else acted on her behalf)
[C'] beloved sets out
[H]   beloved travels
[I]   beloved arrives on persona's birthday
EQ   because beloved has arrived, persona is delighted

In Rossetti's poem as in both Yeats's and Browning's poems, the information that an event has occurred determines not only the function of the represented moment but its position in a unidirectional fabula. Readers who speculate about why the beloved left, how long the beloved had been away, whether the persona knew when, or that, the beloved would return, and so on, may choose to construct fabulas to guide their speculations. Readers may also include in the fabulas they imagine subsequent events in the life of the persona after her beloved returns: their happiness or unhappiness together, conflicts that may arise, and so on. As varied as the fabulas that readers imagine may be, all will include the persona's happiness as subsequent to and a consequence of the beloved's return.

By temporarily withholding information about the beloved's return, Rossetti utilizes the power of language to present a represented scene either as an isolated moment or in relation to another temporal period. In this case the poem guides us to interpret the represented moment initially as the generalized pleasure of an ongoing equilibrium, without foreseeable beginning or end. Then in response to the last line of the stanza, we understand, with a delight that is perhaps not unlike that of the persona, that the moment of happiness that the poem represents is an achieved rather than a less believable, apparently unchanging equilibrium.

In contrast, "She Walks in Beauty," by George Gordon, Lord Byron, does express an apparently enduring equilibrium throughout. I cite the first and last of the poem's three stanzas:

> She walks in Beauty, like the night
> Of cloudless climes and starry skies;
> And all that's best of dark and bright
> Meet in her aspect and her eyes:
> Thus mellowed to that tender light
> Which heaven to gaudy day denies. . . .

And on that cheek, and o'er that brow,
So soft, so calm, yet eloquent,
The smiles that win, the tints that glow,
But tell of days in goodness spent,
A mind at peace with all below,
A heart whose love is innocent! (lines 1–6, 13–18; in
Williams, 125)

The poem depicts an ongoing but unvarying state; there are no
storms, no extremes even of dark and light; nothing happens. Or
rather there is no finite action, only the ongoing action that the
persona interprets as "days in goodness spent." Like the empty
function with which fairy tales often end ("and they all lived happily ever after"), days spent "in goodness" offers an interpretation
without specifying the activities that are being interpreted. Given
this information, we can nonetheless imagine activities in which
the woman the persona describes might happily engage, and other
activities she will happily avoid. To do so we rely on the indexical
information the poem provides.

But in the absence of information about even one singulative
event, if we attempt to construct a fabula we must do so without
the information about sequence that even just one event with consequences can provide. Even with the gaps in information in the
poems by Yeats, Browning, and Rossetti that we may use our
imagination to fill, the fabulas we construct are unidirectional.
Yeats's persona decides to go to Innisfree and then does or does not
do so. Browning's persona was previously in England and now is
not in England. Rossetti's persona was once without her beloved
who now has returned.

But the woman Byron's persona describes may be calm and at
peace because the persona has come to see her and she is pleased
(persona arrives; woman expresses pleasure). Or she may be calm
and at peace because the persona is leaving and she looks forward
to time spent alone or with someone else (persona leaves; woman
expresses pleasure). Or she may be calm and at peace because soon
she is to go to boarding school and she knows that the experience
will enrich her life (woman is at home, then woman is at school).
Or she may be calm and at peace because she has just returned
from boarding school and is pleased to be at home (woman is at
school, then woman is at home).

When no information about an event that changes a situation is
available to guide our interpretations of the position of an event in

a causal chain, the represented isolated moment can be seen metaphorically as a crossroads, or what I call a *hinge* situation or event. A crossroads is a site that many paths cross, and these paths can be traversed in either direction. In response to Yeats's, Browning's, and Rossetti's poems, which provide enough information about an event and its consequences that we can determine the function of the represented moment, we can construct a number of different fabulas which include the represented moment and in which the represented moment expresses the same function as in the poem. But in all the fabulas that (attentive) readers make, the event leads to its consequences; the chronological sequence is unidirectional. In response to Byron's poem we can construct a number of fabulas that include the represented moment and that express the represented moment as an equilibrium. But some of these fabulas are reversible. The represented moment in Byron's poem is a hinge because it can occur in fabulas that like a palindrome can be read as beginning at either end. But unlike a palindrome, which reads identically from either end, a fabula is a sequence of events, and the function of an event depends on its position in a sequence. When a sequence of events that includes a hinge situation or event is reversed, the causal relations that connect event to event change and thus the function of the events changes too.

█

In his comparative study of visual art and literature, Gotthold Ephraim Lessing famously declares that, since a visual artwork "can use but a single moment of an action, [the visual artist] must therefore choose the most pregnant one, the one most suggestive of what has gone before and is to follow" (*Laocoon*, 92). As analyses throughout this book indicate, what has gone before or what is to follow is exactly the information one needs to interpret the function of an event or situation.

Lessing's study takes its title from the ancient sculpture known as the *Laocoon*. The statue represents Laocoon, a priest in Troy during the Trojan War, struggling to save himself and his two sons against serpents that are wrapped around their bodies. Viewers familiar with Laocoon's story, including Lessing, approach the statue knowing that for the three mortals no escape is possible. Virgil, who offers one of the surviving versions of the legend, explains that the "outcome [had] been fated by the gods" (*Aeneid*,

II, 75–76, p. 31). But viewers who approach the statue without knowing the legend will nonetheless probably be able to interpret the situation as Lessing does—with the exception perhaps of the outcome, although even the outcome is strongly implied by the representation. The *Laocoon* provides an example of a visually represented isolated moment that gives viewers the necessary information to be able to interpret the function of the represented moment and to construct a fabula.

Like Yeats's poem, the *Laocoon* guides viewers to recognize the position of the represented event in a causal chain. In Yeats's poem the words the persona speaks inform readers that he is making a function-C decision, and, in response, readers construct a causal chain in which first some situation prompts the persona's decision and then his decision, if it leads to successful action, guides him to Innisfree. In the statue, the position of the men and the serpents informs readers that Laocoon is struggling to disentangle the serpents that have wrapped themselves around the two smaller human bodies and his body. In response, viewers interpret Laocoon's behavior as motivated action undertaken in reaction to the serpents' attack. Because of the degree to which serpents' bodies and humans' arms and legs are intertwined, virtually all viewers will interpret the action as fully under way (function H), long past an initial physical act (function C') that indicates that a decision is being put into effect. (Brackets indicate interpretations of events that precede chronologically the represented moment.)

[A]	serpents attack
[C]	Laocoon decides to do what he can
[C']	Laocoon begins to try to disentangle the serpents
H	Laocoon struggles with all his strength
I or I_{neg}	Viewers responding solely to the statue will assume that, unless intervention occurs, Laocoon will soon succumb. Viewers familiar with the literary accounts know that, since the serpents have been sent by one of the gods, no intervention will occur.

As Lessing understood, a visual representation can provide sufficient information about a motivating situation or a hoped-for outcome to allow viewers to interpret the function of the represented moment and to construct a unidirectional fabula. In fact, the *Laocoon* would seem to give us more information than Yeats's poem does about both the motivation and the outcome of the represented event. For viewers of the statue for whom the legend is familiar, the depiction of three human bodies, one larger than the other two, in conjunction with the serpents, is sufficient to identify the humans as Laocoon and his sons and thereby reveal the events prior and subsequent to the represented moment. For viewers not familiar with the legend, the depicted moment is an event in a recognizable action schema. The presence of the smaller humans along with the fully adult central figure guides understanding that the serpents have attacked the people, rather than that the man has chosen to fight snakes to demonstrate or test his prowess.

Viewers who construct a fabula through iconography and those who do so by recognizing a familiar action schema all see a representation of Laocoon at a moment when he is struggling with all his force. A visual artwork that gives viewers information to construct a fabula has the same power that a lyric has to focus readers' attention on one, rather than another, moment in the sequence. Just as Yeats's poem focuses readers' attention on the persona's function-C decision-making, the statue focuses viewers' attention on Laocoon's function-H struggle. To gauge how great a power this is, we can consider how different our response to Yeats's persona would be if he were shown to us on Innisfree caring for his bean-rows, or to Laocoon if the statue depicted a pair of serpents crawling toward fleeing humans, or showed the serpents entwined on bodies no longer able to stand upright. The visual artist, like the poet, expresses an attitude to a character, a situation, or a set of events through the selection of the moment to be represented as well as through indexical material.

The *Laocoon* guides viewers to construct a fabula that includes several consecutive events. As Browning's and Rossetti's poems show, however, information about just one event and its consequences (or potential consequences if the event is in the process of occurring or has not yet occurred) is enough to allow perceivers to identify the function of the represented moment. Similarly, visual artworks may represent an event that has changed a prior situation or that has the potential to bring change, or a situation that has been changed by an event or that is about to be changed. "Narrative" paintings, for instance, generally offer a recognizable action schema that, perhaps in combination with indexical material, provides enough information about an event and its (potential) consequences to enable viewers to interpret the function of the represented moment. In these instances the fabula we construct may be fragmentary but is nonetheless unidirectional. The event precedes its consequences. In any extended fabula we choose to imagine in response to the artwork, the depicted event precedes its consequences.

Like Byron's poem, however, visual representations sometimes provide no indication of events that are prior or subsequent to a represented situation, or of the causes or consequences (or potential consequences) of a represented event. Indexical material may provide information about the mood, as it does in Byron's poem, or even the identity of a depicted place or personage. But without information about causes or consequences, even if we interpret the visual artwork as an equilibrium we cannot see it as an achieved equilibrium. Nor do we have reason to assume that any one event is more likely to disrupt it than any other event.

Mark Twain writes in *Life on the Mississippi,* in a passage that J. Hillis Miller cites, about his response to a painting that to his eyes depicts a scene that offers no indication of a prior or subsequent event. Miller cites the passage to show that, for Twain, words are more informative than images (Miller, *Illustration,* 61–62). I cite the passage as a demonstration of how a nineteenth-century novelist responded, at least in this one instance, to a visual representation. Twain is describing a painting he was taken to see during a visit to New Orleans:

> a fine oil-painting representing Stonewall Jackson's last interview with General Lee. Both men are on horseback. Jackson has just ridden up, and is accosting Lee. The picture is very valuable, on account of the portraits, which are authentic. But, like many another historical picture, it means nothing without its label. And one label will fit it as well as another:—
>
> > First Interview between Lee and Jackson.
> > Last Interview between Lee and Jackson.
> > Jackson Introducing Himself to Lee.
> > Jackson Accepting Lee's Invitation to Dinner.
> > Jackson Declining Lee's Invitation to Dinner—with Thanks.
> > Jackson Apologizing for a Heavy Defeat.
> > Jackson Reporting a Great Victory.
> > Jackson Asking Lee for a Match.
>
> It tells *one* story, and a sufficient one; for it says quite plainly and satisfactorily, "Here are Lee and Jackson together."

> The artist would have made it tell that this is Lee and
> Jackson's last interview if he could have done it. But he
> could n't, for there was n't any way to do it. A good legible
> label is usually worth, for information, a ton of significant
> attitude and expression in a historical picture. (Twain, *Life*,
> 448 [chapter 44])

From Twain's comments we understand, first, that he values visual representation as a source of indexical information (the picture is valuable because the portraits are authentic), but not as a source of information about the position of the represented moment in a sequence; and, second, that "meaning" ("it means nothing without its label"), in his view, entails positioning an event in a sequence. The first two labels in the list Twain offers do position the represented event in a sequence.

These two labels, which propose that the painting depicts the first *and* the last interview between the two generals, take on added resonance when read as a pre-echo of Hayden White's comment that the "death of the king may be [told by a historian as] a beginning, an ending, or simply a transitional event in three different stories" (*Metahistory*, 7). Twain already understands what White explains more theoretically: that the meaning of an event depends on the set of events in the configuration in which it is perceived and its position in that configuration. In my terms, as I proposed in chapter 6, these are exactly the factors that determine the function of (in White's example) the death of the king or (in Twain's example) the interview between the two generals. For both the novelist and the historian, the meaning of an event depends on its consequences and causes: its function.[8]

White's comments about a (generic, unidentified) king and Twain's comments about Lee and Jackson both refer to historical personages. The events in the lives of historical personages (of anyone in our world, whether famous or not) occur in only one sequence and are not reversible. Although interpretations of the function of a historical event can change, because these interpretations depend on the configuration of prior and/or subsequent events in which the event is perceived, the sequence in which historical events take place is unidirectional. As a result, a depicted historical event is inherently less open to interpretation than a depicted event for which no information about its causes and consequences is available.

In fictional worlds, events can occur in whatever sequence a storyteller indicates.[9] Let us suppose that Twain is looking at a painting of two unidentified men on horseback, one of whom is asking the other for a match. According to one scenario, the men are traveling in opposite directions but stop to talk while they both smoke their pipes. Enjoying each other's company, they decide to take their noon-time meal together at a nearby tavern. According to a second scenario, two men who have stopped at a tavern for a noon-time meal sit at the same table and fall into conversation. After the meal, when they have climbed back on their horses, one asks the other for a match. Enjoying each other's company, they continue their conversation while they both smoke their pipes. Then they separate, riding off in opposite directions.

In one scenario, the first event chronologically is traveling on horseback, which is followed by pipe smoking, and then a meal. In the other scenario, the first event is a meal, which is followed by pipe smoking, and then traveling on horseback. In the first scenario, the men's pleasure in their conversation while they are smoking causes them to share a meal. In the second scenario, their pleasure in their conversation during the meal they share causes them to continue to converse while smoking. Like Byron's poem, a visual representation of two men on horseback, one of them speaking to the other, can be interpreted as a hinge. We can read it as an event in a reversible sequence. When a sequence is reversed, the causal relations among events shift accordingly. Since the function of an event is an interpretation of its consequences or causes, the function of events that in one case precede and in another case follow a hinge event or situation will vary according to which of the two sequences perceivers are interpreting. Many visual representations of an isolated moment, like Byron's poem, give no indication of prior or subsequent events and can be read as hinge situations in a reversible sequence.

Twain, who is of course responding to a painting depicting historical figures, does not interpret the depicted scene as a hinge event in a reversible series. But the labels he lists position the event at moments in the trajectory of the two generals' lives that differ in ways important to novelists: sequence (First Interview between Lee and Jackson, Last Interview between Lee and Jackson), consequence (Jackson Accepting Lee's Invitation to Dinner, Jackson Declining Lee's Invitation to Dinner), and cause (Jackson Apologizing for a Heavy Defeat, Jackson Reporting a Great Victory).

Twain's labels are perhaps most remarkable when read as a document of the novelist's propensity for narrativizing—animating a fixed scene to create a narrative that includes the scene. I have argued throughout this book that whenever our attention is caught by something that happens, in our world or in a representation, we begin to interpret its function by considering its possible causes or consequences. If we are responding to a visually represented scene—and if we express our interpretations in words—we are engaging in *ekphrasis*.

Ekphrasis is the re-representation in words of a visual representation.[10] Both a verbal description of a visual representation and a verbal account that narrativizes, or animates, a represented isolated moment are considered examples of ekphrasis. But in literature, as James A. W. Heffernan shows by analyzing examples of ekphrasis from Homer to John Ashbery, narrativizing a visual representation is a procedure that recurs at every period from Homer's time to our own. In the famous early example of Achilles' shield (*Iliad*, Book 18), Heffernan comments, not only does Homer tell the story of how the shield is made, rather than describing how it looks when completed, but he "animates [individual images on the shield, for example the cattle], turning the picture of a single moment into a narrative of successive actions: the cattle move out of the farmyard and make their way to a pasture ("Ekphrasis and Representation," 301).

Twain's labels narrativize the painting of Lee and Jackson on horseback. Through ekphrasis—that is, using words—Twain offers with each label a sequence of events that includes an isolated moment in which Jackson and Lee are together on horseback. What I find notable in Twain's account, however, is the proliferation of stories in each of which the represented moment occurs. On the one hand, Twain is of course demonstrating the fertility of his novelist's imagination. On the other hand, he is a nineteenth-century novelist who offers these plural and contradictory accounts of a depicted event in the context of a comparative analysis of verbal and visual representation, rather than in a novel. In the next chapter we will look at novels written after the middle of the twentieth century in which plural and contradictory stories—or at least fragments of fabulas—proliferate in response to visual artworks, whether the artwork is recounted through ekphrasis or visually depicted.

CHAPTER 8

NARRATIVE BORDERLANDS II:

The Image Where Stories Proliferate in Novels by Robbe-Grillet and Others

Although the lyric and the discrete image both represent an isolated moment, the image typically cuts the represented event from the temporal continuum even more completely than the lyric does, because the single-scene image generally offers less-precise information about a prior or subsequent event or situation than a lyric can and often does convey. Information about even a single prior or subsequent situation or event, as we saw in chapter 7, is often enough to establish the function of the represented moment. This temporally free-standing condition of the image that can leave the function of the represented moment open to interpretation, I suggest, is the reason that perceivers, including novelists, can so freely narrativize visually depicted scenes, whether by placing the scene in one or more unidirectional sequences or by placing it in a bi-directional sequence.

The polysemy—the many meanings—of the image is well recognized. Roland Barthes goes so far as to argue that a picture "exists only in the *account* given of it; or again: in the total and the organization of the various readings that can be made of it: a picture is never anything but its own plural description" ("Is Painting a Language?," 150). The plural descriptions that Barthes perceives that a painting evokes are comparable, I want to suggest, to the often contradictory descriptions given by witnesses to events in our world, for instance, to an automobile accident. In their multiplicity, plural accounts promote a healthy skepticism about any single account, including one's own, whether of what happened at the moment of the accident in our world or of what is happening at the moment the painting depicts.

The fact that the discrete image represents an isolated moment cut from the temporal continuum and that events in our world may often be perceived as an isolated moment cut from the temporal continuum is not the only reason for the polysemy of both, but it is the one I am emphasizing in this study of how we read narrative causalities. Because visual representations can be viewed repeatedly and at length, while events in our world can be seen only at the moment they occur, analyzing responses to visual representations can inform understanding of how we respond when something that happens attracts our attention. Whether in response to an isolated moment or to a visual representation of an isolated moment, a nonverbal perception is in both cases described in words, and in both cases is often narrativized. In the several fabulas that perceivers construct in response to the visually depicted or experienced scene, even interpretations of the function—the consequences and causes—of the isolated moment will often vary.

Developing Barthes's work on how images are interpreted (and work by Nelson Goodman, Michel Foucault, and others), the psychoanalyst Donald P. Spence considers the similarity between an ekphrastic account of an artwork and the information that a patient on the analyst's couch provides. Spence draws attention "to the fact that visual data are among the primary data of an analysis; that in their natural state they are seen *only* by the patient; and that the large part of an analysis must make do with an approximate and largely makeshift verbal translation. Because the clinical phenomena are never seen by the analyst, he is unusually vulnerable to errors of translation" (*Narrative Truth and Historical Truth*, 56; Spence's emphasis).[1]

The visual data that the patient reports in words to the analyst represent scenes from the patient's life or the patient's dreams, rather than re-representing artworks that the patient has viewed. In this respect, the analyst who listens to the patient's account is in the same position as the investigator, of an accident for instance, who understands that witnesses typically disagree but who has access to only one witness's report. The information available to the analyst (and to the investigator) is comparable, however, as Spence perceives, to the information available to the reader of one—and only one—ekphrastic account of a visual artwork that cannot itself be seen. The analyst, the investigator, and the reader are equally vulnerable to the errors and emphases, first, of perception; second, of translation from one medium to another; and third, of the tendency to narrativize, which introduces one of often several possible interpretations of the function of the perceived scene.

■

When a depiction of an isolated moment, even a moment in our world, represents neither an action schema nor a specific sequence of events—for instance, in a painting of the death of a king, a drawing of a friend's child flying a kite, a photograph of the young John F. Kennedy, Jr., saluting his father's casket—viewers share the historian's power to choose whether to interpret the function of the depicted moment in relation to one, rather than another, sequence of events. The death of the king—or the depicted meeting between Lee and Jackson that inspires Mark Twain's narrativizing, discussed in chapter 7—may be interpreted as the final event, a transitional event, or the first event in a sequence—in other words, the perceiver may interpret the depicted moment in relation to three (or more) different sets of events.[2] In each of these sets of events the sequence is unidirectional. But interpretations of the function of the event will vary according to the set of events in which it is perceived.

In a fictional world, moreover, the sequence of a set of events need not be unidirectional. In Robbe-Grillet's *La Maison de Rendez-vous* (published in French in 1965), a young woman variously referred to as Lauren, Loraine, and Laureen (the letter *L* sounds like the French pronoun *elle,* which translates as "she") appears frequently—whether sitting on a couch, dancing, or acting in private plays—in scenes occurring in Lady Ava's Blue Villa in Hong Kong, which is (perhaps among other things) an expensive house of prostitution. A second character, Georges Marchat, is identified at one point as "Lauren's ex-fiancé who has been wandering around for a long time, constantly ruminating on his lost happiness and his despair" (213).[3] A passage that promises a description of "the scene of Lauren's breakup with her fiancé" (196) describes a man sitting alone and holding a pistol with his finger on the trigger:

> He is sitting alone on a white marble bench, under a clump
> of traveler's palms whose leaves shaped like broad leaves
> [sic] shaped like broad hands hang in a fan around him. He
> is leaning forward. He seems to be staring at his patent

leather shoes, a little darker against the background of pale sand. His hands are resting on the stone bevel on each side of his body. Coming closer, as I continue along the path, I notice that the young man is holding a pistol in his right hand, his forefinger already on the trigger, but the barrel aimed at the ground. (196; see also the description on 141–42)

Given this information, when we learn that Marchat (Marchant) is dead and has committed suicide, most readers, I think, analyze the anecdote according to these functions:

A   Lauren enters the Blue Villa as a prostitute and breaks her engagement to Marchat (for Marchat, an event that disrupts the equilibrium)
C   In despair, Marchat decides to commit suicide (Marchat is the C-actant)
C' Marchat locates or acquires a pistol
H   Marchat commits suicide

According to another passage in the novel, however, the sequence in which these events occur is reversed, and the explanation that the novel offers of why the events occur is altered accordingly:

I was going to say that on that evening, Johnson, who had happened to be the immediate witness of Georges Marchant's tragic end, found dead in his car in Kowloon, not far from the dock where the American arrived a few minutes later to take the ferry to Victoria, that Johnson, then, had upon his arrival at the Blue Villa described the suicide of the businessman, whose action he attributed, along with everyone else, to an excess of commercial scruple, in a deal in which his partners had shown much less integrity. It seems, unfortunately, that his account—as lurid as fertile in emotions—has dramatically affected a young blond girl named Laureen, a friend of the mistress of the house and even, some say, her protégée, who came here precisely to marry this unfortunate young man. From that day on, Laureen changed her life and even her character altogether; formerly docile, studious, and reserved, she flung herself, with a kind of desperate passion, in pursuit of the worst depravities, the most degrading excesses. This is how she became an inmate of the deluxe brothel whose madam is none other than Lady Ava. (244–45)

Given this sequence of events and the attendant interpretation, most readers, I think, analyze the anecdote as follows:

A   Marchat commits suicide (for Lauren an event that disrupts the equilibrium)
B   Johnson tells the group in the Blue Villa, including Lauren, about Marchat's suicide
C   In her bereavement, Lauren decides to enter the Blue Villa as a prostitute (Lauren is the C-actant)
C' Lauren enters the Blue Villa as a prostitute
H   Lauren pursues "the worst depravities"

The two anecdotes have in common two events—Lauren's entering the Blue Villa as a prostitute and Marchat's suicide. In the version we considered first, Lauren's becoming a prostitute precedes and causes Marchat's suicide. In the other version Marchat's suicide precedes and causes Lauren's becoming a prostitute. The shift in sequence brings with it a shift in which event is the cause and which the effect, and a resultant shift in the function we assign to each of the two events. If Lauren's becoming a prostitute is the first event, we interpret it as a function-A event that causes Marchat's suicide. If Marchat's suicide is the first event, we interpret it as a function-A event that causes Lauren to become a prostitute.

But now let us look at one further passage from the novel: a scene in which Lady Ava shows a photograph of Laureen in "the album of girls available" to Sir Ralph: "the photograph in which her latest acquisition appears in the traditional black corset and openwork stockings, with nothing else below or above" (245). In both of the two anecdotes we have analyzed, this photograph depicts the situation that exists between the initial event and the event that it causes. According to one anecdote, first Lauren enters the Blue Villa; then the photograph of Lauren dressed as a prostitute appears in Lady Ava's album; and then Marchat commits suicide. According to the other anecdote, first Marchat commits suicide; then the photograph of Lauren dressed as a prostitute appears in Lady Ava's album; and then Lauren pursues "depravities."

I suggest that through ekphrasis the photograph is narrativized as a *hinge situation* in the two anecdotes we have analyzed. In other words, the isolated moment that the photograph represents provides a crossroads through which a path passes that includes Marchat's suicide and Lauren's becoming a prostitute. That represented moment folds back on itself, like a hinge, creating a bidirectional temporal sequence in which the causal relations among events and the function of events depend on the sequence in which the events are read.

At a colloquium held at Washington University in St. Louis in 1992,[4] Robbe-Grillet mentioned Lewis Carroll as a writer he admired, and he spoke of Carroll's novels, particularly *Through the Looking-Glass,* as an influence on his own work. In that novel, the mirror in Alice's house in which she can see "Looking-Glass House" is a hinge that reverses not only the image it reflects but the sequence in which events occur in the reflection. In Alice's words, "First, there's the room you can see through the glass—that's just the same as our drawing-room, only the things go the other way" (127). And things really do go the other way in the world Alice enters through the mirror. In chapter V, for example, the White Queen begins to scream that her finger is bleeding and in response to Alice's question about whether she has pricked it, "'I haven't pricked it *yet*,' the Queen said, 'but I soon shall'" (177). In Carroll's novel, however, there is only one hinge. Things go one way in Alice's house and the other way in Looking-Glass House.

In Robbe-Grillet's *La Maison de Rendez-vous,* in addition to the photograph of Laureen, which I read as a hinge situation in a reversible sequence, there are other frozen scenes described throughout the novel, which alternate with action in the narrative world. Characters seen in photographs or as statues regularly begin to talk and move, while characters interacting in the narrative world or enacting a play on stage periodically stop talking and are represented as immobile and then later once again begin to move. This alternation in the novel between frozen scenes and action is a well-recognized phenomenon.[5] I suggest that whenever the ongoing action in this novel freezes, the fixed scene offers itself for interpretation as a hinge event or situation; when the action resumes, the scene may be followed by the very events that in another part of the novel preceded it. Hinge events and situations, in this fashion, permit a relatively small number of events to combine and recombine to create many different fragmentary fabulas, or "anecdotes" as Robbe-Grillet calls them, which proliferate throughout the novel.

Studies of Robbe-Grillet's work have drawn attention for some time both to the use of ekphrasis even in the early novels (for instance, in *In the Labyrinth,* published in French in 1959) and to reversible sequences. Of the latter Brian McHale discerns: "One can also 'bend' a sequence back upon itself to form a *loop,* in which one and the same event figures as both antecedent and sequel of some other event. The presence of the same event at two different points in the sequence leaves the reader hesitating between two alternative reconstructions of the 'true' sequence, in one of which event A precedes event B, while in the other event A follows event B" (*Postmodernist Fiction,* 108). Taking as an example the murder of Edouard Manneret in *La Maison de Rendez-vous,* McHale writes:

> Johnson hears of Manneret's murder from the police (and must have known about it already, since he merely 'feigns astonishment' at the news), yet pays a call on him later that same night; so Manneret dies both before and after Johnson's visit. Similarly, Kim discovers Manneret's corpse, then later (having in the meantime remembered, anomalously, that she herself is the one who has killed him!) enters a room where Manneret is waiting for her. (*Postmodernist Fiction,* 109)

Ursula K. Heise cites a passage from Robbe-Grillet's *Topology of a Phantom City* (published in French in 1976) in which she discerns a similar bidirectional sequence or loop. In her words, in that novel the character

> David not only existed long before the invasion of Vanadium, but is in fact parent to all the Amazons that are killed in the battle, whereas the story of the invasion itself suggests that he is an offspring conceived during this battle. Without David, there could be no Amazons; but without the Amazons, David could not have been born: the two versions, reproduction through self-generation and reproduction through violence, entangle the narration in an irresolvable logical and temporal circle. (*Chronoschisms,* 130)

I am drawing a connection between the narrativizing through ekphrasis of a fixed image, even in Robbe-Grillet's early novels, and the bidirectional sequences or loops in *La Maison de Rendez-vous* and later novels. In *La Maison de Rendez-vous*, the hinge situation or event in bidirectional sequences is described often enough as a visual artwork that we can read both sequences as ekphrastic accounts of the same image. In later novels by Robbe-Grillet and in novels by other writers, the hinge event or situation at which a bi-directional sequence folds is sometimes described as a visual representation and sometimes represented as a scene in the narrative world.

Whether it is the result of interpretations of an image or interpretations of an observed scene, a bidirectional sequence demonstrates that the function of an event depends on its position in a sequence. When a sequence folds at a hinge event or situation, the reversal of sequence alters causal relations. As a result, as we have seen, events that express one function in one sequence express another function in another sequence. Whatever the intent of Robbe-Grillet and other writers whose novels offer multiple and contradictory sequences in which a given event or situation recurs, these novels illustrate how subject the isolated moment is, when cut from a continuum of prior or subsequent events, to plural readings of its function and of the configuration of events in relation to which to interpret it. My argument is that an isolated moment is subject to plural readings of its function whether it is perceived in a fictional world or our world or as a visual representation of a fictional world or our world. But visual representations that isolate the moment offer an ideal site to demonstrate the phenomenon.

■

Novelists have found several ways to indicate that the single account of a visual representation is epistemologically suspect. In *La Maison de Rendez-vous* Robbe-Grillet uses ekphrasis to narrativize a given artwork more than once, producing contradictory and sometimes bidirectional sequences in which the artwork serves as hinge. Tamar Yacobi has analyzed another way in which ekphrasis in novels can offer plural and often contradictory accounts. Focusing on works by Isak Dinesen, Yacobi demonstrates that ekphrasis can complicate the message that a narrative communicates because the re-representation of a visual artwork may come "not only in the narrator's own name but through the perspective of fictional observers, dramatized and less than reliable . . . We must then distinguish between two typically narrative and often incompatible viewpoints on the relevant [artwork]:

from within the fictive world and, simultaneously and more intricately, from without, where the storyteller communicates with the reader alone" ("Pictorial Models and Narrative Ekphrasis," 635).

Yet another way that novelists draw attention to the polysemy of the image is by including in their novels visual representations that complement, diverge from, or contradict the message that the verbal text conveys. In Dinesen's novels that Yacobi analyzes, as in Robbe-Grillet's novels that we have looked at thus far, there are no visually represented artworks: readers have access only to the words that through ekphrasis re-represent artworks. For readers, novels that include visually represented paintings or photographs have a different effect on the process of interpreting functions and constructing fabulas than novels that include artworks through ekphrasis do.

In the traditional hybrid forms that combine word and image—illustrations that accompany texts, captions placed under photographs—studies indicate that in most cases the words guide interpretations of the image and thus reduce the polysemy of the image.[6] For instance, A. Kibédi Varga recognizes (as Mark Twain did) that "in the image-title relation, the word explains the image; it restricts its possibilities and fixes its meaning" ("Criteria," 42). In modern art, nonetheless, Kibédi Varga discerns, some "painters have made attempts to free painting from verbal dominance by altering the relation between the title and its visual reference." Of the two methods of freeing painting that he distinguishes, one is to use only uninteresting or generic titles ("landscape," "composition"); the other is the "'poetic' titles that surrealists such as Magritte or Max Ernst gave to their paintings and collages [which] can be seen from our perspective as attempts to establish coordination. The words, far from restricting the meaning of the image, in fact add something to it" ("Criteria," 42–43).

René Magritte is particularly well known for giving his paintings titles that preclude the subordination of image to text that can occur when an image represents what its title says it represents. In his most famous work, which he painted a number of times with minor variations, he includes a text in the painting itself; the painting depicts a very realistically painted pipe above the handwritten words "Ceci n'est pas une pipe" ("This is not a pipe"). The juxtaposition of the two messages forces viewers to ponder the relation between them, discouraging interpretations that would subordinate one to the other, whether by seeing the image as an illustration of the text or the text as a caption explaining the image.

Another painting by Magritte, one that depicts a room in a building that is entirely filled by a single rose blossom, is titled *The Tomb of the Wrestlers*. *The Exception* depicts a cylindrical object that begins on one end as the head of a fish and ends at the other as the ash at the lit end of a cigar. A painting that depicts a neatly coiffed and formally dressed young woman who is eating a bird with its feathers still on it, its blood dripping on her lace collar and cuffs, is called *Pleasure*. There are four paintings by Magritte titled *The Beautiful Captive* (*La Belle Captive*). All four portray a landscape or seascape that includes a painting on an easel; the easel painting in each case depicts—in exactly the same proportions as the rest of the painting—what the rest of the painting leads one to assume one would see if the painting on the easel (and sometimes a curtain behind it) were removed. Because the title does not specify who or what has been captured, but does specify (in French) that she or it is feminine, the title can be read as denoting either "the beautiful captive woman" or, since the word for painting in French is feminine ("la peinture"), as "the beautiful captive painting."

Kibédi Varga suggests that Magritte and Max Ernst may have chosen nonmimetic titles in order to free their paintings from subordination to the words and thereby to increase—rather than to restrict with a title that names what the image represents—the polysemy of the image. During the 1970s Robbe-Grillet published hybrid works which include texts that he wrote along with paintings, photographs, or etchings by artists including Magritte, Jasper Johns, David Hamilton, Paul Delvaux, and Robert Rauschenberg. The most readily available of these hybrid works in English is *La Belle Captive: a novel*, translated by the Robbe-Grillet scholar Ben Stoltzfus.[7] The novel contains reproductions of seventy-seven paintings by Magritte, chosen and ordered by Robbe-Grillet, along with a text written by Robbe-Grillet. In the novel as in Magritte's paintings titled *La Belle Captive*, the title can refer to a beautiful captive female (several are depicted in the paintings and described in the text) and to a beautiful captive painting (in Robbe-Grillet's novel, Magritte's paintings held captive).

In this novel and in all his pictonovels and photonovels, Robbe-Grillet replicates in his text some details of the visual artworks, but contradicts other details of the artworks and introduces objects and events that the artworks do not include. His purpose, he says, is the same purpose that Kibédi Varga suggests is

Magritte's and Max Ernst's: to avoid the subordination of image to text that the term "illustrated text" conveys. Robbe-Grillet writes:

> [T]he existence of images in the text is problematical. And it is as far as there are problematical images appearing in the text that the text is interesting with regard to images. When . . . I placed a text next to images that existed already as, for example, with the photographs of Hamilton or the paintings of Magritte, I was interested, to be precise, in presenting as a problem those elements that appear in images. So that when we look at these works, and compare the texts and the images that are next to one another, we realize that there are indeed effects of resemblance but that there are above all effects of distance. As a result, the work in its totality, the work that contains both an image and the text is going to be not an illustrated text, but an ensemble of contradictions in which the text and the images are going to play antagonistic roles. ("Images and Texts," 39)

Important hybrid novels that have been published more recently than Robbe-Grillet's pictonovels and photonovels include Mario Vargas Llosa's *In Praise of the Stepmother* (published in Spanish in 1988 and in English translation in 1990) and W. G. Sebald's *Austerlitz* (2001). Vargas Llosa's *In Praise of the Stepmother* includes color reproductions of six oil paintings that hang in museums in our world by artists including Fra Angelico, Titian, François Boucher, and Francis Bacon. These paintings exist in the narrative world as well as in our world; reproductions are included in Don Rigoberto's collection of erotic art, and the characters discuss the paintings. Six chapters (chapters 2, 5, 7, 9, 12, and 14) offer first-person ekphrastic accounts that narrativize these paintings. Although these accounts of what is happening in the paintings are nominally told by a character depicted in the painting, these stories are in most cases introduced in the preceding chapter as the sexual fantasies either of Don Rigoberto or of his second wife, who learns to share his pleasure in his collection. The other eight chapters and an epilogue, which are told by an unidentified narrator, report interactions in the narrative world between Don Rigoberto and his wife, many of which are inspired by the paintings—and describe the inception, development, and finally the disclosure of intimacy between the new wife and her schoolboy stepson.

For the plot that the boy admits in the Epilogue to having devised and carried out—to rid himself of an unwanted stepmother by seducing her, and then making sure his father finds out—readers cannot be certain whether he was inspired by a painting or did not need a painting for inspiration. The painting that most closely resembles the boy's actions—a Bronzino that depicts a very young Cupid kissing Venus and fondling her breast—appears on the cover but not inside the novel. Thus the painting is in our world for readers to see, but, since none of the characters mention it, we cannot know whether it is also in the narrative world and included in Don Rigoberto's collection, where the boy could see it. As a result, readers can create two contradictory fabulas. In both, the boy is unhappy about the introduction of a stepmother (for the boy, function A). If the Bronzino is in his father's collection and he has seen it, it serves as the function-F empowerment that allows the boy to achieve his purpose.

A   father remarries, boy has stepmother
C   boy decides to remove stepmother from the house
C' in public, boy is careful to behave appropriately, while waiting to devise a plan
F   boy is inspired by the Bronzino
H_1 boy seduces stepmother
H_2 boy makes sure father finds out
I   boy succeeds in getting his stepmother out of the house

In the other interpretation (the Bronzino does not exist in the narrative world), the boy is sexually precocious—a trait perhaps inherited from his father—and does not need the Bronzino or anything else as empowerment.

A   father remarries, boy has stepmother
C   boy decides to remove stepmother from the house
C' boy devises plan, is careful to behave appropriately in public
H_1 boy seduces stepmother
H_2 boy makes sure father finds out
I   boy succeeds in getting his stepmother out of the house

The difference between the two interpretations is not insignificant because it affects what we think of the boy and how we judge the father. If the boy has seen the painting and is blithely replicating the actions of the sweet-looking little Cupid it depicts, we are much more apt to think of the boy as a mischievous but innocent child than if we assume that he has been capable of developing his plan entirely on his own. For his father too, if his comfortable second marriage falls apart because he has not kept his collection of erotica out of the hands of his young son, some readers may want to think that he deserves his punishment. But if his son has destroyed his father's marriage through a plot that is entirely his own idea, some readers will have visions of the monstrous child who is a feature of a number of myths and horror films, and whom no parent deserves.

Sebald's *Austerlitz* includes scores of black-and-white photographs, which are unidentified and without captions. Often a photograph is placed in the text shortly after a description of a place or a character or an object that the photograph resembles. A report of the narrator's having observed a raccoon, for instance, is followed by a photograph of the face of a raccoon. A description of a specific tower in the Rhine River is followed by a photograph of a cylindrical structure in a large river. A description of a photograph of "the girl sitting in a chair in the garden with her little dog in her lap" (52) is followed by a photograph (53) of a girl in a chair with a dog on her lap and a doll, or several dolls, propped up at her feet. Probably readers cannot proceed from the account in the text to the photograph that follows it without the description's influencing what they see in the photograph and the photograph's affecting the image they have already begun to construct in response to the description. Most readers, in fact, in the process of constructing the narrative world as they move through the novel, probably rely equally on the photographs and the text.[8]

But readers looking at the photographs will not all see even the same objects, and for two reasons. First, the photographs appear to be old and faded, and the process by which they are physically reproduced on the page leaves many of the details indistinct, at least in part because the photographs are reproduced on paper that absorbs ink, rather than photographic paper. Second, because one's individual interests guide which aspects of a visual representation attract and hold one's attention, readers looking at the photographs pay attention to various different elements. When looking at the photograph of the little girl with a dog in her lap, for instance, some readers will be curious about the doll or dolls and wonder whether the girl positioned the doll(s) at her feet before guiding the dog to her lap or whether someone else, perhaps the photographer, has arranged the position of the doll(s) and perhaps also of the dog and the girl. Other readers will examine the stone façade of the house in the background, perhaps attempting to identify when it might have been built. Still other readers may be curious about the season, considering the apparently lush grass and the bush in bloom to the girl's right, while the larger bush behind her and to her left seems to consist entirely of branches, with no sign of leaves. Although the questions that I raise about the photograph of the girl may seem less crucial to interpreting the novel than the question about whether the boy's actions in *In Praise of the Stepmother* were inspired by the Bronzino painting, *Austerlitz* includes scores of photographs, in response to each of which similar questions can be raised.

Both Robbe-Grillet's *La Belle Captive: a novel* (in the original French edition, in which many of Magritte's paintings are reproduced in color) and Vargas Llosa's *In Praise of the Stepmother* include detailed, clear reproductions of the paintings along with a text that offers one narrativized account of the depicted scenes—an account that in Robbe-Grillet's novel always contradicts the depicted scene in one or more details and that in Vargas Llosa's novel is to such a degree a personalized interpretation by one of the characters that most readers will recognize that other accounts of what is happening in the depicted scene are equally plausible. In both novels, in effect, the presence of an attractively reproduced painting along with a narrativized account of it encourages readers to reinterpret the paintings themselves. Sebald's novel, I think, works more subtly and even insidiously, first to allow readers to see in the faded photographs whatever elements they choose and then to incorporate whatever they have seen in the photographs into the narrative world they are constructing as they read. I say insidiously because, in response to Robbe-Grillet's and Vargas Llosa's hybrid novels, readers can probably, if they choose, distinguish between a reading of the words only and a reading of the words in relation to the paintings. With Sebald's novel, in contrast, because the design of the pages places the photographs so close to the words that name something depicted, and because the words do not contradict but also do not specify the rest of what the photograph depicts, readers cannot escape incorporating whatever details they see in each of the photographs in the narrative world they are constructing.

The polysemy of the visually represented isolated moment provides a theoretical explanation for the widespread fascination with visual representation in Western cultural productions, including novels, since about the middle of the twentieth century, and for the practice of novelists who introduce images into their novels, either through ekphrasis or, in hybrid novels, by juxtaposing paintings or photographs with verbal texts, whether the words precede, follow, surround, or are superimposed upon the painting or photograph. Novels like Robbe-Grillet's *La Maison de Rendez-vous* demonstrate through ekphrasis that a visual artwork can inspire several fragmentary narratives which contradict each other and in which the function of the visually represented scene may vary from one to another. Hybrid novels that include visual artworks multiply the possible interpretations of the verbal account in several ways. First, the visual representation offers, in addition to the narrator's, a second and often contradictory perspective (that of the painter or photographer). Second, the visual representation introduces an event or situation—whatever event or situation the reader-viewer interprets it as depicting, an interpretation that may vary from perceiver to perceiver. Third, as interpreted, the depicted event or situation may reinforce or complement or contradict the set of events that the verbal account reports. In short, while ekphrasis offers examples of interpreting and reinterpreting artworks, hybrid novels offer readers the experience of interpreting and reinterpreting the artworks, and in the context of a verbal text that problematizes their interpretations. Both the images and the ekphrastic accounts of images open the novels that contain them to plural accounts of what the images depict and to contradictory interpretations of the function of depicted events.

■

David Herman describes what he terms an "ethics of representation." Referring to fiction in which characters and events "*prima facie* seem distinct, but that then turn out to be analogues of one another, morphed, integrated, retransformed," he concludes that these fictions "suggest that human beings should try to represent a thing not by isolating and defining it once and for all, but rather by contextualizing it through any number of possible analogues, by establishing precedents for future paraphrases, additional versions, of what they are trying to represent" ("Lateral Reflexivity," 298). Similarly, the novels we have considered in this chapter, by offering several interpretations of visual representations or by presenting contradictory information in two media, suggest that a

single account of a visually represented isolated moment is epistemologically suspect.

Moreover, as I have argued throughout this chapter, an interpretation of a visually represented isolated moment is not unlike
an interpretation of a visually perceived isolated moment. Fiction
that demonstrates the polysemy of the image encourages readers
to recognize the many possible interpretations not only of the
visually represented isolated moment, but also, by extension, of
the isolated moment that attracts our attention in the world. By
offering plural accounts, the novels we have considered in this
chapter, like the fiction Herman analyzes, make the experience of
reading (viewing) similar to the experience of perceiving and interpreting events in our world. Plural accounts in fiction teach readers that if we rely on the single interpretation—whether the interpretation is reported to us or is our own response to an observed
scene—we put ourselves in a position not unlike that of the investigator who has access to only one of several accounts of an accident or the psychoanalyst who hears only the patient's verbal
account of his or her visual memories.

In chapter 7 we noted the many fragmentary fabulas that Mark
Twain offered in response to the painting of Jackson's interview
with Lee. In this chapter we traced the numerous fragmentary fabulas—some of them even reversible at hinge moments—in Robbe-
Grillet's *La Maison de Rendez-vous.* What both Twain's statements and Robbe-Grillet's and similar novels suggest is that one
technique fiction writers use is to respond to an observed isolated
moment (in our world, imagined, or visually represented) by placing it in first one and then another position in one or another configuration of events, to consider possible interpretations of its
function.[9] Of course Mark Twain in his novels, like the majority
of novelists even today, selected one interpretation of the function
of the observed event and represented the event accordingly in one
position in one configuration. A novel like *La Maison de Rendez-
vous,* on the other hand, illustrates how we in our own lives—just
like Twain and Robbe-Grillet—construct first one story and then
another, placing observed events in first one and then another
position in one or another configuration, in an attempt to interpret the function of events in our world.

We began with the idea that interpretations of the function of a
given event, like interpretations of the color of a given pigment in
Josef Albers's experiments, depend on the context—the other
events, the other pigments—in which it is viewed. Throughout this

book we have looked at examples in literature that demonstrate that the configuration in which an event is perceived and its temporal position in that configuration determine interpretations of its function. In chapters 7 and 8 we have looked at responses to the visually depicted isolated moment cut from the temporal continuum: the plural interpretations of its function that it evokes and the proliferating stories viewers construct to interpret it.

Information about events comes to us either as a report from someone else or through our own observation. When we observe an event ourselves, as I think the novels we have looked at in this chapter indicate, we interpret its function—its causes and consequences—in relation to other events that we supply from our individual store of knowledge. Once we recognize the polysemy of the isolated moment, we need to consider—as the foundation for a complement to the ethics of representation that Herman perceives—an ethics of observing. As we have seen in chapters 7 and 8, we can place an isolated moment in first one sequence and then another, sometimes even considering the moment as a hinge in a reversible sequence. We may entertain simultaneously two or more interpretations of the function of an event we observe.

A narrative places a given event in a specific chronological position in relation to a configuration of other events, and relates these events sequentially. As we have seen throughout this book, the configuration of events in which a given event is perceived affects readers' and listeners' interpretations of its function, and the sequence in which events are told affects interpretations of the given event's function by determining which events are included in the configuration at each stage as the narrative unfolds. Any single account—any narrative—reports the events in one, rather than another, sequence and places the event in a configuration that is finite. In other words, any narrative influences readers' (listeners', viewers') interpretations of the function of reported events.

Modes of sequential representation on the narrative borderlands—plural ekphrastic accounts of visual representations, hybrid novels that juxtapose a text to images it contradicts, the fictions Herman analyzes and others that are not narratives because they offer multiple and contradictory accounts—reflect the experience of perceivers who recognize, and offer their readers the experience of recognizing, the polysemy of the isolated event. An ethics of representation that values plural accounts has as its foundation an ethics of observing and experiencing. What is at stake is recognizing that any interpretation of the consequences and causes—the function—of an isolated moment is at best one among other possible interpretations and that any narrative, because it offers one rather than another configuration of events and reports these events in one rather than another sequence, is guiding readers' (listeners', viewers') interpretations of the causes and consequences— the function—of reported events.

GLOSSARY

This glossary is designed to complement, and to collect in one place, information that is distributed throughout these chapters. Included in this list are two categories of terms: (1) those specific to function analysis, for which I supply definitions that summarize or repeat those provided in the chapters in which the terms are introduced; and (2) familiar terms in narrative studies that will be found in this volume. For the latter, for many of which several definitions exist, the definitions I give reflect my usage, and in some cases differ from other theorists' usage. For standard definitions, and for information about the many important terms that narrative theory offers that are not included here, a succinct and always reliable source is *A Dictionary of Narratology* by Gerald Prince.

A-experiencer. The character or characters who are affected by a function-A or function-a event.

bracketed function. An interpretation of an event that the interpreter infers as having occurred but that is not scenically represented, whether the event is revealed only by its consequences (e.g., a function-C decision, revealed by action that it motivates), or the event precedes or follows (in the chronology of fabula) the duration dramatized in the representation (from the initial scene to the concluding scene).

C-actant. A character, or group of characters, who decides to act to try to alleviate a function-A (or function-a) situation. For the duration of any one sequence, the role of the C-actant is filled by a single character (or a single group of characters acting together). In narratives containing more than one sequence, the role of the C-actant in one sequence may be filled by a different character from the one playing the C-actant role in a second sequence.

character narrator. A narrator who is an inhabitant of the same narrative world as the characters whose activities she or he recounts.

donor functions. See **functions D, E, F.**

ekphrasis. The re-representation in words of a visual representation.

empty function. An interpretation of an unspecified event. An empty function interprets an event in the narrative world that is suppressed in the representation except for its consequences—e.g., *they lived happily ever after.* At the end of a film, a fadeout accompanied by triumphal music, a scenic view in pleasant weather (sunlight on a body of water, snow-covered mountains, a sunset), or the image of a scene previously identified as "home," similarly conveys an interpretation without specifying the events interpreted. An empty function stands in contrast to an **uninterpreted event.**

EQ. The equilibrium that is disrupted by a function-A (or function-a) event, or reestablished—whether by a C-actant's action or some other means (e.g., there is nothing further that can be done that will alleviate the function-A situation; the function-A situation disappears with the passage of time). An **achieved equilibrium** is the consequence of a function-I event and is finite in duration (it begins when the function-I event occurs). See **situation.**

fabula. A chronologically ordered abstraction of the events, and the identity of the agents that perform them, that a **representation** either explicitly represents as having occurred, or provides information that permits a given reader (listener, viewer) to deduce as having occurred. A fabula is a concept, without material form and not manifest in any medium. As I use the term, a fabula is made by a perceiver (reader, listener, viewer). A fabula is made from information found in a representation—or, by extension (in my usage), from information perceived in our world. See **representation.**

focalizer. A character whose perceptions and conceptions readers (listeners, viewers) of narratives are given. The older term *perspective* does not distinguish between, on the one hand, whose sensory perceptions and thoughts (often in response to those perceptions) are reported (the focalizer), and, on the other hand, whose words report that information (the voice). The distinction was introduced by Gérard Genette (*Narrative Discourse,* primarily chapters 4 and 5). See **voice.**

function. A position (site, stage) in a causal sequence. Functions represent events that change a prevailing situation and initiate a new situation. See **situation.**

function A.   A destabilizing event.

function a.   A reevaluation of a situation that reveals an instability not previously perceived.

function-A (or function-a) situation.   A situation caused by a function-A (or function-a) event.

function B.   A call for help; specifically, a request that someone alleviate a situation that the requester interprets as a function-A (or function-a) situation.

function C.   A decision to act to try to alleviate a function-A (or function-a) situation. By performing function C, a character becomes a C-actant.

function C' (pronounced "C prime")   The initial action that a C-actant takes, after performing function C, to attempt to alleviate a function-A (or function-a) situation.

functions D, E, F (donor functions).   Events that provide experiences that, if successful, may allow a C-actant to develop or acquire empowerment (qualifications, attributes, information, possessions) necessary to accomplish a function-H endeavor. Function D represents a testing of the C-actant by a potential **donor;** function E represents the C-actant's behavior in response to the test; function F represents the C-actant's acquisition of some form of power that will help her or him carry out the function-H event successfully. Although logically function D leads to function E, which leads to function F, it is not unusual in narratives to find only one or two of these three functions expressed.

function G.   The arrival of the C-actant at the place or time (or both) where function H will take place.

function H.   The C-actant's primary action to alleviate a function-A (or function-a) situation.

function I (or function I_{neg}).   The success (or failure) of a function-H action.

functional polyvalence.   The principle that explains that the function of an event—its causes and consequences—changes according to the configuration of events in which it is perceived and the chronological position of the event in that configuration. Because events are functionally polyvalent, an event can—and often does—express one function in one narrative and another function in another narrative. Moreover, interpreters may disagree about the function of an event, and may change their interpretation of the function of an event in response to new information.

hinge situation or event. A situation or event that folds back on itself, like a hinge, creating a bidirectional temporal sequence in which the causal relations among events and the function of events depends on the sequence in which the events are read.

interpretive site. One of the ten positions or stages I identify in a narrative sequence that begins at the onset of a problem and leads to its resolution.

narratee. The one (or more than one) whom the narrator addresses, overtly or otherwise, conceived as in the text and at the ontological level of the narrator (see Gerald Prince, "Introduction to the Study of the Narratee").

narrative. A sequential representation of a sequence of events. According to this definition, a narrative is a representation in any medium (words, film, ballet, sequential photographs) that shows (drama) or recounts (stories) fictional or nonfictional events.

narrative ambiguity. A structural pattern in which one representation reveals two mutually exclusive fabulas (see Shlomith Rimmon-Kenan, *The Concept of Ambiguity*).

narrative sequence. The movement from an equilibrium (EQ), through a period of imbalance (a function-A or function-a situation), to another equilibrium (EQ). In a complete narrative sequence, in response to a function-A or function-a situation, a C-actant decides to take action (function C) that begins (function C'), continues (function H), and concludes (function I or function I_{neg}).

narrative world. The represented world: the world where characters act and interact.

narrativize. To animate a fixed scene by creating a narrative that includes the scene.

negative function. A function that represents a specified event that does not occur.

primacy effect. Our tendency to accept as valid the information we are initially given, even when that information is contradicted later in the same message.

protagonist. The main character in a narrative—often the C-actant or, if there are several, one of the C-actants; sometimes an A-experiencer (also see Tamar Yacobi, "Hero or Heroine?").

representation. A manifestation of sequential events in any medium (in words, for example, or film or dance); comparable to "discourse" (in the paired trajectories *story/discourse* in Seymour Chatman's terminology) and to "sju et" (in *fabula/sju et,* the Russian Formalist terminology). As I use the term, a representation includes, in addition to the components of the medium, the shaping of the reported events (the sequence, duration, and frequency of the events in the manifestation and the focalization, which may conceal or reveal motivation, as well as other aspects of the narrative world). See **fabula.**

situation. Either (1) an ongoing equilibrium (a situation that one interprets as an equilibrium without considering whether it was caused by an event or, if so, by what event) or (2) the consequence of a function: for example, a function-A situation (a situation that is the consequence of a function-A event) or an achieved equilibrium. See **EQ.**

uninterpreted event. A specified event to which no function has been assigned. An uninterpreted event stands in contrast to an **empty function.**

voice. The source of the words in which a focalizer's perceptions and conceptions are reported in a narrative. See **focalizer.**

NOTES

Note to Preface

1. In addition to the many paintings he made of squares superimposed on squares, Albers described and published his findings in *Interaction of Color* in 1963. The original edition is in the form of a box containing some 150 color illustrations in several dozen folders, and an eighty-page book. Later editions include reproductions of only a few of the illustrations.

Notes to Chapter 1

1. According to Turner, "It is not possible for a human infant to fail to achieve the concept of a container, for example, or liquid, or pouring, or flowing, or a path, or movement along a path, or the product of these concepts: the small spatial story in which liquid is poured and flows along a path into a container" (*The Literary Mind*, 14).

2. For Meir Sternberg, the defining characteristic of narrativity is the interplay between the two temporal sequences: "actional and communicative, told and telling/reading . . . that generates the three universal narrative effects/interests/dynamics of prospection, retrospection, and recognition—suspense, curiosity, and surprise, for short" ("How Narrativity Makes a Difference," 117). Compare to Gerald Prince's perhaps more familiar definition of narrative as "the representation of at least two real or fictive events (or one situation and one event)" (*A Dictionary of Narratology*, rev. ed., 58). While Prince, in earlier work (e.g., in the first edition of his *A Dictionary of Narratology*, 58), defines *narrative* as a "recounting" of events (in other words, he requires that, in narratives, events must be reported by a narrator rather than enacted as in drama), in the 2003 revised edition he changes "recounting" to "representation." Thus Prince, like Sternberg (116), now defines enacted events, as well as reported events, as narratives—a position that facilitates comparisons between narrative (a sequential representation of sequential events) and life (a sequential perception of sequential events). Both theorists recognize that the medium of the recounting may include, in addition to oral and written language, sequential images, gestures, and sounds. In sum, the two theorists' definitions differ primarily in emphasis (see chap-

ter 7) and are in agreement on the core requirement: sequential events, sequentially represented.

3. "Une nouvelle coïncide souvent, mais non toujours avec une séquence: la nouvelle peut en contenir plusieurs, ou ne contenir qu'une partie de celle-ci" ("La Grammaire du récit," 101). My translation, here and elsewhere unless otherwise specified. See also Todorov's comments on this topic in his *Grammaire du Décaméron,* p. 20.

4. Although I have derived the ten functions in my model by considering which of Propp's thirty-one functions interpret events in the narratives from various periods that I read and teach, I draw attention to similarities between the functions I select and those in two of the three five-function logically ordered sequences A.-J. Greimas uncovered in his analysis of Propp's morphology (Greimas, "Searching for Models of Transformation," 228), as well as those in the three core sequences in Paul Larivaille's extension of Greimas's model (Larivaille, "L'Analyse (morpho)logique du récit," 376, 383). A sophisticated five-function model developed by William O. Hendricks from Propp's work (the idea that narratives trace syntagmatic patterns) and Greimas's (envisioning the forces of change synchronically in the semiotic square) is more abstract than earlier models and thus more versatile, but represents situations rather than the processes that change them ("'A Rose for Emily': A Syntagmatic Analysis," 262–64, 291). Of the models with which I am familiar, the one to which mine is closest in spirit is the concise five-category plot-grammar devised by Thomas Pavel (*The Poetics of Plot*), which convincingly depicts causal relations among represented events as interconnected trees. My model differs from all these in that it is designed to analyze, and to compare, the effects of sequence in (a) the sequence of perception of events in our world, (b) the sequence of a representation, and (c) the chronological sequence that we construct in response to a perceived or represented sequence.

5. I am grateful to James Phelan and David Herman, who helped me formulate the distinction between what a function is and how it is used.

6. Although Propp's purpose is generally understood to be to demonstrate the generic identity of a category of Russian fairy tale, Propp does not claim that the one hundred tales he analyzed are identical in form. He recognizes, as I do, that not every function is represented in every sequence, and that narratives differ according to which functions they represent and according to the number of sequences they contain and the combinatory pattern in which multiple sequences are arranged. The question is whether Propp's purpose—"a description of the tale according to its component parts and the relationship of these components to each other and to the whole" (*Morphology of the Folktale,* 19)—is to define a genre by revealing a pattern to which a set of narratives conform, or to reveal the differences that characterize an individual narrative.

Claude Bremond and Jean Verrier have claimed not only that Propp's project was the former but that he failed to accomplish it. After analyzing French translations of the eight stories for which Propp provides a formal representation, they conclude that four of the eight "cannot be reduced to the Proppian sequence without severe mutilations which destroy essential aspects of the plot" ("Afanasiev and Propp," 192–93), and report what they perceive as "Propp's blindness or indifference before the resistance his corpus offered to the analytical framework he attempted to impose on it" (193). Whatever Propp's purpose was, his recognition that a number of different events can express the same function, and that a function can represent a number of different events, is a major contribution to understanding how a narrative communicates.

7. Propp too, after specifying that "[t]he sequence of functions is always identical" in each of the set of fairy tales he studied, immediately explains "that by no means do all tales give evidence of all functions. But this in no way changes the law of sequence. The absence of certain functions does not change the order of the rest" (*Morphology of the Folktale*, 22). My theory explains the invariant sequence Propp perceived as a logical necessity: at each stage in a sequence that begins at the onset of a problem and leads to its resolution, only events with certain outcomes (e.g., events that fill a specific one or two functions) can move the situation closer to resolution.

William O. Hendricks, who analyzes (in "On the Notion 'Beyond the Sentence'") "the criteria by which it is determined where to draw the line separating work which may legitimately be considered an attempt to extend linguistic science from that which may not be so considered," proposes that "the drawing line between what constitutes a legitimate extension of linguistics beyond the sentence and that which does not be determined by this criterion: wherever a gap exists between the structural unit and the basic units (phonological, morphological, and syntactic) of the language, linguistics has not been extended, but on the contrary abandoned" (40, 43). For Hendricks, "Vladimir Propp's morphological analysis of Russian fairy tales . . . essentially straddles the border between what does, and what does not, constitute a legitimate extension of linguistics" (40).

On the one hand, in Hendricks's words, "each function refers to a class of actions rather than to one specific action"; the function "is a sort of equivalence class" (41). On the other hand, however, a function is "not so much a class of verbs as it is of 'actions,' i.e., the classes are established primarily on semantic grounds" (41). Furthermore, Hendricks notes that "at one point Propp equates verbs of sentences with the constant aspects of tales . . . but the labeling of the functions actually implies the 'doer' (grammatical subject) and the 'receiver' of the action (grammatical object). For instance, the function Victory actually refers to 'victory of the hero over the villain' . . . It would thus seem that the function corresponds to the sentence rather than to the sub-sentence unit" (42).

But Propp, Hendricks continues, "is concerned with 'actions,' not with sentences. That is, not only is the relation notional (one of chronology), but the entities so related are notional also (actions, rather than sentences)." And in folktales, "the relation between 'actions' . . . and individual sentences is not one-one. That is, a given action may in fact be signified by a series of sentences" (42).

In sum, for Hendricks, Propp does not "specify the exact relation between his structural unit, the function, and its linguistic manifestation (in terms of sentence constituency, etc.). Indeed, one of the variables of tales, according to Propp, is the choice of linguistic means to realize the tale" (43). As I use the term, a function is a semantic rather than a linguistic unit, and no one-to-one relation between a function and a linguistic unit (sentence, paragraph, etc.) is suggested. I am grateful to David Herman, who brought Hendricks' study to my attention.

8. A negative function represents a specified event that does not occur; function I_{neg} marks the recognition that a function-H endeavor will not reach a successful conclusion. Theoretically, a negative version of every function can be conceived. In practice, however, if a function-A or function-a event, for instance, does not occur, then the prevailing equilibrium (EQ) remains unbroken. With the exception of function I_{neg}, the non-occurrence of an event that, had it occurred, would have changed the prevailing situation can be omitted in a function analysis except in instances in which the perceiver considers it worth including. For examples of analyses that do include the non-occurrence of specified events, see chapters 2, 5, 6, and 7.

9. Compare *representation* and *fabula* to the terms *discourse* and *story* made familiar by Seymour Chatman (*Story and Discourse*). For my purposes *representation* is preferable to *discourse,* because it allows me to talk about representations in any medium without needing to explain that a film, for instance, or a ballet is in effect a discourse. By using the Formalist term *fabula* to denote the conceptual construct that readers (listeners, viewers) make from a representation, I reserve the word *story* to name examples of the short-story genre: the stories we read or hear or tell.

Among theorists writing about narrative, there is wide variation in the names chosen to denote the interrelated trajectories I call *representation* and *fabula,* and in the definitions provided. As I use the terms, *fabula* includes the reported events, chronologically ordered, and the identity (but no other characteristics) of the agents who perform them. I include as aspects of *representation* both the manifestation (in words, for example, or film) and the shaping of the material (through perspective, for instance, which may or may not reveal motivation, and including the sequence, duration, and frequency of events in the representation).

Some theorists see the shaping and the manifestation as separate categories (and in addition to the category of unshaped events I call *fabula*). Other theorists include the shaping as an aspect of what I call *fabula,* and reserve the category I call *representation* for issues pertaining to medium. For a comprehensive analysis of variations among narrative theorists in the terminology they choose, the definitions they provide, and the aspects of narratives and narrative theory they address in their work, see Shlomith Rimmon-Kenan's "A Comprehensive Theory of Narrative." Claude Bremond was the first to describe what I term *fabula* as medium-free ("Le Message narratif," 4).

10. In work that has helped me understand this distinction, Tzvetan

Todorov discerns two levels where what I call functional polyvalence may create ambiguity: (1) Within a fictional world, what he calls "propositional ambiguity" (*l'ambiguïté propositionnelle*) arises when two characters interpret a given event as an element in different sequences, or at different positions in a sequence. My example is a feud; one of his examples is a murder—which one character interprets as a punishment and another character interprets as a crime to be punished. (2) For readers of narratives, what he calls "sequential ambiguity" (*l'ambiguïté séquentielle*) arises in response to a narrative that is told first from one character's perspective and then shifts to another character's perspective (*Grammaire du Décaméron*, 64–68).

11. Marie-Laure Ryan explains that fictional texts each refer to a world of their own, and cannot be validated externally because other texts do not share their reference world. For nonfiction, in contrast, "[t]he reader evaluates the truth value of the text by comparing its assertions to another source of knowledge relating to the same reference world. This source of knowledge can range from sensory experience to information provided by other texts." Her argument, which she develops by extending her earlier work on possible worlds, is that "[w]hether accurate or inaccurate, texts of nonfiction stand in a competitive relation with other texts and other representations because to the reader they offer versions of the same reality [whereas] fictional texts do not share their reference world with other texts" ("Postmodernism and the Doctrine of Panfictionality," 166–67).

As successfully as in my judgment Ryan salvages the theoretical distinction between fiction and nonfiction, when the need arises to gauge whether a given narrative is nonfiction or fiction or exemplifies an intermediate position between, the criteria available to guide us are less precise than one could wish. The best to date that I have seen are those offered by Dorrit Cohn in *The Distinction of Fiction*, especially chapter 2. In chapter 6 I take up again the similarities and differences between fiction and nonfiction.

12. A picaresque novel is told from the perspective of the protagonist: the rogue. From the perspective of the townspeople, of course, the rogue's arrival and disruptive behavior is a function-A disruptive event. Thus the town responds by trying to catch the rogue (function C') and punish him, for instance, by putting him in prison (function H), thus succeeding (function I) in establishing a new equilibrium.

13. A new sequence is most commonly indicated by an event that is interpreted either as function A (or a), or as function C. The hermeneutic relationship between these two functions is complementary; an interpretation of an event as expressing either function will reinforce an interpretation of an event as expressing the other function. If we tentatively interpret something that happens as disruptive (as potentially a function A), then a character's decision (function C) to attempt to ameliorate the effects of the event we thought disruptive will tend to convince us that the event was in fact disruptive. Similarly, if we are made aware that a character has decided to attempt to ameliorate a given situation, we will ten-

tatively interpret the situation, or the event that caused it, as function a or function A. The hermeneutic relationship between function C and function A is developed in chapter 4.

Readers' decisions about where a sequence begins are influenced by characteristics of the reader (the reader's individual sensitivities and historical period; the reader's degree of involvement in the reported events, presuppositions, and degree of attentiveness to the details of the representation; and the reader's purpose: a local-level or a global-level analysis), and also by characteristics of the narrative being read: both the fabula (some reported events are more obviously destabilizing than others, although historical shifts in what is considered acceptable behavior also come into play), and the representation (the perspective from which a representation is told, the sequence of the telling, which elements are revealed and which withheld, where emphasis is placed, and how—and how directly—a C-actant's decision is indicated).

I am grateful to David Herman, who, in response to my earlier work on functions, suggested that I directly address the question of how, and according to what signposts, readers decide whether to interpret a local-level action as a sequence, or to reserve the sequence to represent global-level change.

14. In John Barth's novella "Dunyazadiad" (in *Chimera*), which is inspired by both the fabula and the shape of *The Arabian Nights,* the character known as the Genie has read *The Arabian Nights* and thus can tell Scheherazade the stories that she will tell the king. Recounting to Scheherazade her story for the third night, Barth's character the Genie "recited the opening frame of the Fisherman and the Genie, the simplicity of which he felt to be a strategic change of pace for the third night— especially since it would lead, on the fourth and fifth, to a series of tales-within-tales, a narrative complexity he described admiringly as 'Oriental'" (31). Famously, early stories in Arabic often present complex forms of embedding.

Barth's novella begins where the frame story of the ancient text ends, with the double marriage of Scheherazade to the king and of her sister Dunyazade to the king's brother, which marks for Scheherazade the successful conclusion (function I) of her long endeavor to amuse the king sufficiently with her storytelling to keep from being executed. Barth's novella reinterprets the wedding as initiating, for Dunyazade, the function-a situation (after her 1001 nights listening and watching in Scheherazade's bedroom, what bridal behavior is still available to Dunyazade?) that motivates his novella. A functionally polyvalent event (or events) often serves as the bridge between a familiar story and a Postmodern retelling.

15. Roy Jay Nelson defines causality in fiction as a hypothesis made by readers ("a readerly hypothesis about a relationship of derivativeness between two observed phenomena"), and in the larger context sees "causation as a subjective pattern, as a model of some practical utility in the specific situations of everyday life, but meaningless as a scientific or philosophical generality" (*Causality and Narrative in French Fiction,*

xxv, xxvii). In general agreement with Nelson's definitions, I have developed the idea of functions to be able to talk about and compare hypotheses about causality, both those made by readers of fiction (Nelson's focus) and those that everyone makes in trying to understand the world we inhabit.

In contrast to both Nelson's study and my own, the intellectual historian Stephen Kern's *A Cultural History of Causality: Science, Murder Novels, and Systems of Thought* offers a comparative analysis of "the nature of causal explanation across two ages—Victorian to modern" (26). Although Kern draws some of his examples from murder novels (in addition to philosophy, the history of science, and other disciplines), for him the novels serve as sources of information about the explanations for criminal behavior commonly provided at a given historical moment: genetic inheritance, childhood experience, education, psychological state, social pressure, etc. Where Kern uses novels to analyze society's shifting explanations of (generally) aberrant human behavior, I use novels and stories as representations of finite sets of specific events in order to analyze readers' (and characters' and narrators') interpretations of causes and effects among events perceived as related. I am grateful to Brian McHale for bringing to my attention Kern's study, which, in addition to its inherent interest, allows me to define my focus more precisely through the contrast with his.

16. Just as not every narrative (a sequential representation of sequential events) includes indications of causality, not every narrative is high in narrativity ("the degree . . . to which that narrative fulfills a receiver's desire" [Prince, *A Dictionary of Narratology,* 2nd ed., 65]). For Sternberg (see note 2 above), narrativity is an effect of the interplay between what I call the representation and the fabula, which generates prospection, retrospection, and recognition ("How Narrativity Makes a Difference," 117). While information about what is going to happen (prospection) or what has happened (retrospection and recognition), which allows us to construct a chronological fabula, does not necessarily thereby reveal causal relations, I argue that one of the ways that narratives most readily satisfy our desire is by explaining, or at least suggesting, why one event follows another.

Notes to Chapter 2

1. Hans Christian Andersen published "The Princess and the Pea" ("Prindsessen paa aerten") in 1835, in his first collection of stories. Although Andersen wrote original fairy tales as well as retellings of folk tales, he identifies "The Princess and the Pea" as one of the latter: a tale he "had heard as a child, either in the spinning room or during the harvesting of the hops" ("Notes," 1171). Jacob and Wilhelm Grimm collected, edited, and published seven editions of fairy tales from 1812 to 1857. "The Pea Test" ("Die Erbsenprobe") is included in the fifth edition, published in 1843. According to Jack Zipes, "The Pea Test" was

omitted from later editions because of its similarity to Andersen's story (2: 396).

2. In order to analyze the functional polyvalence of events, I need to be able to differentiate between the events (included in a fabula) and the varying interpretations of the events (as functions) that multiple perspectives bring. To do this, I define fabula in my work as including the reported events, chronologically ordered, and the identity of the agents. I include as aspects of the representation, in addition to information about events and agents, both the disclosure of information about motivations and (characters' and narrators') speculations about motivations, as well as all other aspects of the shaping of the material and its manifestation (in words, for instance, or film).

3. Unless the pea has been stolen. In comments on an earlier version of this chapter, Peter J. Rabinowitz points out that "the stability of the equilibrium at the end of the story depends crucially on how seriously you take the possibility that the pea has been stolen. For if it has, the prince will *not* always have access to it." In Rabinowitz's reading, the story is being told during the prince's lifetime; if the pea is stolen, the prince loses his access to it. In my reading, the reported events are being told long after they occurred; the possible (and recent) theft of the pea affects only the listeners, who would no longer be able to see it. Both readings seem to me valid and, by disagreeing, illustrate that gaps (in this case, about the relation between the time of the telling and the time of the reported events) are filled in differently by different readers. In both readings, equilibrium in the narrative world has been achieved. But in Rabinowitz's reading—unlike mine—a potential disruption has been foreseen. The effects of temporary and permanent gaps on function analysis will be considered in chapters 5 and 6.

4. Gérard Genette (*Narrative Discourse*) distinguishes three categories of relations between a sequential representation and the chronological fabula that perceivers construct from it. In addition to *order* (the sequence in which events are reported in relation to the chronological sequence of fabula), and *duration* (the relation between the percent of a report devoted to a given event, and the percent of time in a complete fabula that the event occurs), the third is *frequency* (the relation between the number of times an event is reported and the number of times the event occurs in the fabula). In Andersen's story, the importance accorded to the prince's real efforts to find a princess is de-emphasized by the reduction in the representation to a single summarized account (in the first paragraph) of the many occasions in the fabula in which the prince found princesses who were not real princesses.

Notes to Chapter 3

1. The distinction between *focalization* and *voice*, which was introduced by Gérard Genette (*Narrative Discourse*, primarily chapters 4 and 5), has been the subject of much commentary. As I use the terms, the *voice* is the source of the words we read (e.g., a narrator); the *focaliza-*

tion is the source of the perceptions and conceptions (e.g., the character whose perceptions and resultant conceptions the voice reports). According to the description of Genette's position by Gerald Prince, from whom I learned in a conversation many years ago how to use this distinction, focalization is "the perceptual or conceptual position in terms of which . . . the narrated situations and events are rendered" (*Dictionary*, 31). Genette's idea of subdividing *perspective* (the older term, perhaps more familiar to nonspecialists) into its components, voice and focalization, is particularly useful in two situations: (1) in narratives like "The Assignation," in which, as we shall see, the words (the voice) and the perceptions and conceptions (the focalization) are those of the same character (the narrator) but at different times in his life span; and (2) in narratives like many of Henry James's in which one character's perceptions and conceptions (focalization) are represented in the words of someone else—in James's case, a narrator who is not the focalizer. According to the definition of *fabula* and *representation* that I use, focalization is an element of the representation in any medium; voice is a component of the representation in media that incorporate language.

2. For the narrator and for first-time readers, Aphrodite's words to the stranger at this early point in the story are incomprehensible. After watching the ensuing events play out, both the narrator and (much more slowly) readers come to understand the message that Aphrodite, by speaking these words, communicates to the stranger. Moreover, perhaps much later, readers recognize that the stranger immediately understands the message that Aphrodite's words convey—and that he could not do so unless the two of them had had an earlier conversation in which the stranger proposed ("*thou* hast conquered," she says; my emphasis) that a joint suicide was the only way they would be able to be together. Apparently Aphrodite demurred, perhaps suggesting that they wait to see if some other solution became available; she is telling him now that she will do what he has asked. Only if a conversation on this topic has occurred can the stranger understand from Aphrodite's words that she is going to poison herself the next morning. For readers, the stranger's understanding of Aphrodite's message is an important part of the evidence that the relationship between the stranger and Aphrodite precedes the scene in which the stranger saves the child.

3. Both focalization and voice are retrospective in the opening paragraph, but split in the second paragraph: the source of the words remains at the later time of retrospection; the focalization shifts (through a very heightened form of memory) from the narrator's "confused recollection" (Poe, 193) to his perceptions and conceptions at the time of the events. Because the initial indications of retrospection are so clearly established, however, and the split so subtly crafted, few readers will be aware of it, the first time they read the story, until the final paragraph.

I am indebted to James Phelan, who accepted an early version of this analysis of "The Assignation" (which was also my first presentation outside the classroom of function analysis) for a session sponsored by the Society for the Study of Narrative Literature at the 1991 MLA

Convention, both for his interest in the theory I was developing and for guiding my understanding of the "paradox in the retrospective nature of the telling. The knowledge that the narrator achieves at the end of the time of the action, which is of course before the time of the narration, doesn't inform that narration" (letter dated April 5, 1991).

4. In every classroom and conference session in which I have participated in a discussion of "The Assignation," someone has suggested that Aphrodite intentionally drops the baby in the water to test the stranger. As I understand the story, this is a possible but not a necessary reading. My own preference is to consider the means by which the baby "slip[s] from the arms of its own mother" (194) as being equally unimportant as the baby apparently is to everyone in the story, except perhaps the narrator. Whether Aphrodite drops the baby intentionally or unintentionally, her gaze that is "riveted" on the "gloomy niches" of the building that "yawns right opposite her chamber window" (195) indicates that she assumes (or knows, or hopes) that the stranger is there, and that she expects him to try to save the baby. In other words, as I read the story, by staring at the stranger's hiding place Aphrodite is testing him (function D), whether she has dropped the baby intentionally or not. A second question that often arises is whether the father of the child is Aphrodite's husband, the Marchese Mentoni, or the stranger. On this issue, the story seems to me ambiguous.

5. The *narratee* is the one whom the narrator addresses, overtly (as here) or otherwise, conceived as in the text and at the ontological level of the narrator. The term was introduced by Gerald Prince ("Introduction to the Study of the Narratee").

6. In a dramatic monologue, the restriction of voice and focalization to one character requires readers to "adopt [the speaker's] viewpoint as our entry into the poem," as Robert Langbaum notes as early as 1957 (*The Poetry of Experience*, 78). Langbaum's recognition of a causal relationship between, on the one hand, one of the defining characteristics of the genre, and, on the other, the experience of readers as they read the opening lines, is not invalidated by arguments against his further claim that the genre incites sympathy for the speaker to the degree that readers "suspend moral judgement" (83), which, as Wayne Booth perceives, "seriously underplays the extent to which moral judgment remains even after psychological vividness has done its work" (*The Rhetoric of Fiction*, 250n6).

7. Tamar Yacobi draws attention to the effect of the even longer delay before readers are told the identity of the narratee. In response to Robert Langbaum's assertion that "the duke determines the arrangement and relative subordination of the parts" (83) of the poem, Yacobi argues convincingly that "the Duke deserves credit for engineering the gradual and indirect emergence of the message, but surely not for (say) the shock given us by the last-minute discovery of the messenger's identity [since the Duke] of course knows all along whom he is addressing" ("Narrative Structure," 344).

8. In comments on an earlier version of this chapter, James Phelan

argues that "the Duke isn't worried about negotiating [with the narratee the] terms for his next marriage . . . Rather than negotiating terms, the Duke is sending a warning to the next Duchess via the narratee because sending the warning himself would be stooping and 'I choose never to stoop.'" I find Phelan's reading ingenious and think that like all good readings it enriches the poem. But I insist that nominally the Duke is negotiating his marriage contract, whatever individual readers think his covert purposes are. One of the reasons that readings vary as much as they do is that readers each fill gaps in their own ways—and often without recognizing which elements of our reading we have been given and which are our assumptions based on information we have been given. In this case, whether we interpret as function H the Duke's negotiating (my reading) or the Duke's sending a message (Phelan's reading), Phelan and I agree that the Duke's confidence indicates that he will succeed (function I), even if success may mean that the Duke will marry (my reading, which is bad enough) or that the Duke will marry a bride who has been warned that her life depends on reserving her smiles for her husband (Phelan's reading, which of course is worse).

9. The Russian terms can be transliterated as *sju et* and *fabula*. According to the accounts I have read, credit for introducing the term *sju et* is given to Viktor Shklovsky, and for developing definitions to distinguish between the two trajectories primarily to Boris Tomashevsky and Juri Tynyanov. (See Tzvetan Todorov, "Some Approaches to Russian Formalism," and D. W. Fokkema and Elrud Kunne-Ibsch, *Theories of Literature in the Twentieth Century*.)

10. My view of narrative is that it is a semiotic system structured like language. As Ferdinand de Saussure discerned (in lectures from 1906–11, published posthumously under the title *Course in General Linguistics*), the sound of the word "horse" (the signifier) is meaningless except to those who, when they hear it, think about their concept (the signified) of what a horse is like. The two together—the sound and the concept, the signifier and the signified—comprise a two-part sign that represents a horse. Similarly, a narrative representation (written, oral, filmed, danced) guides readers (listeners, viewers) to construct (some would say "reconstruct") a fabula. The two together—the representation that has material form and the fabula that exists only as a concept in a perceiver's mind—represent a narrative world. Nonfiction represents our world, fiction represents a fictional world.

In taking this position I am arguing against Dorrit Cohn's theory (*The Distinction of Fiction*, particularly chapter 7, "Signposts of Fictionality") that historical accounts differ from fiction in that only the former have a referential level (they refer to our world). In disagreeing with Cohn on this point by maintaining that fictional narratives represent fictional worlds, I am influenced by possible worlds theory, particularly Marie-Laure Ryan's *Possible Worlds, Artificial Intelligence, and Narrative Theory*.

11. Seymour Chatman recognizes and explains that the paired trajectories of narrative are illuminated by—and enable—the translation of a fab-

ula from one medium to another: "One of the most important observations to come out of narratology is that narrative itself is a deep structure quite independent of its medium. In other words, narrative is basically a kind of text organization, and that organization, that schema, needs to be actualized: in written words, as in stories and novels; in spoken words, combined with the movements of actors imitating characters against sets which imitate places, as in plays and films; in drawings; in comic strips; in dance movements, as in narrative ballet and in mime; and even in music, at least in program music of the order of *Till Eulenspiegel* and *Peter and the Wolf*.

"A salient property of narrative is double time structuring. That is, all narratives, in whatever medium, combine the time sequence of plot events, the time of the *histoire* [fabula] with the time of the presentation of those events in the text, which we call 'discourse-time' [representation]. What is fundamental to narrative, regardless of medium, is that these two time orders are independent. . . . This is true in any medium: flashbacks are just as possible in ballet or mime or opera as they are in a film or novel. Thus, in theory at least, any narrative can be actualized by any medium which can communicate the two time orders" ("What Novels Can Do That Films Can't," 121–22).

12. Seymour Chatman, writing in response to Culler's argument, emphasizes that "[f]rom the theoretical point of view, narratology is resolutely synchronic. It does not assume that either telling or told 'precede' each other: they are coexistent, cotemporal parts of the model" ("On Deconstructing Narratology," 14). Ruth Ronen considers the possibility that the status of fabula is different in fiction and nonfiction: "In extrafictional contexts chronology is an essentialist concept accounting for the 'natural' concatenation of events independent of any perspectival interference (whether such a chronology of events in reality is accessible or not is a question of a different sort); in fictional contexts the chronology of reported events is the outcome of the order and mode of their presentation. There is no order prior to the perspectivally determined mode of telling. . . . Fictional discourse constructs temporal relations in the narrative world, it does not *reveal* these relations" (*Possible Worlds in Literary Theory,* 215–16, 217; her emphasis).

13. Roy Jay Nelson, in his fine book on causality in fiction (*Causality and Narrative in French Fiction*), provides the clearest statement I have seen of the two related but separable causal sequences that I have come to think that Culler in this instance has confused. Whereas Culler's methodology is to attempt to weaken the fabula at the expense of the representation, Nelson retains the two traditional trajectories and includes in addition the third element that Gérard Genette calls *narration* (often translated as "narrating"; Genette, *Narrative Discourse,* 27 and 27n2). In Nelson's definition, "*narration,* as the productive act per se, is the realm of the author[:] not a persona but rather those elements of a supposed authorial thought process or intention which can be inferred from the existence and nature of texts themselves" (13; I reiterate that Nelson is analyzing narrative fiction). Nelson discerns that readers of fiction

infer causes and effects at all three levels. Like most theorists, he sees that the sequence of the representation reveals, rather than contradicts, the chronological sequence of fabula. In the process of planning a narrative, he recognizes, decisions about an outcome do often precede decisions about the events and situations that will allow that outcome to seem appropriate. In Nelson's words, "If . . . 'realistic' fiction [is impelled] to provide the causes before revealing the effects in the *récit* [representation] and the *histoire* [fabula], the *narration* has the effect 'in mind,' and invents the cause afterward so that the effect may occur" (93).

Of course, as Nelson well understands, nothing in this account subverts the relation between chronology and causality. If it may seem at first thought that the same set of events—but in a different sequence, and with different causal interrelations—occurs in the authorial thought process and in the characters' lives, I argue that the events at the two sites are not the same. The two sets of events cannot be the same events because they take place in ontologically disparate realms: one set in the mental world in which the authorial thought process occurs, and one set in the represented world in which the characters act. Functional polyvalence explains that interpretations of causality depend on the configuration in which an event is perceived and its chronological position in that configuration. Since the events take place in configurations in different worlds, and the sequence of events in the authorial process is most often different from the sequence in which the characters act, there is no reason that interpretations of the causality of the events can be expected to be the same in the two configurations.

14. Although Prince's categories are pertinent in the instances I cite, the distinction between the relation that in this instance he is analyzing (between a narrative text and the narrative world that it describes) and the relation I am analyzing (between a representation [e.g., Poe's and Browning's narrative texts] and the fabula that readers construct in response to it) is important to maintain.

Notes to Chapter 4

1. In the terms of function analysis, doers whose actions are motivated by someone else are donors, whose actions (function F) empower C-actants to achieve their objectives. In the case of armed forces, the government or individual who acquires their services is the C-actant who determines their objective. In the case of chain gangs, the governing body or the individuals who manage the prison are the C-actants who determine their objectives.

2. I am grateful to David Herman, who drew my attention to the parallels between Turner's argument and my own.

3. Broadcast on the local NPR station on May 21, 1996. Because I did not hear the beginning of the commentary and the speaker was not identified during the portion I heard, I do not know who was speaking.

4. In "In a Grove," one of the two stories by Akutagawa on which the

film *Rashomon* is based, the wife says that she "plunged the dagger through his [her husband's] blue kimono and into his chest" (176). She claims responsibility for killing her husband, however, only in the story. In the film, Kurosawa softens the wife's role in the version she narrates: she approaches her husband dagger in hand, but claims that she faints then, and that he is dead when she regains consciousness. In both the story and the film, the bandit and the husband each declare themselves responsible.

5. The comments by Thomas Pavel that I cite are part of an argument he develops about the history of structures: a "gradual specialization of genres [that he envisions], thanks to which tragedy begins to eliminate its epic openings." Drama, he proposes, develops from narrated accounts of events: "just as Renaissance comedy is still under the influence of medieval romances and pastoral prose, so the tragedies still bear the unmistakable stamp of the historical narrative, the folktale and the novella" ("Racinian Spaces," 120–21).

6. Citations of *Hamlet* are from the Arden edition, edited by Harold Jenkins.

7. One might interpret Polonius's death as itself a function-A event, rather than as merely ensuring Hamlet's already probable forced departure from Denmark. According to that interpretation, Polonius's death would be the one function-A event that Hamlet causes, however unintentionally. From the perspective of an interpreter considering the play in its entirety, including its ending, it would be easy to argue that Polonius's death, avenged by Laertes, is the cause of Hamlet's death. I have not included Polonius's death as a function-A event because I think that as we watch or read the play, we tend to interpret the function of events as Hamlet does. As I interpret Hamlet's interpretation, Polonius's death does not disrupt his situation in the way that all the function-A events I list do.

8. Laertes, who wants to kill Hamlet to avenge his father's and his sister's deaths, and Claudius, who has been plotting against Hamlet since Act 2, conspire to use against Hamlet a poisoned sword and poisoned drink. A function analysis from the perspective of Claudius and Laertes (at the end of Act 4) looks like this:

A   Hamlet must die (for Claudius, to protect his throne; for Laertes, for revenge)
C   Claudius and Laertes decide to kill Hamlet
C' Claudius and Laertes make plans to murder Hamlet
F_1 Laertes has "bought an unction of a mountebank" (4.7.140)
F_2 Claudius counts on a servant or courtier ("I'll *have* prepar'd him / A chalice" [4.7.158–59; my emphasis])
G   the duel that Claudius will organize is the time and place where Hamlet is to be killed

9. Here and throughout, I cite the translation of Racine's *Phèdre* by John Cairncross: *Phaedra*. Because Cairncross's translation has the same

number of lines as Racine's French, anyone wanting to locate the passages in French can do so easily. (By convention in French classical drama, lines are numbered consecutively throughout the play. Because scenes are shorter in French drama than in English drama—in French drama, a new scene begins whenever someone enters or leaves the stage—reference to a scene is generally sufficient information to locate a specific passage.)

10. Racine's sources include, in addition to Euripides' *Hippolytus,* the accounts in Greek mythology of Phaedra and her family. When Phaedra refers to the torments visited by Venus on her "race" (*sang* [literally, "blood"]; 1.3.278), in the passage I cite, one thinks among other examples of the experience of her mother Pasiphaë, who, after her Venus-driven encounter with the white bull presented by Neptune to her husband Minos, gave birth to the half-bull, half-human monster known as the Minotaur.

11. In the Preface to *Phaedra,* Racine describes her as "involved by her destiny, and by the anger of the gods, in an unlawful passion" (Racine, translated by Cairncross, p. 145).

12. Roland Barthes explains that "Oenone's ruse consists not in *retracting* Phaedra's confession, in annulling it, which is impossible; but in *reversing* it: Phaedra will accuse Hippolytus of the very crime she herself is guilty of; speech will remain intact, simply transferred from one character to the other" (*On Racine,* 120–21).

13. Since Hippolytus has not previously demonstrated interest in any women (nor does he in Euripides' play), Phaedra has not assumed that he loved her, but she has not even considered that he might love someone else. Although Racine does not invent the character Aricia, who appears in several ancient accounts, the subplot in his play of a relationship between Hippolytus and Aricia that torments Phaedra is not an element in Euripides' play.

14. Careful readers may recognize that this function analysis is less detailed than many in this book. In analyzing *Phaedra,* my goal is to show as clearly as possible the causal chain that leads from an initial function-A situation to Phaedra's function-C decision intended to resolve it, but which leads to action that causes a further function-A situation, etc., throughout the play. To do this I have not bracketed the three functions that interpret events preceding the opening scene of the play (functions A_1, C_1, C'), and I have eliminated donor functions and function-H events by characters other than Phaedra. In a function analysis as in any form of analysis, sometimes detail is useful and sometimes not.

For readers interested in the process of function analysis I draw attention to function a_5 as a good example of a lower-case function-a event. The narrative world has not changed; Hippolytus loves Aricia (and playgoers know it) when the play begins. But for Phaedra the information is new—and disruptive; it changes her interpretation of the narrative world.

15. In fact, as James Phelan points out in comments on an earlier version of this chapter, a C-actant's decision, in instances when it puts the C-actant in peril, regularly incites in viewers (readers, listeners) a variety of emotions quite other than comfort—anxiety and fear, for example.

Moreover, as Phelan perceptively notes, "[t]he degree and kind of discomfort [that perceivers feel] is related to the audience's inferences about the genre of the particular narrative. Scary movies go for one kind of discomfort, tragedies another, romantic comedies still another."

16. Although I adopt for my analysis of *Daisy Miller* two of Tamar Yacobi's findings about the novella—the division among readers in the protagonist they identify and the fact that that division occurs along historical lines—in the present context I cannot do justice to the complexity of the process she demonstrates that we engage in in determining a protagonist. I encourage readers to consult her important article ("Hero or Heroine?").

17. Throughout this section on interpretations of *Daisy Miller*, in which I analyze and indicate as functions the causal relations that I think that other writers' recorded interpretations reveal, only I can be held responsible. To interpret an interpretation, and in a terminology unknown to the initial interpreter, is dangerously close to attempting to portray how Rembrandt's artworks would have looked if he had worked, for instance, in a digital medium.

18. One could argue, moreover, that Winterbourne's inaction is less the result of his inability to decide whether he wants a relationship with Daisy, than to determine what kind of offer it is appropriate to make her. I cite in support of this reading the passage in which Winterbourne thinks that if it were "impossible to regard her as a wholly unspotted flower [it would] much simplify the situation to be able to treat her as the subject of one of the visitations known to romancers as 'lawless passions'" (59).

19. In fact, their ability to communicate deteriorates as their relationship progresses. Daisy's first request is that Winterbourne stay with her brother Randolph so that she and her mother can visit the Château de Chillon, to which Winterbourne manages to respond by indicating that he would prefer to accompany Daisy to Chillon (19). Two results ensue: the trip to Chillon, but also Mrs. Costello's refusal to meet Daisy. When Daisy makes her second request to Winterbourne that evening, that he take her boating, she has already learned from him that his aunt refuses to meet her. Although neither Winterbourne nor readers have access to Daisy's motivations beyond what she says and what she does, we can speculate that this social rebuff may motivate Daisy, who walks away after Winterbourne offers to go boating, with no explanation except that she wanted "a little fuss" (38).

Thereafter, Winterbourne's responses to her requests seem increasingly rude. At Chillon, when Daisy suggests that Winterbourne join their party and travel with them, Winterbourne responds that he has prior engagements. When she asks him to visit her in Rome, he tells her he is going to Rome to visit his aunt, and when Daisy insists, "'I want you just to come for me'" (44), he refuses to say more than that "at any rate he would certainly come" (44). In Rome, although readers are informed that Winterbourne has traveled there with "the zeal of an admirer" (51), Daisy, who meets him at Mrs. Walker's by chance, is not. When she asks him to escort her to meet Giovanelli he agrees, but he leaves her when

Mrs. Walker demands that he get into her carriage (63). Their final mis-understanding is the recurring conversation in the final pages of the novella about whether Daisy is engaged to Giovanelli (84, 88–89, 91).

20. Roman Jakobson's analysis of the constituent elements of verbal communication ("Closing Statement: Linguistics and Poetics") is funda-mental to my understanding of what is required for a message to be received.

21. By "relatively traditional" I indicate what (as I understand him) Roland Barthes calls the "moderately plural (i.e., merely polysemous)" (*S/Z: An Essay,* 6), exemplified by Balzac's *Sarrasine:* one can construct a fabula from the information that the representation provides. For analy-sis of less traditional forms on the narrative borderlands, see chapter 8. I also draw attention to Yacobi's suggestion that James may have been "trying out not just a new, 'international' matter but also a new manner: the consistently self-limited mode of narration" ("Hero or Heroine?" 31).

Notes to Chapter 5

1. Gérard Genette's terms *voice* and *focalization* (*Narrative Discourse,* esp. chapters 4 and 5) differentiate, but more clearly, what James differ-entiates by redefining the word *narrator* and creating the term *center of consciousness:* two distinct activities, both of which, in many narratives, are assigned to a narrator who is the source of language but also of per-ceptions and conceptions.

2. My reading of Strether's behavior in Paris, in light of its conse-quences, as function F reflects recent scholarship on *The Ambassadors* in which Strether's personal growth is a recurrent theme. James Phelan ana-lyzes the decisive role of language in "the way James describes Strether's internal action [which] enables us to see and participate in the complex moral and psychological growth Strether experiences" (*Worlds from Words,* 58). Marianna Torgovnick finds that the contrast between Strether's behavior in the early scenes and the deftness he displays in the final scene, in which "he is Maria's equal in conversation . . . supports the reading of the novel that finds Strether, at novel's end, a more mature, sensitive, self-aware man than he had earlier been" (*Closure in the Novel,* 140). According to Joyce A. Rowe, "[a]t fifty-five, Strether has complet-ed his initiation" (*Equivocal Endings in Classic American Novels,* 77). For Jeanne Campbell Reesman, the conclusion "firmly suggest[s]" that Strether has "nothing but knowledge by the end" although, in her opin-ion, "this knowledge is very dangerous" (*American Designs,* xiii).

Readers of fairy tales will remember that the characteristic triplifica-tion is often seen at exactly this point in the sequence. The hero is tested, responds to the test, and gains (or fails to gain) empowerment, and then all three stages are repeated a second and a third time. If we represent the triple testing of many fairy tales as $(D\ E\ F)^3$, then Strether's testing should be rep-resented as $(D\ E\ F)^n$ to indicate that each of countless experiences draws from him a response that enhances his personal growth.

3. The exposition of *The Ambassadors*—the events that are prior chronologically to "that point in time which marks the beginning of the *fictive present*" in the representation (Meir Sternberg, *Expositional Modes,* 21)—includes everything that happens prior to Strether's inquiry at the hotel about Waymarsh (the initial scene of the representation). This means that the material that James's representation relegates to exposition includes the events that in the novel's fabula express the primary motivating event (function A) and the initial actions of the C-actant (functions C and C'). Although *The Ambassadors* is by no means the first narrative, nor James the first writer to consign primary motivating events to exposition, I draw attention to this feature of the novel because it is the major element in the construction of the text that leads readers to shift their interpretation of the opening scene so many times.

4. Lubomír Dole el distinguishes between the absolute authentication authority of the anonymous third-person narrator and the lower degree of authentication authority of the first-person narrator. In Dole el's theory, "[a]uthentication [in fiction] is a special illocutionary force analogous to the force of performative speech acts described by [J. L.] Austin [in *How to Do Things with Words*]. The analogy is based on the fact that the performative illocutionary force is carried only by speech acts uttered by speakers who have the necessary authority." Dole el cites as one of Austin's examples of a performative speech act the naming of a ship, which only the person authorized to do the naming can accomplish. In fiction, Dole el argues, "the 'speaker' properly authorized to authenticate motifs is the anonymous Er-form [third-person] narrator." The first-person narrator, like the anonymous third-person narrator, Dole el recognizes, "assumes the role of constructing the narrative world. However, the theory of authentication should assign a lower degree of authentication authority to the Ich-form [first-person] narrator than the absolute authority of the Er-form narrator. The world constructed by the Ich-form narrator is *relatively* authentic. It is not the world of absolute narrative facts, rather [it is] an authentic belief-world of the Ich-narrator" ("Truth and Authenticity in Narrative," 11–12, 17; Dole el's emphasis). See Dole el's full description of binary and non-binary authentication models, which I summarize only in part. I am grateful to David Herman, who drew this essay to my attention.

5. Jeanne Campbell Reesman, who perceptively discerns that Maria Gostrey's "frequent repetition of Strether's words forces him to reexamine them in a dialogical context," draws attention to the correlations between Maria Gostrey's role and the reader's: "She is enacting the same process the reader is experiencing, the attempt to understand Strether, and her allowing Strether his personal freedom to develop his thoughts becomes the reader's hermeneutic model as well" (*American Designs,* 79).

6. Marianna Torgovnick, whose discussion of conventional endings and James's "delightfully pejorative" comments on them (*Closure in the Novel,* 122) has influenced my thinking, concludes, "'Where [Strether] is' at novel's end is obscure neither to Strether, nor . . . to the reader, despite

some readers' feelings that he ought to be somewhere else—for instance, preparing to stay in Paris and marry Maria" (140–41). Although I too regret that Maria Gostrey should be made to relinquish a future that she envisions as enhanced by Strether's presence, I am arguing, in agreement with Torgovnick, that Strether's logic, in the final scene, leaves his view of the appropriateness of his departure in no doubt. Moreover, for us to know "where Strether is" at the end of the novel requires, as James Phelan perceptively recognizes, that the final scene be represented in dialogue, which permits Maria to speak in her own voice. According to Phelan, "[I]f we are to interpret Strether's refusal [of Maria's offer] as a final victory, James must plausibly represent Maria herself acknowledging it as a victory" (*Worlds from Words*, 60). This she does—although the pain she is suppressing in doing so is left to the reader to imagine.

7. Dorothea Krook, who defines "Jamesian ambiguity" as "leav[ing] the reader faced with two and only two interpretations of the data" ("*The Ambassadors:* Two Types of Ambiguity," 154), agrees that "*The Ambassadors* as a whole is by no means ambiguous," although she discovers "one great 'pocket' of this kind of ambiguity" (151): the status of Chad's transformation. Arguing that "Chad cannot both be and not be transformed," she traces "the evidence of the witnesses, which may be read both ways, as confirming one interpretation (Strether's—that Chad is transformed) and disconfirming the other (the Pococks'—that Chad is not transformed), or confirming the Pococks' and disconfirming Strether's" (154). In chapter 6 I take up the issue of Jamesian ambiguity again.

8. Although Kafka incorporates the text of "Vor dem Gesetz" in the penultimate chapter of *Der Prozeß* (*The Trial*), the completeness of the story as a narrative unit is not affected because the story is embedded in the novel in its entirety and as a narrated text, in the form of an exemplum that the priest tells K. Moreover, since the ensuing conversation between the priest and K. includes conflicting exegeses for which no hierarchy is established, the embedding of the story in the novel invites, more than it precludes, analysis of the story as a separate unit.

On the other hand, whereas a very short story may seem a less appropriate choice for comparison to *The Ambassadors* than Kafka's novel *Das Schloß* (*The Castle*), which also opens with the arrival of the protagonist at the locus of the action, the novel is unfinished, and, even though Max Brod provides a summary of the concluding situation as Kafka described it to him, an unfinished narrative does not lend itself to a function analysis. The final pages of *The Ambassadors* demonstrate the degree to which the specific words of a completed representation can govern readers' interpretations of the function of events.

9. The translations of "Vor dem Gesetz" that I cite are by Willa and Edwin Muir.

10. See chapter 7 for a consideration of the effect of indexical information on readers' and viewers' interpretations of the function of events and situations.

11. For this pertinent citation from Jurij Lotman's study of plot typolo-

gy, I am indebted to Teresa de Lauretis, who cites the passage I cite, along with Lotman's further specification that "closed space [in] the elementary sequence of events in myth . . . can be interpreted as 'a cave,' 'the grave,' 'a house,' 'woman,' [and] entry into it is interpreted on various levels as 'death,' 'conception,' 'return home' and so on; moreover all these acts are thought of as mutually identical" ("The Origin of Plot," 168). In a particularly famous passage in the canon of feminist narrative studies, de Lauretis concludes: "In this mythical-textual mechanics, then, the hero must be male, regardless of the gender of the text-image, because the obstacle, whatever its personification, is morphologically female and indeed, simply, the womb" (*Alice Doesn't,* 118–19).

12. McHale's argument is that Postmodern fiction can be distinguished from Modernist fiction by the greater importance of ontological issues in the former and of epistemological issues in the latter (see esp. chapter 1).

13. Similarly, in both "The Assignation" and "My Last Duchess" (as we saw in chapter 3), information about causal events that are chronologically prior to the initial event in the representation is temporarily withheld, although, as in *The Ambassadors,* information that permits readers to identify the events and to interpret their functions is gradually revealed. The difference to which I draw attention between the two narratives analyzed in chapter 3 and *The Ambassadors* is that in the latter the sequence is cut off before it concludes, whereas in Poe's story the events to complete the sequence—and in Browning's poem the events to complete the primary sequence—are revealed. As a result, while the representations of Poe's and Browning's narratives effectively produce in readers an emotional response, they do not finally (after one has read and analyzed them) create the epistemological doubt that James's novel and, even more so, Kafka's story do.

14. Gerald Prince's path-breaking analysis in "The Disnarrated" of areas of disjuncture between a representation and the world it represents has guided my analysis of the status of events and functions in the segments that precede and follow the two representations, and underlies my idea of empty functions and negative functions. In his terms, the events that precede the man's arrival are, I suggest, "unnarrated"—events that are omitted because of the focalizer's concentration on the task at hand.

15. Admittedly, the suppression of the events (particularly the events to fill functions A and C) encourages multiple interpretations in a way that the information we learn in *The Ambassadors*—that Strether has agreed to go to Europe to bring Chad home—does not. Peter J. Rabinowitz points out, for instance, in comments on an earlier version of this chapter, that "it's possible that the story begins in equilibrium (the man lives in a world where, in the normal state of affairs, people can go to the law whenever they want); in this case, it's the doorkeeper's refusal that's the motivating disruptive event." In that case, depending on one's interpretation of "waiting," one might read the man's response either as (1) function C_{neg} (the man does not decide to act) or as (2) a decision to wait (function C) followed by the act of waiting (function C'). In either case, nothing is accomplished. If the doorkeeper's refusal is the motivating disruptive event, the man does not succeed in overcoming it.

16. The "double-bind" that Jacques Derrida perceives in this story is, similarly, a motivated not-doing, which in my terminology, could be interpreted as a function E_{neg} or H_{neg}, depending on its consequences: "The [doorkeeper's] discourse operates, not directly to prohibit, but to interrupt and defer passage, or permission to pass. The man has at his disposal the natural or physical liberty to enter the premises, if not the law. So he must . . . forbid himself to enter. He must constrain himself, issue to himself, not the order to assent to the law, but the order not to ascend [accéder] to the law, which, in short, has him informed or lets him know: do not come to me, I command that you do not yet come to me. It is there and therein that I am the law and that you will accede [accéderas] to my demand. By not having access [accéder] to me" (183; my translation).

Notes to Chapter 6

1. Gérard Genette, who notes with approval Sternberg's use of these two terms to distinguish between types of omniscient narrators, adds that the terms are equally applicable to "focalized narratives" (*Narrative Discourse Revisited*, 78n8), which of course they are.

2. The two books address different issues: Shlomith Rimmon-Kenan defines a specific form of structural ambiguity available to narrative, which she locates in certain late works by Henry James, and Meir Sternberg explores the artistic effects of the placement of expositional material in a representation. The similarity between the two books, and between the two theorists' work, is that both theorists analyze relations between representations and fabulas to explain the effects of specific narratives, and both illuminate relations between representations and fabulas by investigating gaps.

3. In later work Sternberg discerns that, for readers, temporary gaps and permanent gaps raise disparate questions. In response to a temporary gap, readers ask these questions, he writes: "Why has the narrative chosen to distribute the information that belongs together, to deform a coherent plot only to reform it into proper chronology at a later stage? In short, why fabricate an ambiguity destined for resolution, and why conceal and reveal the truth at exactly these stages?" But in response to a permanent gap, readers ask a different question—in his words: "Why has the narrator chosen to omit this information altogether?" (*The Poetics of Biblical Narrative*, 240).

4. The historian Peter Burke perceives that "[a] narrative history of the First World War, for example, will give one impression if the story ends at Versailles in 1919, another if the narrative is extended to 1933 or 1939," and suggests that it "might be worth following the example of certain novelists, such as John Fowles, and providing alternative endings" ("History of Events and the Revival of Narrative," 240).

5. The set of functions that Propp discerned includes preparatory functions that represent events which by changing a preliminary situation weaken its stability and enable a subsequent and more serious function-

A event to occur. Among these "preliminary" misfortunes is the departure or death of a family member. By extension, then, the death of a king can be interpreted either as a function-A event in itself or as merely a preliminary event that leaves the kingdom vulnerable to a function-A event. I have not included preliminary functions in my model, largely because living beings are always so very vulnerable to disruptive events, and yet the specific vulnerability that will lead to disaster can be determined only in hindsight, after the disruptive event has occurred. In contrast, the ameliorative move (from a function-A situation to a new equilibrium) can be perceived as it develops, whether or not it is successful. In addition to the reasons proposed in chapter 4, perhaps this too is a reason that literary narratives and narratives about events in our world so often trace the ameliorative move.

6. The other two modes that Mink proposes in his early and very interesting essay on the relations between history and fiction are the *theoretical* (in which a number of objects are comprehended "as instances of the same generalization") and the *categoreal* (in which a number of objects are comprehended "as examples of the same category") ("History and Fiction as Modes of Comprehension," 550).

7. Mink argues that the distinction between anticipation and retrospection may be more than the mere difference in temporal perspective: "We know that the difference between past and future is crucial in the case of moral and affective attitudes; we do not fear something that is over and done with, nor feel regret for something not yet undertaken. My thesis is that the difference is crucial as well for cognition: at least in the case of human actions and changes, to know an event by retrospection is categorically . . . different from knowing it by prediction or anticipation. It cannot even, in any strict sense, be called the 'same' event, for in the former case the descriptions under which it is known are governed by a story to which it belongs, and there is no story of the future" (546).

8. Although the governess writes her account after the fact, in a past tense, the focalization is hers at the time that the events are occurring.

9. An uninterpreted event (a specified event whose causes and consequences have not been interpreted) stands in contrast to an empty function (an interpretation of the causes and consequences of an unspecified event).

10. Gérard Genette comments that "to [his] knowledge . . . the situation of a *double narrator* occurs only . . . in *Sarrasine.*" In his terminology, "the extradiegetic narrator [of the framing narrative] himself becomes intradiegetic narrator [of the contained narrative] when he tells his companion the story of Zambinella" (*Narrative Discourse*, 229n42).

11. In agreement with Barthes, Ross Chambers comments that "in *Sarrasine,* the contract is as close to being explicit as decorum allows: in accepting the very intimate circumstances of the rendezvous in which the narrator reveals the secret she wishes to learn . . . Mme de Rochefide accepts her part of the bargain" ("*Sarrasine* and the Impact of Art," 218). The setting that Mme de Rochefide arranges—a small salon in her home, softly lit and with a fire in the fireplace; she is seated on a sofa, the

narrator on cushions at her feet—indicates to me both that she has agreed to the bargain and that the narrator, who describes the setting, interprets the setting as signifying her agreement.

But then, like many, I come to *Sarrasine* through Barthes; my reading of the story is strongly influenced by his. A recent study by Claude Bremond and Thomas Pavel, *De Barthes à Balzac,* takes as its highly appropriate aim "to extricate *Sarrasine* from Barthes's grasp in order to defend it and to emphasize precisely the aspect that Barthes did his utmost to undervalue: its intelligibility" ("de dégager *Sarrasine* de l'étreinte barthésienne pour en défendre et mettre en valeur précisément le trait que Barthes s'évertuait à déprécier: son intelligibilité" [10]). In their reading, "the interpretation that would have the transaction between the narrator and the young woman be an exchange (a night of love for a good story) betrays both the spirit and the letter of the text. The narrator is not in a position to negotiate these stakes" ("l'interprétation qui veut que l'objet de la négociation entre le narrateur et la jeune femme soit un troc [une nuit d'amour contre une belle histoire] trahit aussi bien l'esprit que la lettre du texte. Le narrateur n'est pas en position de négocier un tel enjeu." [254]). In support of this position they cite lexia #144 (the narrator has just offered to call the next evening to reveal the mystery): "She smiled and we parted; she just as proud, just as forbidding, and I just as ridiculous as ever. She had the audacity to waltz with a young aide-de-camp; and I was left in turn angry, pouting, admiring, loving, jealous" (Balzac, 234, #144; quoted by Bremond and Pavel, 253). Bremond and Pavel conclude, "In a fit of fleeting lucidity, the narrator knows at that moment that he has lost the wager" ("Dans un accès de lucidité passagère, le narrateur sait à ce moment qu'il a perdu la parti." [253]).

Although the narrator's thoughts at that moment are far less transparent to me than to Bremond and Pavel, particularly since in the next lexia Mme de Rochefide parts from the narrator saying "'till tomorrow'" (Balzac, 234, #145), their larger argument—that the narrator gravely misunderstands the young woman's character, thinking her more a coquette than a serious thinker (253–54)—forces a reconsideration of the story (a reconsideration that is useful in the present context because it indicates how differently Mme de Rochefide's response at the end of the story can be interpreted when viewed in a configuration that includes all of Balzac's fiction and traditional readings of his work, than when viewed—as Barthes does—ahistorically and without reference to Balzac's corpus.

According to Bremond's and Pavel's interpretation, Mme de Rochefide is a spokesperson for Balzac, and the judgment she pronounces at the end of the story reflects "one option, the rejection of the world, whose legitimacy Balzac understands and respects" ("une option, le rejet du monde, dont Balzac comprend et respecte la légitimité" [260]): "From the scandalously happy fate of the Lanty family, the young Parisian woman passed judgment on the Paris of 1830; from the scandalously unhappy fate of the sculptor Sarrasine, she passed judgment on the passions and particularly, to be sure, on love" ("Du destin scandaleusement

heureux de la famille Lanty, la jeune Parisienne conclut en effet à la condamnation du Paris de 1830; du destin scandaleusement malheureux du
sculpteur Sarrasine, elle conclut à la condamnation des passions et
surtout, bien sûr, de l'amour" [194]).

12. I cite passages from *Sarrasine* in English translation only, and give
page numbers that refer to the fine translation by Richard Miller that is
part of his translation of Roland Barthes's *S/Z*. But to facilitate locating
citations in French, I also include the lexia numbers (preceded by an
asterisk) that Barthes assigns to the fragments I cite.

13. Whether the information that the narrator reveals is indeed about
events he knows to have occurred, or whether he begins at this moment
to invent a story to tell his companion, to earn her gratitude, is another
question. Readers of Balzac's story who have seen the film *L'Année
dernière à Marienbad* (*Last Year at Marienbad*), with screenplay and dialogue by Alain Robbe-Grillet, may find suspicious the narrator's pause—
his hesitation before he provides even the most general information.

Henrik Ibsen's *The Master Builder* raises similar suspicions in the
scene near the end of Act I when Solness finally acquiesces to Hilda's
claim that he kissed her ten years before, then asks what happened next.
In all three works a character attempts a seduction by telling a story
about previous events that may or may not have occurred in the potential seducer's world.

At the beginning of the twenty-first century, we cannot escape the
effects of "reading backwards" when we return to nineteenth-century
narratives. While I cannot read Ibsen's play or Balzac's story without
wondering whether Hilda and the narrator of *Sarrasine* are storytellers
who use their stories to accomplish their goals, both narratives are
ambiguous in this respect and can be read—or in the nineteenth century
could have been read—with less skepticism.

14. Although my emphasis here is on the ways in which this passage
defers readers' understanding of the narrator's desire for Mme de
Rochefide, her primary role in this extremely beautifully constructed
story *is,* I suggest, to serve as a lens through which to show how horrifying the events of the narrator's story appear to a first-time listener.

15. As Ross Chambers discerns, the narration is not fully restricted to
Sarrasine's focalization all the way to the end of the telling. Chambers
locates the change as beginning after the narrator's companion's second
interruption, after which she and readers are "free[d] . . . from absolute
subjugation to Sarrasine's point of view" ("*Sarrasine* and the Impact of
Art," 228). His example, two paragraphs later in Balzac's text, is the
response to Vitagliani's telling Sarrasine, "Go ahead; you need fear no
rivals here" (Balzac, 243, *331). Chambers perceives, and draws attention to, "the shift in narrative point of view which is now able to notice
(although Sarrasine does not) the malicious smiles which accompany
Vitagliani's equivocal remark" (Chambers, 229).

Sarrasine illustrates both situations in which the distinction
between voice and focalization seems most useful: where one character's
conceptions and perceptions are revealed in someone else's words (in

Sarrasine, in the contained narrative), and where a character's perceptions and conceptions at the time of an ongoing set of events are revealed in that character's words *at a later time* (in *Sarrasine,* in the framing narrative, in which the narrator maintains suspense by revealing no more than he knew at the time of the events he describes).

16. Meir Sternberg, in his analysis of the interplay between narrative's two sequences (representation and fabula), discerns three possible effects: suspense, curiosity, and surprise. The latter two, he notes, "involve manipulations of the past, which the tale communicates in a sequence discontinuous with the happening. Perceptibly so, for *curiosity:* knowing that we do not know, we go forward with our mind on the gapped antecedents . . . For *surprise,* however, the narrative first unobtrusively gaps or twists its chronology, then unexpectedly discloses to us our misreading and enforces a corrective rereading in late re-cognition" ("How Narrativity Makes a Difference," 117). The long-deferred information about la Zambinella's early life exemplifies "surprise."

17. I cite the early version of this essay because in the revised version (in *Expositional Modes and Temporal Ordering* [1978, 218]) Sternberg leaves out the phrase in which he suggests that a quasi-mimetic explanation for gaps may be motivated by a desire to keep readers satisfied, which is an important idea in the argument I am developing.

18. Often, in plays and films, a character tells a story, or the contents of a letter, a diary, or a message left on an answering machine are revealed (examples of what Perry describes as "a block of information transmitted from one character to another" [39–40]). Sometimes, in plays and films, characters who identify themselves as narrators appear in the opening scene (indicating that everything subsequent is narrated) or in the concluding scene (indicating that everything preceding has been narrated). In addition to relatively simple examples like these, the ontological status of the source of the narration in film and drama, as well as specific strategies for skewing information from one character's perspective rather than another, has received much sophisticated treatment and been the subject of arguments that I need not enter here.

19. For an analysis of borderline cases—sequels and prequels, characters who migrate from one writer's novel to another writer's novel—see, for example, "Epilogue: Fictional Worlds in Transduction: Postmodern Rewrites" in Lubomír Dole el's *Heterocosmica.*

20. Perry continues: "it is not only the relative weight of items in the following stages which is affected. . . . The details of the sequel are assimilated as best they can into a prepared framework where they undergo an assimilative change of meaning: had this material *stood on its own* it would have had other implications than those now activated" ("Literary Dynamics," 50; his emphasis). An "assimilative change of meaning," I suggest, is a way of describing the effect of a configuration on interpretations of events that are perceived in relation to it.

Roy Jay Nelson describes a process of decision-making that affects further decision-making even at later stages in one's reading: "In midnovel, already a sizable portion of the *histoire* [fabula] exists for readers, while a large segment of the *récit* [representation] is still 'inexistent,' unknown to them. The *histoire* which exists for us at the midpoint of a novel is, of course, still fluid, subject to revision as we alter our hypotheses on the basis of later data. But all our efforts will be bent toward making it congeal, and to that end we will be building a *lecture* [interpretation], also fluid, hypothetical, aimed at grasping the purposes behind the *histoire*. . . . To be sure, the *lecture* needs the data from [the fabula we construct] to exist, but it does not require all the data and may begin growing from a very few early events. As it begins to solidify, making the reader 'closed-minded,' it influences the mental elaboration of the *histoire* (*Causality and Narrative in French Fiction*, 222).

21. There is of course also a recency effect, but its influence seems more readily understood, and thus less pernicious, than that of the primacy effect.

22. In a study that looks at how readers of news reports update information in response to subsequent reports of the same event, Herre van Oostendorp cites earlier researchers' findings indicating that "audiences tend to hear what they want to hear" and that "readers have difficulty eliminating incorrect or obsolete information," and summarizes the results of his own research which "suggest that it is very difficult to completely discredit an old perspective, and to exchange that for a new perspective. Readers seem to prefer to skip the information that is needed in order to update their old model or perspective" ("Holding onto Established Viewpoints," 175, 187).

23. Per Nykrog asks in addition two related questions: for whom does the narrator write, and why does the narrator gives Mme de Rochefide the last word ("On Seeing and Nothingness: Balzac's *Sarrasine*," 439)? Of course Nykrog recognizes (as do I) that the story we read was written not by the narrator but by Balzac, which in no way lessens the interesting speculation his questions raise about the character narrator's motivation.

24. "Un roman: c'est un miroir qu'on promène le long d'un chemin," cited by Henri Beyle, who published his major novels under the pseudonym "Stendhal," as the epigraph to chapter 13 of his novel *Le Rouge et le noir* (1830). Although Stendhal attributes the epigraph to "Saint-Réal," scholars have been unable to locate the source and generally assume that Stendhal wrote it himself.

25. In *The Postmodern Condition*, Jean-François Lyotard posits and analyzes "grand" narratives of legitimation. These master-narratives (abstract but pervasive sets of judgments or worldviews) can influence readers' interpretations of written narratives, as well as individuals' interpretations of events perceived in the world.

26. The primacy effect may even come into play to preserve the new interpretation. The psychoanalyst Donald P. Spence points to the effects of formulating an interpretation in words as a way to explain that a memory—even an altered memory or a memory of an event that did not occur—once accepted as factual often persists, even if further pertinent information is acquired: "[T]he analyst's construction of a childhood

event can lead the patient to remember it differently if he remembered it at all; and if he had no access to the event, to form a new memory for the first time. Within his private domain, the newly remembered event acts and feels like any other memory; thus it becomes true. Once this kind of memory has been created, its roots in the patient's historical past become almost irrelevant, and even if it were objectively disconfirmed (by, for example, discovering an old letter or hearing from a long-lost neighbor), its subjective truth value would probably continue" (*Narrative Truth and Historical Truth*, 166–67).

27. See Marie-Laure Ryan's *Possible Worlds, Artificial Intelligence, and Narrative Theory*, especially chapter 6. Ryan introduces the idea that narrative worlds are modally stratified and include, in addition to the domain regarded as actual by the characters, the modalized worlds (wishes, dreams, etc.) of individual characters. Ryan's recognition of these strata guides my understanding of what readers (listeners, viewers) need to be able to distinguish to construct a fabula.

Notes to Chapter 7

1. Not all the novels that make it impossible for readers to construct a chronological fabula include images or narrativized accounts of images. See, for example, the catalog that Brian Richardson offers in "Between Story and Discourse" of strategies that violate realistic temporality. Richardson concludes his analysis by proposing that "[t]he most urgent task of narrative theory is to construct a poetics of nonmimetic fiction that can finally do full justice to the literature of our time" (59). My hope is that the theory I introduce in this chapter and the next will contribute to that endeavor.

2. In other words I am analyzing a single discrete image (rather than a film, a collection of photographs, or a photonovel) that represents one event or situation (rather than a multi-episodic artwork—a painting or drawing that depicts on one surface two or more events). For a fine analysis of the narrativity of multi-episodic paintings, see Wendy Steiner's *Pictures of Romance*.

3. In an earlier article I argued that the single scene that a painting or photograph offers can be understood as a compressed discourse (or "compressed sju et" in the terminology of that article) because it influences interpretations even more strongly than the initial scene in a narrative does. In a narrative, the importance of the first scene is heightened for interpreters through the primacy effect: our tendency to accept as valid the information we are initially given, even when that information is contradicted later in the same message (see chapter 6). When we read narratives, however, the effect of the initial information may gradually weaken as we amass further information during our progress through the text. Because paintings and photographs, in contrast, remain frozen before our gaze, the primacy of the visually represented moment retains a dominance that cannot be undermined by information presented subsequently, since

the information a painting offers is presented in its entirety all at once ("Implications of Narrative in Painting and Photography").

4. Göran Sonesson describes, as one among other varieties of pictorial narrativity, the "single, static picture [that is] recognizable as a possible intermediary scene of whole classes of (usually trivial) *action schemes*." Further, in his fine article on the discrete image considered from the perspective of narrative theory, he argues that several of the features that have been thought to enhance narrativity (that make us judge a story a *good* story) are displayed at least as effectively through visual as through verbal representation: external rather than internal events, actions rather than happenings, events involving an agent and a patient, even disnarrated elements (events that could have happened but did not—since images in a series can lead viewers to understand what is happening in one scene in a way that a later scene indicates retrospectively to have been inaccurate) ("Mute Narratives," 245, 246)

Werner Wolf explains that captions can refer to "a cultural 'script' which supplies the temporal dimension necessary for a narrative interpretation." An example he offers is "the script 'Saint Nicholas's Feast.' As an expression of the Christian concept of personal responsibility for one's acts to a metaphysical agency it involves a pre-history (the previous year), an expectation and an 'event,' in which the reward for, and/or punishment of, the behaviour in the 'pre-history' is administered by the 'saint'— and hence this script contains the central narratemes in the field of 'narrative forms of experience': chronology, causality and teleology." ("Narrative and Narrativity," 191)

5. See also Mark D. Stansbury-O'Donnell's analysis of how Barthes's concept of indices proper and informants translate to visual art (*Pictorial Narrative in Ancient Greek Art*, 20–21). Stansbury-O'Donnell's book offers an excellent detailed analysis of the process of responding to a visual artwork by constructing a narrative—and then often reconstructing it differently if new information becomes available or because cultural expectations change.

6. For Roland Barthes, a depicted scene can suggest a fragmentary fabula even without indications of a human or anthropomorphic being—if he can imagine himself in the scene: "For me, photographs of landscape (urban or country) must be *habitable*, not visitable. This longing to inhabit . . . is fantasmatic, deriving from a kind of second sight which seems to bear me forward to a utopian time, or to carry me back to somewhere in myself . . . Looking at these landscapes of predilection, it is as if *I were certain* of having been there or of going there" (*Camera Lucida*, 39–40; Barthes's italics).

7. Brian McHale draws attention, in comments on an earlier version of this chapter, to "a linguistic detail that [the poems by Yeats and Browning] share and that in both cases (though in different ways) reveals the speakers' situations: 'there' in Yeats, 'there' vs. 'this' ('this gaudy flower') in Browning. Powerfully, though almost subliminally, the deictics establish the speakers' positions relative to what once was (Browning) or what will be (Yeats) in an elsewhere that each poem specifies."

8. As Peter J. Rabinowitz correctly notes in comments on an earlier version of this chapter, in White's example a single event is viewed in different sequences, whereas in Twain's example a single painting is interpreted as representing several different events. While the historian maintains the identity of the event, the novelist narrativizes the represented scene. Both nonetheless recognize the correlation between the meaning of an event and its position in a sequence.

9. Ruth Ronen draws upon possible-world theories to explain the range of possibilities fiction offers: "Fictional worlds allow, in principle at least, radical deviations from the regularities of time in the actual world. That is, fictional worlds do not necessarily obey rules of the physical operation of time in 'the world as it is.' Thus, fictional worlds can include time paradoxes where time is presented as reversible or bilateral" (*Possible Worlds*, 202). I am grateful to Brian Richardson for drawing my attention to this passage, part of which he cites ("Beyond Story and Discourse," 48).

10. Tamar Yacobi draws attention to the prior representation that an ekphrastic account re-represents by speaking of ekphrasis as a *re-presentation*: "The one work's representation of the world then becomes the other's re-presentation, a mimesis in the second degree" ("Pictorial Models," 600). On the effects of re-representing in one medium an artwork in another medium, see Kafalenos, "The Power of Double Coding."

Notes to Chapter 8

1. Intriguingly, Spence explains in detail the stages of the interpretative process through which a patient transforms a visually remembered scene or a dream into the ekphrastic account told to the analyst. He reminds us that Barthes describes the photograph as a "continuous message": a message that comes to us uninterpreted by the brush or pencil marks that already partition a drawing or painting into discrete units and thereby guide what viewers see (Barthes, "The Photographic Message," 17–20; "Rhetoric of the Image," 43). Patients' visual memories of past events and of dreams, Spence suggests, resemble photographs. How the patient partitions the visual memory is "capricious and selective" and will affect the associations it suggests. Once a partitioned element is named, the word that is chosen will arouse its own network of associations. Moreover, these associations, Spence argues, "if they are sufficiently compelling, will tend to supplant the image" (*Narrative Truth*, 67, 57).

2. See Kafalenos, "Reading Visual Art."

3. The page numbers of Robbe-Grillet's novel that I cite here and subsequently are from the edition of Richard Howard's translation presently in print: *La Maison de Rendez-Vous* and *Djinn: Two Novels*, published in one volume by Grove. Anyone having access to the first edition of the translation can find these passages on pp. 83, 66 (see also 11–12), 114–15, and 115. Those reading the initial French edition (Les Editions de Minuit, 1965) will find the equivalent passages on pp. 119–20, 97–98

(see also 25–26), 161–62, and 162. In my analysis of these passages I treat as interchangeable the names Lauren, Loraine, and Loreen, and the names Marchat and Marchant. In doing so I am oversimplifying a narrative world in which, as Jean Ricardou describes it (referring to *La Maison de Rendez-vous* and a novel by Pinget), "[w]hat is commonly *unique* (a given character, a given event) is subjected to the *dislocation* of contradictory variants; what is ordinarily *diverse* (several characters, several events) is subjected to the *assimilation* of odd resemblances. The fiction excludes perfect singularity as well as absolute plurality" (*Pour une théorie*, 262; my translation, Ricardou's emphasis).

4. "Robbe-Grillet at Seventy," organized by Michel Rybalka, October 9–11, 1992.

5. Brian McHale demonstrates moreover that still scenes, when animated, often illicitly transgress ontological boundaries. In *La Maison de Rendez-vous,* for instance, in one of McHale's examples, "a magazine-cover illustration in the hands of a street-sweeper develops into an apparently 'real' scene at Lady Ava's luxurious villa." Similarly, he points out, "dynamic episodes which have evolved illicitly from static representations often collapse back into 'stills'" (*Postmodernist Fiction,* 118). Lubomír Dole el includes shifting ontological orders in his summary of the contradictions the novel constructs: "(1) one and the same event is introduced in several conflicting versions; (2) a place (Hong Kong) is and is not the setting of the novel; (3) the same events are ordered in reversed temporal sequence (A precedes B, B precedes A); and (4) one and the same world entity recurs in several modes of existence—as a literary fictional fact, as a theater performance, as a sculpture, as a painting" (*Heterocosmica,* 164).

6. In an analysis of hybrid messages that contain both images and words, Roland Barthes says that "all images are polysemous; they imply, underlying their signifiers, a 'floating chain' of signifieds, the reader able to choose some and ignore others." The linguistic message, he continues, provides *anchorage:* "the text *directs* the reader through the signifieds of the image, causing him to avoid some and receive others; by means of an often-subtle *dispatching,* it remote-controls him towards a meaning chosen in advance" ("Rhetoric of the Image," 39–40; Barthes's emphasis).

7. Published in 1975 under the title *La Belle Captive: roman* (Brussels: Cosmos Textes), the French edition includes color reproductions of a number of Magritte's paintings. In the English translation, published by the University of California Press in 1995, Magritte's paintings are all in black and white. For detailed information about the making of this novel and Robbe-Grillet's other collaborative hybrid works from the 1970s, as well as the so-called assemblage novels in which Robbe-Grillet republished the texts of the hybrid works but this time without the images, see Bruce Morrissette, *Intertextual Assemblage in Robbe-Grillet from Topology to the Golden Triangle.*

8. Logically, because the visual artworks in Sebald's novel are photographs, rather than paintings or drawings, they cannot represent the same places, objects, and beings as the text of the novel does. As a result

of the photographic process and unlike other forms of visual representation, a photograph attests to the past existence *in the same world* of the referent of which it is an emanation. A photograph that we can see in our world requires a referent in our world; Sebald's novel is said to be fiction—that is, a representation of a narrative world that is not our world. Thus the referents of the photographs and of the words exist in different worlds—our world for the photographs and a fictional world for the text. Even when the text describes a photograph of a girl with a dog in her lap, the photograph that follows it that shows a girl with a dog in her lap is not that photograph. The photograph that we see is of a girl who once existed in our world. The photograph described in the text is of a girl who once existed in the narrative world. In fiction, a photograph of a character (or an object or a place) in the narrative world can be viewed by characters in the narrative world; it can be represented in a novel through ekphrasis, but it cannot be viewed by readers in our world.

9. In Roland Barthes's terms, the writer, like the *bricoleur*, sees the meaning [*le sens*] of events by relating them: "by *trying* fragments of events together . . . by tirelessly transforming these events into functions" ("Literature and Discontinuity," 182; his emphasis). Narrative can be considered a procedure for interpreting events by perceiving them in a sequence.

WORKS CITED

Akutagawa, Ryunosuke. "In a Grove" (1915). Translated by Virginia Marcus. In *Made Into Movies: From Literature to Film*. Edited by Stuart Y. McDougal. New York: Holt, Rinehart, and Winston, 1985. 172–78.

Albers, Josef. *Interaction of Color*. New Haven: Yale University Press, 1963.

Andersen, Hans Christian. *The Complete Fairy Tales and Stories*. Translated by Erik Christian Haugaard. Garden City, NY: Doubleday, 1974.

Balzac, Honoré de. *Sarrasine* (1830). Translated by Richard Miller. In *S/Z* by Roland Barthes. 221–54.

Barth, John. *Chimera* (1972). Greenwich, CT: Fawcet Crest, 1973.

Barthes, Roland. *Camera Lucida* (1980). Translated by Richard Howard. New York: Hill and Wang, 1981.

———. *Image—Music—Text*. Translated by Stephen Heath. New York: Hill and Wang, 1977.

———. "Introduction to the Structural Analysis of Narratives" (1966). In *Image—Music—Text*. 79–124.

———. "Is Painting a Language?" (1969). In *The Responsibility of Forms: Critical Essays on Music, Art, and Representation*. Translated by Richard Howard. New York: Hill and Wang, 1985. 149–52.

———. "Literature and Discontinuity" (1962). In *Critical Essays*. Translated by Richard Howard. Evanston: Northwestern University Press, 1962. 171–83.

———. *On Racine* (1960). Translated by Richard Howard. New York: Hill and Wang, 1964. Reprint, Berkeley: University of California Press, 1992.

———. "Rhetoric of the Image" (1964). In *Image—Music—Text*. 32–51.

———. *S/Z: An Essay* (1970). Translated by Richard Miller. New York: Hill and Wang, 1974.

———. "The Photographic Message" (1961). In *Image—Music—Text*. 15–31.

Beidler, Peter G. "A Critical History of *The Turn of the Screw*." In *Henry James: The Turn of the Screw*. Edited by Beidler. Case Studies in Contemporary Criticism. Boston: St. Martin's Press, 1995. 127–51.

Booth, Wayne C. *The Rhetoric of Fiction*. Chicago: The University of Chicago Press, 1961.

Borges, Jorge Luis. "Pierre Menard, Author of the *Quixote*." In

Ficciones. Buenos Aires: Emecé Editores, 1956. Translated by James E. Irby. In *Labyrinths: Selected Stories and Other Writings*. New York: New Directions, 1964. 36–44.

Bremond, Claude. "Le Message narratif." *Communications* 4 (1964): 4–32.

Bremond, Claude and Thomas Pavel. *De Barthes à Balzac: Fictions d'un critique, Critiques d'une fiction*. Paris: Albin Michel, 1998.

Bremond, Claude and Jean Verrier. "Afanasiev and Propp." Translated and with an introduction by Thomas G. Pavel and Marilyn Randall. *Style* 18,2 (Spring 1984): 177–95.

Brooks, Peter. *Reading for the Plot: Design and Intention in Narrative*. New York: Alfred A. Knopf, Inc., 1984.

Browning, Robert. "My Last Duchess" (1842). In *Bells and Pomegranates I–VI*. Edited by Ian Jack and Rowena Fowler. Oxford: Clarendon-Oxford University Press, 1988. 186–88. Vol. 3 of *The Poetical Works of Robert Browning*, edited by Ian Jack and Margaret Smith.

Burke, Peter. "History of Events and the Revival of Narrative." In *New Perspectives on Historical Writing*. Edited by Burke. University Park: Pennsylvania State University Press, 1992. 233–48.

Carroll, Lewis. *Alice in Wonderland and Other Favorites* (including *Through the Looking-Glass*). New York: Washington Square Press-Pocket Books, 1951.

Chambers, Ross. "*Sarrasine* and the Impact of Art." *French Forum* 5 (1980): 218–38.

Chatman, Seymour. "On Deconstructing Narratology." *Style* 22, 1(1988): 9–17.

———. *Story and Discourse: Narrative Structure in Fiction and Film*. Ithaca: Cornell University Press, 1978.

———. "What Novels Can Do That Films Can't (and Vice Versa)." *Critical Inquiry* 7, 1 (1980): 121–40.

Cohn, Dorrit. *The Distinction of Fiction*. Baltimore: The Johns Hopkins University Press, 1999.

Culler, Jonathan. "Story and Discourse in the Analysis of Narrative." In *The Pursuit of Signs: Semiotics, Literature, Deconstruction*. Ithaca: Cornell University Press, 1981. 169–87.

de Lauretis, Teresa. *Alice Doesn't: Feminism, Semiotics, Cinema*. Bloomington: Indiana University Press, 1984.

Derrida, Jacques. "Devant la loi." In *Philosophy and Literature*. Edited by Phillips Griffiths. Cambridge: Cambridge University Press, 1984. 173–88.

Dole el, Lubomír. *Heterocosmica: Fiction and Possible Worlds*. Baltimore: The Johns Hopkins University Press, 1998.

———. *Occidental Poetics: Tradition and Progress*. Lincoln: University of Nebraska Press, 1990.

———. "Truth and Authenticity in Narrative." *Poetics Today* 1, 3 (1980): 7–25.

Fiedler, Leslie A. *Love and Death in the American Novel* (1960). Revised edition. New York: Stein and Day, 1966.

Fokkema, D. W. and Elrud Kunne-Ibsch. *Theories of Literature in the Twentieth Century: Structuralism, Marxism, Aesthetics of Reception, Semiotics* (1978). New York: St. Martin's Press, 1986.

Genette, Gérard. *Narrative Discourse: An Essay in Method* (1972). Translated by Jane Lewin. Ithaca: Cornell University Press, 1980.

———. *Narrative Discourse Revisited* (1983). Translated by Jane E. Lewin. Ithaca: Cornell University Press, 1988.

Gorman, James. "Which Wizard Beats 'Em All?" *The New York Times.* Friday, January 11, 2002. National edition: B1, B37.

Graham, Kenneth. "*Daisy Miller:* Dynamics of an Enigma." In *New Essays on* Daisy Miller *and* The Turn of the Screw. Edited by Vivian R. Pollak. Cambridge: Cambridge University Press, 1993. 35–63.

Greimas, A.-J. "Searching for Models of Transformation" (1966). In *Structural Semantics: An Attempt at a Method.* Translated by Daniele McDowell, Ronald Schleifer, and Alan Velie. Lincoln: University of Nebraska Press, 1983. 222–56.

Grimm, Jacob and Wilhelm. *The Complete Fairy Tales of the Brothers Grimm.* Edited and translated by Jack Zipes. New York: Bantam, 1987. 2 vols.

Heffernan, James A. W. "Ekphrasis and Representation." *New Literary History* 22 (1991): 297–316.

Heise, Ursula K. *Chronoschisms: Time, Narrative, and Postmodernism.* Cambridge, UK: Cambridge University Press, 1997.

Hendricks, William O. "'A Rose for Emily': A Syntagmatic Analysis." *PTL: A Journal for Descriptive Poetics and Theory of Literature* 2 (1977): 257–95.

———. "On the Notion 'Beyond the Sentence.'" *Linguistics* 37 (1967): 12–51.

Herman, David. "Lateral Reflexivity: Levels, Versions, and the Logic of Paraphrase." *Style* 34, 2 (Summer 2000): 293–306.

Howells, W[illiam] D[ean]. *Heroines of Fiction.* 2 vols. New York: Harper and Brothers Publishers, 1901.

Hoxie, Elizabeth F. "Mrs. Grundy Adopts Daisy Miller." *New England Quarterly* 19 (December 1946): 474–84. Reprinted in Stafford. 125–30.

Jakobson, Roman. "Closing Statement: Linguistics and Poetics." In *Style in Language.* Edited by Thomas A. Sebeok. Cambridge, MA: MIT Press, 1960. 350–77.

James, Henry. *The Ambassadors.* Vols. 21 and 22 of *The Novels and Tales of Henry James.* New York Edition. New York: Scribner's, 1909. 26 vols. 1907–17.

———. *The Aspern Papers, The Turn of the Screw, The Liar, The Two Faces.* Vol. 12 of *The Novels and Tales of Henry James.* New York Edition. New York: Scribner's, 1908. 26 vols. 1907–17.

———. Daisy Miller, Pandora, The Patagonia, *and Other Tales.* Vol. 18 of *The Novels and Tales of Henry James.* New York Edition. New York: Scribner's, 1909. 26 vols. 1907–17.

Kafalenos, Emma. "Implications of Narrative in Painting and Photography." *New Novel Review* 3,2 (Spring 1996): 53–64.

————. "The Power of Double Coding to Represent New Forms of Representation: *The Truman Show, Dorian Gray,* "Blow-Up," and Whistler's *Caprice in Purple and Gold.*" *Poetics Today* 24, 1 (2003): 1–33.

————. "Reading Visual Art, Making—and Forgetting—Fabulas." *Narrative* 9, 2 (2001): 138–45.

Kafka, Franz. "Before the Law." In *The Metamorphosis, The Penal Colony, and Other Stories.* Translated by Willa and Edwin Muir. New York: Shocken, 1975. 148–50.

Kern, Stephen. *A Cultural History of Causality: Science, Murder Novels, and Systems of Thought.* Princeton, Princeton University Press, 2004.

Kerrigan, William. *Hamlet's Perfection.* Baltimore: The Johns Hopkins University Press, 1994.

Kibédi Varga, A. "Criteria for Describing Word-and-Image Relations." *Poetics Today* 10, 1 (1989): 31–53.

Krook, Dorothea. "*The Ambassadors:* Two Types of Ambiguity." *Neophilologus* 74 (1990): 148–55.

Kurosawa, Akira. *Rashomon.* Daiei Company, 1950.

Langbaum, Robert. *The Poetry of Experience: The Dramatic Monologue in Modern Literary Tradition* (1957). New York: Norton, 1963.

Larivaille, Paul. "L'Analyse (morpho)logique du récit." *Poétique* 19 (1974): 368–88.

Lessing, Gotthold Ephraim. *Laocoon* (1766). Translated by Ellen Frothingham. New York: Noonday, 1957.

Lotman, Jurij M. "The Origin of Plot in the Light of Typology." *Poetics Today* 1, 1–2 (1979): 161–84.

Lyotard, Jean-François. 1984 [1979]. *The Postmodern Condition: A Report on Knowledge* (1979). Translated by Geoff Bennington and Brian Massumi. Minneapolis: University of Minnesota Press, 1984.

McHale, Brian. *Postmodernist Fiction.* London: Routledge, 1989.

Miller, J. Hillis. *Illustration.* Cambridge: Harvard University Press, 1992.

Mink, Louis O. "History and Fiction as Modes of Comprehension." *New Literary History* 1, 3 (1970): 541–58.

Morrissette, Bruce. *Intertextual Assemblage in Robbe-Grillet from Topology to the Golden Triangle.* Fredericton, NB, Canada: York Press: 1979.

Nelson, Roy Jay. *Causality and Narrative in French Fiction from Zola to Robbe-Grillet.* Columbus: The Ohio State University Press, 1990.

Nykrog, Per. "On Seeing and Nothingness: Balzac's *Sarrasine.*" *Romanic Review* 83, 4 (1992): 437–44.

Oostendorp, Herre van. "Holding onto Established Viewpoints during Processing News Reports." In *New Perspectives on Narrative Perspective.* Edited by Willie van Peer and Seymour Chatman. Albany: State University of New York Press, 2001. 173–88.

Pavel, Thomas G. *The Poetics of Plot: The Case of English Renaissance Drama.* Minneapolis: University of Minnesota Press, 1985.

————. "Racinian Spaces." *Thematics: New Approaches.* Edited by

Claude Bremond, Joshua Landy, and Thomas Pavel. Albany: State University of New York Press, 1995. 113–26.

Perry, Menakhem. "Literary Dynamics: How the Order of a Text Creates Its Meanings [With an Analysis of Faulkner's 'A Rose for Emily']." *Poetics Today* 1, 1–2 (1979): 35–64, 311–61.

Phelan, James. *Worlds from Words: A Theory of Language in Fiction.* Chicago: University of Chicago Press, 1981.

Poe, Edgar Allan. "The Assignation" (1834). In Stern 1977 [1945]: 192–207.

Prince, Gerald. *A Dictionary of Narratology.* First edition. Lincoln: University of Nebraska Press, 1986.

———. *A Dictionary of Narratology.* Revised edition. Lincoln: University of Nebraska Press, 2003.

———. "The Disnarrated" (1988). In *Narrative as Theme: Studies in French Fiction.* Lincoln: University of Nebraska Press, 1992. 28–38.

———. *Narratology: The Form and Functioning of Narrative.* Berlin: Mouton, 1982.

———. "Introduction to the Study of the Narratee" (1973). Translated by Francis Mariner. Reprinted in *Reader-Response Criticism.* Edited by Jane P. Tompkins. Baltimore: The Johns Hopkins University Press, 1980. 7–25.

Propp, Vladimir. *Morphology of the Folktale* (1928). 2nd edition. Translated by Laurence Scott. Revised by Louis A. Wagner. Austin: University of Texas Press, 1968.

Racine, Jean. *Iphigenia / Phaedra / Athaliah.* Translated by John Cairncross. Harmondsworth and New York: Penguin Books Ltd., 1963. Revised edition 1970.

Reesman, Jeanne Campbell. *American Designs: The Late Novels of James and Faulkner.* Philadelphia: University of Pennsylvania Press, 1991.

Ricardou, Jean. *Pour une théorie du nouveau roman.* Paris: Editions du Seuil, 1971.

Richardson, Brian. "Beyond Story and Discourse: Narrative Time in Postmodern and Nonmimetic Fiction." In *Narrative Dynamics: Essays on Time, Plot, Closure, and Frames.* Edited by Brian Richardson. Columbus: The Ohio State University Press, 2002.

———. *Unlikely Stories: Causality and the Nature of Modern Narrative.* Newark, University of Delaware Press, 1997.

Rimmon[-Kenan], Shlomith. "A Comprehensive Theory of Narrative: Genette's *Figures III* and the Structuralist Study of Fiction." *PTL: A Journal for Descriptive Poetics and Theory of Literature* 1 (1976): 33–62.

———. *The Concept of Ambiguity—the Example of James.* Chicago: University of Chicago Press, 1974.

Robbe-Grillet, Alain. "Images and Texts: A Dialogue." Translated by Karlis Racevskis. In *Generative Literature and Generative Art: New Essays.* Edited by David Leach. Fredericton, NB, Canada: York Press, 1983.

———. *La Belle Captive: a novel* (1975). Translated by Ben Stoltzfus. Berkeley: University of California Press, 1995.

————. *La Maison de Rendez-vous.* Translated by Richard Howard. In *La Maison de Rendez-vous and Djinn: Two Novels.* New York: Grove Press, 1987. 129–284.

Ronen, Ruth. *Possible Worlds in Literary Theory.* Cambridge: Cambridge University Press, 1994.

Rowe, Joyce A. *Equivocal Endings in Classic American Novels.* Cambridge: Cambridge University Press, 1988.

Ryan, Marie-Laure. *Possible Worlds, Artificial Intelligence, and Narrative Theory.* Bloomington: Indiana University Press, 1991.

————. "Postmodernism and the Doctrine of Panfictionality." *Narrative* 5, 2 (1997): 165–87.

Saussure, Ferdinand de. *Course in General Linguistics.* Edited by Charles Bally and Albert Sechehaye in collaboration with Albert Riedlinger. Translated by Wade Baskin. New York: McGraw Hill, 1959.

Sebald, W. G. *Austerlitz.* Translated by Anthea Bell. New York: Random House, 2001.

Shakespeare, William. *Hamlet.* Arden Edition. Edited by Harold Jenkins. London: Methuen, 1982.

Sonesson, Göran. "Mute Narratives: New Issues in the Study of Pictorial Texts." In *Interart Poetics: Essays on the Interrelations of the Arts and Media.* Edited by Ulla-Britta Lagerroth, Hans Lund, and Erik Hedling. Amsterdam and Atlanta, GA: Rodopi, 1997. 243–51.

Spence, Donald P. *Narrative Truth and Historical Truth: Meaning and Interpretation in Psychoanalysis.* New York: Norton, 1982.

Stafford, William T. *James's Daisy Miller: The Story, the Play, the Critics.* New York: Charles Scribner's Sons, 1963.

Stansbury-O'Donnell, Mark D. *Pictorial Narrative in Ancient Greek Art.* Cambridge, UK: Cambridge University Press, 1999.

Steiner, Wendy. *Pictures of Romance: Form against Context in Painting and Literature.* Chicago: University of Chicago Press, 1988.

Stern, Philip Van Doren, ed. *The Portable Poe* (1945). New York: Penguin-Viking, 1977.

Sternberg, Meir. *Expositional Modes and Temporal Ordering in Fiction.* Baltimore: The Johns Hopkins University Press, 1978. Reprinted Bloomington: Indiana University Press, 1993.

————. "How Narrativity Makes a Difference." *Narrative* 9, 2 (2001): 115–22.

————. *The Poetics of Biblical Narrative: Ideological Literature and the Drama of Reading.* Bloomington: Indiana University Press, 1985.

————. "Temporal Ordering, Modes of Expositional Distribution, and Three Models of Rhetorical Control in the Narrative Text: Faulkner, Balzac, and Austen." *PTL: A Journal for Descriptive Poetics and Theory of Literature* 1 (1976): 295–316.

Todorov, Tzvetan. "Les Catégories du récit littéraire." *Communications* 8 (1966): 125–51.

————. *Grammaire du Décaméron.* The Hague: Mouton, 1969.

————. "La Grammaire du récit." *Langages* 12 (1968): 94–102.

———. "Some Approaches to Russian Formalism" (1971). In *Russian Formalism: A Collection of Articles and Texts in Translation*. Edited by Stephen Bann and John E. Bowlt. Edinburgh: Scottish Academic Press, 1973. 6–19.

———. "Structural Analysis of Narrative." *Novel: A Forum on Fiction* (Fall 1969): 70–76. Reprinted in *Contemporary Literary Criticism*, edited by Robert Con Davis. New York: Longman, 1986. 323–29.

Torgovnick, Marianna. *Closure in the Novel*. Princeton: Princeton University Press, 1981.

Turner, Mark. *The Literary Mind*. New York: Oxford University Press, 1996.

Twain, Mark. *Life on the Mississippi*. The Oxford Mark Twain. New York: Oxford University Press, 1996.

Vargas Llosa, Mario. *In Praise of the Stepmother* (1988). Translated by Helen Lane. New York: Penguin-Viking, 1991.

Virgil. *The Aeneid of Virgil*. Translated by Allen Mandelbaum. New York: Bantam-Doubleday, 1981.

Walsh, W. H. "'Plain' and 'Significant' Narrative in History." *The Journal of Philosophy* 55, 11 (May 22, 1958): 479–84.

White, Hayden. *Metahistory: The Historical Imagination in Nineteenth-Century Europe*. Baltimore: The Johns Hopkins University Press, 1973.

———. "The Value of Narrativity in the Representation of Reality." *Critical Inquiry* 7, 1 (1980): 5–27.

Williams, Oscar, ed. *The Mentor Book of Major British Poets: From William Blake to Dylan Thomas*. New York: Mentor-New American Library, 1963.

Wilson, Edmund. 1948 [1934]. "The Ambiguity of Henry James". In *The Triple Thinkers: Twelve Essays on Literary Subjects*. Revised and enlarged edition. New York: Oxford University Press, 1948. 88–132.

Wolf, Werner. "Narrative and Narrativity: A Narratological Reconceptualization and its Applicability to the Visual Arts." *Word & Image* 19, 3 (July–September 2003): 180–97.

Yacobi, Tamar. "Hero or Heroine? *Daisy Miller* and the Focus of Interest in Narrative." *Style* 19, 1 (Spring 1985): 1–35.

———. "Narrative Structure and Fictional Mediation." *Poetics Today* 8, 2 (1987): 335–72.

———. "Pictorial Models and Narrative Ekphrasis." *Poetics Today* 16, 4 (1995): 599–649.

Zipes, Jack, translator. *The Complete Fairy Tales of the Brothers Grimm*. 2 vols. New York: Bantam, 1988.

INDEX

action schema, 160, 174, 181

Akutagawa, Ryunosuke. *See* "In a Grove"

Albers, Josef, vii, xi, 126, 155, 194, 203n1 (Preface). *See also* functional polyvalence

alternating sequences, 22, 146

Ambassadors, The (James), xi, 105–15, 116, 117, 118, 121–25, 136

Andersen, Hans Christian, 27, 209n1. *See also* "The Princess and the Pea"

Anna Karenina (Tolstoy), 22

Arabian Nights, The (anonymous), 23

"The Assignation" (Poe), x–xi, 46–53, 54, 57, 60, 222n13

Austerlitz (Sebald), 189, 191–92, 232–33n8

Balzac, Honoré de. See *Sarrasine*

Barth, John. *See* "Dunyazadiad"

Barthes, Roland, 121–22, 141, 144, 155, 160, 179, 217n12, 219n21, 224–25n11, 230n5, 230n6, 231n1, 232n6, 233n9. *See also* indexical information

Belle Captive: a novel, La (Robbe-Grillet), 188, 192, 232n7

"Before the Law" (Kafka), xi, 105–6, 115–25

Beidler, Peter G., 138

Beyle, Henri. *See* Stendhal

Bildungsroman, 18–21, 29

"Birthday, A" (Rossetti), 169–70, 171, 174

Booth, Wayne C., 88, 95–96, 100, 212n6

Borges, Jorge Luis. *See* "Pierre Menard, Author of the *Quixote*"

bracketed function, 13, 29, 37, 46, 47, 56, 60, 107, 108, 116, 165, 167, 169–70, 173, 197

Bremond, Claude, 204–5n6, 206n9, 225–26n11

Brooks, Peter, 69

Browning, Robert. *See* "Home-Thoughts from Abroad"; "My Last Duchess"

Burke, Peter, 223n4

Byron, Lord George Gordon. *See* "She Walks in Beauty"

Cairncross, John, 216–17n9

Canterbury Tales, The (Chaucer), 23

Carroll, Lewis. See *Through the Looking-Glass*

Chambers, Ross, 224n11, 226n15

Chatman, Seymour, 201, 206n9, 213–14n11, 214n12

Clemens, Samuel. *See* Twain

Cohn, Dorrit, 207n11, 213n10

contained focalization, 50, 55

context, effects of. *See* Albers; functional polyvalence

Culler, Jonathan, 58–60, 214n12, 214n13. *See also* hierarchical relationship between a representation and its fabula

Daisy Miller (James), xi, 71, 87–102

Decameron (Boccaccio), 4–5

243

definition of fiction, 148–49
de Lauretis, Teresa, 221–22n11
Delvaux, Paul, 188
Derrida, Jacques, 223n16
detective fiction, 70, 74
disnarrated, 60
Dole el, Lubomír, 6, 220n4, 227n19, 232n5
Don Quixote (Cervantes), 20–21
"Dunyazadiad" (Barth), 208n14

ekphrasis, 178, 180, 185, 186–87, 193, 195, 198; and narrativizing, 178, 183–84, 185–86, 189–91, 193
embedded sequences, 22–23, 146
empty function, 114, 124, 125, 165, 171, 198, 224n9
epistemological doubt, 123–24, 125
epistemological issues, in first-person narration, 112, 137; for protagonists, 125; for readers, 115, 125, 147, 150–54; in third-person narration, 112, 117; of what we can know, ix, 193–94
equilibrium, achieved, 169, 170, 175, 198; as defined by Todorov, 4
Ernst, Max, 187, 188
events, defined, vii, 1
exposition, 52–53, 94, 129–30, 220n3

Fiedler, Leslie, 89–90
Fokkema, D. W., 213n9
function, defined, ix, 3, 5–6, 45, 157, 168, 198; information required to interpret, 159–60, 179. *See also* ten-function chart
function C, as a hermeneutic device, 62, 67–71, 78–79, 80, 86, 92, 100, 101–3, 104, 112, 163–64, 165, 207–8n13; as a thematics, 62, 66–67, 69–71, 78–79, 86–87, 92, 100, 102–3, 164–65

functional polyvalence, x, 6, 16–17, 21, 25, 45, 53, 60, 148, 199, 208n14, 210n2, 215n13; and context/configuration, 126, 132, 148, 155, 176, 194–95; and narrativizing, 180–81, 184, 186, 192, 193, 195, 196. *See also* Albers
functions, conflicting interpretations of, ix, 151–52, 154, 180, 183, 186, 193, 195. *See also* functional polyvalence; hinge situation or event

gaps, 128, 137–38, 140–41, 147, 148; relation between temporary and permanent, 128–29, 148–53, 223n3
Genette, Gérard, 2, 198, 210n4, 210–11n1, 214n13, 219n1, 223n1, 224n10
Gorman, James, 67
Graham, Kenneth, 96–97
Greimas, A.-J, 204n4
Grimm, Jacob and Wilhelm, 9, 27, 209n1. *See also* "The Pea Test"; "A Third Tale"

Hamilton, David, 188
Hamlet (Shakespeare), xi, 71–79, 84–86, 102
Haugaard, Erik Christian, 28
Heffernan, James A. W., 178
Heise, Ursula K., 185
Hendricks, William O., 204n4, 205–6n7
Herman, David, 193, 194, 195, 204n5, 208n13, 215n2, 220n4
hierarchical relationship between a representation and its fabula, 58–60
hinge situation or event, xi–xii, 177, 184, 186, 194, 195; defined 172, 200
Hippolytus (Euripides), 217n10
"Home-Thoughts from Abroad" (Browning), 166–69, 170, 171, 174

Howells, William Dean, 88, 92–95
Hoxie, Elizabeth F., 89

Ibsen, Henrik. See *The Master Builder*
"In a Grove" (Akutagawa), 66–67, 215–16n4
In Praise of the Stepmother (Vargas Llosa), 189–91, 192
indexical information, 121–22, 160–61, 163, 164, 166, 167–68, 169, 171, 174, 175, 176, 221n10, 230n5
interpretation, defined, 1

Jakobson, Roman, 219n20
James, Henry, 71, 87, 93–94, 211n1, 219n1, 220n3. See also *The Ambassadors; Daisy Miller; The Turn of the Screw*
Johns, Jasper, 188

Kafka, Franz, 221n8. *See also* "Before the Law"
Kern, Stephen, 209n15
Kerrigan, William, 71
Kibédi Varga, A., 187, 188
Krook, Dorothea, 221n7
Kunne-Ibsch, Elrud, 213n9
Kurosawa, Akira, 216n4. See also *Rashomon*

Lakoff, George, 65
Langbaum, Robert, 212n6
LeGuin, Ursula K., 67
"Lake Isle of Innisfree, The" (Yeats), 163–66, 167, 168, 170, 171, 173, 174
Laocoon (Lessing), 172–74
Larivaille, Paul, 204n4
Last Year at Marienbad (Robbe-Grillet), 226n13
Lessing, Gotthold Ephraim, 172, 173. See also *Laocoon*
Liaisons dangereuses, Les (Laclos), 23
Lotman, Jurij M., 122, 221–22n11

Lyotard, Jean-François, 228n25
lyric poetry, xi, 155, 157–72, 179; and function interpreted by the persona, 162

Magritte, René, 187–88
Master Builder, The (Ibsen), 226n13
McHale, Brian, 123, 185, 209n15, 222n12, 230n7, 232n5
Maison de Rendez-vous, La (Robbe-Grillet), 181–84, 185, 186, 193, 194, 231–32n3
meaning, defined, 1, 23
Miller, J. Hillis, 175
Miller, Richard, 226n12
Mink, Louis O., 131–32, 224n6, 224n7
Morrissette, Bruce, 232n7
Muir, Willa and Edwin, 221n9
"My Last Duchess" (Browning), x–xi, 54–58, 60, 222n13

narrative, defined, vii–viii, 2–3, 155–56, 157, 158, 200, 203–4n2
narrative ambiguity. *See* structural ambiguity
narrative competence, 2, 17, 25
"narrative" painting, 174. *See also* action schema
narrativizing, defined 178. *See also* ekphrasis; functional polyvalence
narrators, omnicommunicative and suppressive, 128
negative function, 30, 47, 99, 120–21, 125, 134, 139, 145, 165–66, 200, 206n8
Nelson, Roy Jay, 208–9n15, 214–15n13, 227–28n20
nonchronological narration, 44–45, 46, 52–54, 61, 128; in *The Ambassadors*, 124; quasi-mimetic sources of, 46, 147, 148; and sequential perception, 126–28, 141–43, 144–45, 146–48, 151, 154

Nykrog, Per, 228n23

Oostendorp, Herre van, 228n22

Pavel, Thomas G., 71–72, 204n4, 216n5, 225–26n11
"Pea Test, The" (the Brothers Grimm), 33–43, 167, 209–10n1
Perry, Menakhem, 46, 50, 147, 150–51, 227n18, 227n20
Phaedra (Racine), xi, 71–72, 79–87, 91, 102
Phelan, James, 204n5, 211–12n3, 212–13n8, 217–18n15, 219n2, 221n6
photographs, 232–33n7. See also *Austerlitz*
picaresque novel, 18–22, 29, 207n12
"Pierre Menard, Author of the *Quixote*" (Borges), 152
Poe, Edgar Allan, 50. *See also* "The Assignation"
Portrait of the Artist as a Young Man, A (Joyce), 21
prejudice, 154
primacy effect, 151, 152, 153, 154, 155, 200, 228n21, 228n26
Prince, Gerald, 59–60, 66, 158, 159, 197, 200, 203–4n2, 209n16, 211n1, 212n5, 215n14, 222n14. *See also* dis-narrated; unnarratable; unnarrated
"Princess and the Pea, The" (Andersen), 28–33, 35, 36, 37, 39–42, 209n1
Propp, Vladimir, 4, 5–6, 8, 40, 204n4, 204–5n6, 205–6n7, 223–24n5
psychoanalysis, 154, 180

Rabinowitz, Peter, 210n3, 222n15, 231n8
Racine, Jean, 217n11, 217n13. See also *Phaedra*

Rashomon (Kurosawa), 66, 215–16n4
Rauschenberg, Robert, 188
real-world danger, ix, 103
real-world events, interpretations of, ix, x, 1–2, 44, 62–71, 80, 103, 104–5, 127–28, 130, 132, 148–50, 154–55, 157, 158, 161, 179, 180, 186, 194
real-world purposes, of function analysis, ix; of narratives, 67, 233n9
Reesman, Jeanne Campbell, 219n2, 220n5
Ricardou, Jean, 232n3
Richardson, Brian, 23–24, 229n1, 231n9
Rimmon-Kenan, Shlomith, 114, 128–29, 136–37, 200, 206n9, 223n2. *See also* structural ambiguity
Robbe-Grillet, Alain, 184, 188–89, 194. See also *La Belle Captive: a novel; Last Year at Marienbad; La Maison de Rendez-vous; Topology of a Phantom City*
Ronen, Ruth, 214n12, 231n9
Rossetti, Christina. *See* "A Birthday"
Rowe, Joyce A., 219n2
Russian Formalists, 58
Ryan, Marie-Laure, 148–49, 207n11, 213n10; and modally stratified worlds, 229n27. *See also* definition of fiction
Rybalka, Michel, 232n4

Saussure, Ferdinand, 213n10
Sarrasine (Balzac), xi, 132–33, 140–48, 150, 153–54, 155, 219n21
Sebald, W. G. See *Austerlitz*
Shakespeare, William. See *Hamlet*
"She Walks in Beauty" (Byron), 170–72, 175, 177
Sherwood, Mrs. John, 89
Shklovsky, Viktor, 213n9

Sonesson, Göran, 230n4
Spence, Donald P., 180,
   228–29n26, 231n1
Stansbury-O'Donnell, Mark D.,
   230n5
Stendhal (Henri Beyle), 154,
   228n24
Steiner, Wendy, 229n2
Stern, Philip Van Doren, 50
Sternberg, Meir, 2, 52–53, 88,
   128–30, 147, 151, 158,
   203–4n2, 209n16, 220n3,
   223n1, 223n2, 223n3, 227n16,
   227n17. See also exposition;
   gaps; narrators, omnicommunicative and suppressive
Stoltzfus, Ben, 188
structural ambiguity, 114–15, 136,
   137, 156, 200, 221n7

ten-function chart, 7
"Third Tale, A" (the Brothers
   Grimm), 9–10, 12–17
Through the Looking-Glass
   (Carroll), 184
Todorov, Tzvetan, 4–5, 10, 22–23,
   44, 64, 146, 204n3, 206–7n10,
   213n9. See also embedded
   sequences
Tomashevsky, Boris, 213n9
Topology of a Phantom City
   (Robbe-Grillet), 185
Torgovnick, Marianna, 219n2,
   220–21n6
Turn of the Screw, The (James),
   xi, 132–40, 146, 152–53, 156
Turner, Mark, 1–2, 64–65, 203n1
   (chapter 1)
Twain, Mark, 175–76, 177–78,
187, 194
Tynyanov, Juri, 213n9

uninterpreted event, 138, 201,
   224n9
unnarratable, 59–60
unnarrated, 59, 222n14

Vargas Llosa, Mario. See In Praise
   of the Stepmother
Verrier, Jean, 204–5n6
Virgil, 172–73
visual representation, xi, 155,
   157–62, 172–78, 179, 180–81,
   187–88, 191–92, 195; in novels, xii, 161–62, 178, 179,
   183–84, 185, 186–93, 194

Walsh, W. H., 24–25
White, Hayden, 130–31, 149,
   150, 176
Wilhelm Meister's Apprenticeship
   (Goethe), 20
Wilson, Edmund, 134–35
Wolf, Werner, 230n4

Yacobi, Tamar: and ekphrasis,
   231n10; and ekphrasis in narrative, 186–87; and James's
   mode of narration, 219n21;
   and the identity of the protagonist in narratives, 87–88, 95,
   100, 200, 218n16; and "My
   Last Duchess," 212n7
Yeats, William Butler. See "The
   Lake Isle of Innisfree"

Zipes, Jack, 9, 33, 209–10n1